Gospel
For the Law

A daily devotional for law enforcement

Mike Poole

Gospel
For the Law

A daily devotional for law enforcement

Mike Poole

Scripture quotations are from the New Revised Standard Version Bible, Copyright © 1989, by the Division of Christian Education of the National Council of Churches of Christ in the United States of America.

PUBLISHED BY:
BRENTWOOD CHRISTIAN PRESS
4000 BEALLWOOD AVENUE
COLUMBUS, GEORGIA 31904

DEDICATION

This book is dedicated to my wife, Leslie, and my two sons, Chris and Sean; who had to endure the life of a cop right along with me.

Special thanks to the men and women of the Hilliard (OH) Police Department, the New Orleans (LA) Police Department and the United States Army Military Police Corps for being the inspiration behind this book.

JANUARY 1

In the Beginning God created the heavens and the earth, the earth was a formless void and darkness covered the face of the deep, while the spirit of God swept over the face of the waters. The God said, "Let there be light"; and there was light.

Genesis 1:1–2

As God created the heavens and earth, God also created us. God created us for a specific vocation, to be law enforcement officers. Look back on the beginning of your career, no matter how long ago that was in your life. Think about what brought you to a law enforcement career. God brought you to this job for a purpose. Allow the Spirit of God, the third person of the Trinity, to work through you, everyday, in your chosen profession. On this New Year's Day, take a moment to think about your beginnings.

Almighty God, we thank you for Your creation, for creating us in Your Image. Allow the Holy Spirit to work through me when I am at work. During the times of difficulty, remind me that You created all people, and I should act accordingly, to further Your kingdom. On this New Year's Day, bless this new year. Amen.

JANUARY 2

The words of the wise: Incline your ear and hear my words, and apply your mind to my teaching;

Proverbs 22:17

We take an oath to serve and to protect. We are called to take actions that may go against someone's wishes. Even in these confrontations, we need to remember God's teaching. When we assume the role of an adversary, we need to hear God's words and follow God's teachings. We are not exempt just because we have a job to do.

Heavenly Teacher, I look to you to show me how to act. Allow me to hear your words. Give me the strength to follow your way, even in difficult situations. Amen.

JANUARY 3

O LORD, who may abide in your tent? Who may dwell on your holy hill? Those who walk blamelessly, and do what is right, and speak the truth from their heart; who do not slander with their tongue, and do no evil to their friends, nor take up a reproach against their neighbors;

Psalm 15:1-3

Being a law enforcement officer can be a very difficult job. Not only do we have to take negative treatment from the people on the street, but also we have problems with the people in our own department. We have to learn not to blame others for our own actions. In a profession like ours, we need to set the example. Don't get into a "do as I say, not as I do" mindset. We need to refrain from gossiping about each other. This is a big problem. We always want to talk negatively about other people. We need to be careful not to separate our partners, because there are times that you may only have each other. You do not want backbiting to stand between officers in stressful situations. We need to build up and take care of each other.

Dear Lord, watch over me today. Give me the guidance to know what is right, and to stay on that path. Fill my heart with the truth. Give me the strength to support all those around me, even those with whom I disagree. Allow us to find some common ground to work out our problems.

JANUARY 4

If in my name you ask me for anything, I will do it.

John 14:14

Be careful what you pray for, you might just get it! The way we ask God for something is through prayer. But we should be asking for guidance, not outcomes. Don't ask God to make you number one on the promotional exam, but pray for guidance in decisions, strength and support in studying, and that God's will be done, not your will. If we turn these decisions over to God, we will find that everything in our careers, family, home, and personal life, will work better than we could ever imagine.

Dear God, we realize that if we ask, you will give. Help us to focus ourselves in the proper direction. The ancient Hebrews did not speak your name, because they knew the great power of asking anything in your name. Help us to remember that you will provide for us. Hear us even when we are afraid to ask. All of this we ask in your name. Amen.

JANUARY 5

He (Jesus) called the crowd with his disciples, and said to them, "If any want to become my followers, let them deny themselves and take up their cross and follow me. For those who want to save their life will lose it, and those who lose their life for my sake, and for the sake of the gospel, will save it. For what will it profit them to gain the whole world and forfeit their life? Indeed, what can they give in return for their life? Those who are ashamed of me and of my words in this adulterous and sinful generation, of them the Son of Man will also be ashamed when he comes in the glory of his Father with the holy angels."

Mark 8:34-38

Today the church remembers Kaj Munk. Kaj Munk was a Danish Lutheran pastor and playwright. Munk was also an outspoken critic of the Nazis who occupied Denmark during WWII. His plays frequently highlighted the eventual victory of the Christian faith despite the church's weak witness during that time. The Nazis, because of his sermons and articles that strengthened the resistance, feared Munk. Munk was martyred by the Nazis in 1944. His life and death invites us to think about the power of the Gospel in the midst of social and political conflicts. We, too, need to take a stand when we know that people in power are acting contrary to what God has taught us is true.

God of all power, we give you thanks for inspiring people like Kaj Munk, who stand up for the Gospel. We offer our prayers for all who face persecution and those who resist and challenge tyranny. Send your Holy Spirit to each one of us that we may also take a stand against those who are not acting according to your word. Amen.

JANUARY 6

In the time of king Herod, after Jesus was born in Bethlehem of Judea, wise men (or Magi) from the east came to Jerusalem, asking "Where is the child who has been born king of the Jews? For we observed his star at its rising, (or in the East), and have come to pay him homage." When King Herod heard this, he was frightened, and all Jerusalem with him; and calling together all the chief priests and scribes of the people, he inquired of them where the Messiah was to be born. They told him, "In Bethlehem of Judea; for so it was written by the prophet: 'And you, Bethlehem, in the land of Judah, are by no means least among the rulers of Judah; for from you shall come a ruler who is to shepherd (or rule) my people Israel.'" Then Herod secretly called for the wise men and learned from them the exact time when the star had appeared. Then he sent them to Bethlehem, saying, "Go and search diligently for the child; and when you have found him, bring me word so that I may also go and pay him homage." When they had heard the king, they set out; and there, ahead of them, went the star that they had seen at its rising, until it stopped over the place where the child was. When they saw that the star had stopped, they were overwhelmed with joy. On entering the house, they saw the child with Mary his mother; and they knelt down and paid him homage. Then, opening their treasure chests, they offered him gifts of gold, frankincense and myrrh. And having been warned in a dream not to return to Herod, they left for their country by another road.

Matthew 2:1-12

Today, the church celebrates Epiphany. We hear the story of the wise men. The Magi left all they had to follow the star. They also had the mindset to do what was right, even going against the king. We should have the mindset to do police work. If you do not have the mind to do what it takes, it is time to get out and do something else. That does not mean that you necessarily have a negative attitude at work. It means that you have to be in the proper mindset. You need to leave your home and personal life at home. You also should leave work at work, and not bring it home. Bringing all the emotions home that are not dealt with can cause problems with your family and friends. We need to constantly evaluate our own frame of mind. We also need to listen to those around us that may see us in a different perspective.

Dear Lord, we ask that you clear our minds of all the non-essentials while we are at work. Allow us to be a people with the mind to work. Be with us in our struggles that we may be able to sort everything out. May we be like the magi in making the proper decisions, and following the course you have laid out for us. Amen.

JANUARY 7

Now when all the people were baptized, and when Jesus had also been baptized and was praying the heaven was opened, and the Holy Spirit descended upon him in bodily form like a dove. And a voice came from heaven, "You are my Son, the Beloved (my beloved Son); with you I am well pleased."

Luke 3:21-22

Do you remember your baptism? It was a time when you were made a part of the body of Christ. Once we are baptized, all we do should be the work of the church. We are to proclaim the Gospel even in our jobs. The Holy Spirit fills you with the ability to do the work of the church. Even though others may see us as the bad side, as long as we are acting out our Christian walk, we are attempting to further the church.

God, Brightness of Faithful Souls, send the Holy Spirit to us to lead us along the Christian path. Be with us at work, as we try to further the body of Christ through our jobs. Amen.

JANUARY 8

And I was overjoyed to find some of your children walking in the truth, just as we have been commanded by the Father. But now, dear lady, I ask you, not as though I were writing you a new commandment, but one we have heard from the beginning, let us love one another. And this is love, that we walk according to his commandments; this is the commandment just as you have heard it from the beginning – you must walk in it.

II John 1: 4 – 6

Sometimes it is difficult for us as police officers to determine the truth. Everyone we talk to has his or her own agenda. But, we are called to walk in the truth. We need to get as close to it as we can, then make the appropriate decision. We are going to upset some people. We can't please everyone. But, if we love everyone, and base our decisions in the truth, we can feel assured that we are walking in the way of God.

Dear Father, we continue to try to stay on the path of truth. Support us as we try to love everyone as Christians, even in difficult situations. Guide us in making proper decisions. Allow your will to work through us. Amen.

JANUARY 9

And now faith, hope, and love abide, these three; and the greatest of these is love.

I Corinthians 13: 13

These are the three great lights or pillars of the Christian faith. We need to carry these with us wherever we go. We become cynical in this profession. After a while, we look at what we see everyday, and think that things will never get better. Then we just give up. Sometimes, people call it burnout. That may not be the proper term. It is a feeling that nothing we do matters. But we need to prop ourselves up on the "big three". We need to realize that there is a greater plan. We need to have faith in God, hope that everything will work out in the end, and love everyone, no matter what.

Dear God, sometimes the world seems like it is on a continual downward spin. We trust that you are in control. Build our faith in you. Allow us to have hope that it will all work out. Guide us to love you, love our neighbors, and love ourselves. We pray to the One who is our faith, the Source of hope, and the Greatest Love. Amen.

JANUARY 10

The eyes of the LORD are in every place, keeping watch on the evil and the good.

Proverbs 15:3

We need to remember that God sees everything, no matter if anyone is around or not. God sees how we handle each situation. God sees what we do when no one is watching. When you think about taking things out of buildings while doing a search, no matter how small, He is watching. When you think about hiding from the Sgt. to get some sleep on 3RD shift, He is watching. When you are meeting with people you should not be, He is there. Whenever you look around to see if anyone is watching, remember that God is!

Dear All-Seeing Eye, be with us in those times of temptation. Remind us that you are always watching. That also means that you are always with us, and we are not alone. Amen.

JANUARY 11

Even fools who keep silent are considered wise; when they close their lips, they are deemed intelligent.

Proverbs 17:28

The police department is one of the most gossipy places that exist. Everyone talks behind everyone else's back. Everybody knows everybody else's business. The problem is that everyone talks. You feel obligated. Someone tells you something, so you have to give him or her a bit of information in return. Even if we just listen, and say nothing, we are contributing to the gossip. We should learn to keep our mouths shut. Whenever we start to open our mouths to gossip, we should think how we feel when others talk about us, because they do. We should be intelligent and just tell people that we are not interested.

Dear Wisest of All, help me to keep silent. Remove gossip language from my lips. Teach me that I do not need to know everything about everybody. Assist me not being foolish, but intelligent and wise. All of this we ask in the Name of you who does know all. Amen.

JANUARY 12

And I heard a voice from heaven saying, "Write this: Blessed are the dead who from now on die in the LORD." "Yes," says the Spirit, "they will rest from their labors, for their deeds will follow them."
Revelation 14:13

Why do we spend so much effort on the funeral of a police officer? This is a difficult subject for us. We realize that the officer gave the ultimate sacrifice. Many times it seems that the only people that we have is each other. No one outside of law enforcement can understand us. We can be comforted that the fallen brother or sister IS in a better place. God tells us this is so. Even though here on earth, we realize the Thin Blue Line just got a little thinner. The officer is finally at rest.

Dear LORD, we ask you to watch over each one of us. Keep us safe from harm. Take care of the officers who have given the sacrifice of life, for they are truly saints. All of this we ask in your everlasting love.

JANUARY 13

Be silent before the Lord GOD! For the day of the LORD is at hand; the LORD has prepared a sacrifice, he has consecrated his guests.

Zephaniah 1:7

Today the church remembers George Fox. Fox was the founder of the Society of Friends, commonly known as the Quakers. The Quakers are known for the long periods of silence in their meetings. How difficult is it for us to continually fill the silence in our lives. We always have the radio, television, stereo or something going all the time. In the cruisers, we always have noises going on around us. We have forgotten how soothing silence may be for us. Today, try to have as much silence in your life as possible. Listen to the sounds that naturally occur around you. Use the time to reflect, pray, or listen.

God, Giver of peace, we thank you for the silence in our lives. Assist us to use these times to grow in our own lives. Hear us when we pray. Be with us as we reflect upon our lives. Show us the paths we should travel. Amen.

JANUARY 14

He (Jesus) said to him (Simon Peter) the third time, "Simon son of John, do you love me?" Peter felt hurt because he said to him the third time, "Do you love me?" And he said to him, "Lord, you know everything; you know that I love you." Jesus said to him, "Feed my sheep..."

John 21:17

Today the church remembers Eivind Josef Berggrav who was elected the Bishop of Norway and became the head of the State religion in 1937. In 1940, Berggrav was asked to negotiate with the Nazis to find out what their intentions were as far as the social and religious life issues for the people of Norway. He rejected the compromises of the occupying Nazi regime. He demanded that the Nazis recognize the rights of the Jewish people and the autonomy of the Christian Church. He was stripped of his title and was arrested in 1942. Bergrrav escaped and remained in hiding in Oslo, Norway until the end of the war. During this season of Epiphany, we see how Christ's light shines as a witness throughout the world. Would you be willing to lose your job, power, prestige and authority as a law enforcement officer to speak for those who are oppressed? Would you risk all that to seek the truth in the middle of the issues that trouble the world today? We come across oppression and injustices almost everyday in our jobs. We need to be faithful to Christ's light and shine to these people in the darkness of these situations.

God of light, we give you thanks for all those who stand up against oppression and wrong doing in this world. We ask that you inspire us to take up for those who need our help. Send the Holy Spirit to us so that we may burn with the light of Christ in the darkness of this world. Amen.

JANUARY 15

"But I (Jesus) say to you that listen, Love your enemies, do good to those who hate you, bless those who curse you, pray for those who abuse you. If anyone strikes you on the cheek, offer the other also; and from anyone who takes away your coat do not withhold even your shirt. Give to everyone who begs from you; and if anyone takes away your goods, do not ask for them again. Do to others as you would have them do to you...."

Luke 6:27-31

Today, the church remembers Martin Luther King, Jr. King is remembered as one who worked for non-violent resistance to racism in the U.S. We look to him as a pastor whose faith empowered his yearning for justice. Preaching non-violence, he pointed us to the lesson that we should always return love for hate. He was awarded the Nobel Peace Prize for his efforts. He was assassinated for his beliefs. We celebrate his birthday as a holiday in the U.S. on the third Monday in January. But how do we perform in the face of hatred? By the very nature of our jobs, many do not like us, what we have to say, or the tasks we must complete. Do we offer love in return to resistance? Today, strive to control your anger, and offer a sense of love whenever you encounter any type of negative emotion to you. Remember, someone may show you an act of love when you offer hate.

God, Giver of love, we give you thanks for sending peace-makers into this world. Send your Holy Spirit to us so that we may follow your son's words in loving our enemies. Remove the hatred from our hearts. Inspire us to give love in response to hate. Amen.

JANUARY 16

Oppression upon oppression, deceit upon deceit! They refuse to know me, Says the LORD.

Jeremiah 9:6

As agents of a governmental agency, we need to make sure that we do not serve as oppressors of specific classes of people. Sometimes, we may even oppress others subconsciously. We need to make sure that we are taking action on the enforcement of the law, not just coming down hard on people.

Redeemer of the oppressed, watch over us to see that we do not serve as oppressors. Give us the wisdom to know the difference between enforcement and oppression. Be with all those who suffer oppression, that they may be freed. Amen.

JANUARY 17

The spirit of the Lord GOD is upon me, because the LORD has anointed me; he has sent me to bring good news to the oppressed, to bind up the brokenhearted, to proclaim liberty to the captives, and release to the prisoners; to proclaim the year of the LORD's favor, and the day of vengeance of our God; to comfort all who mourn; to provide for those who mourn in Zion – to give them a garland instead of ashes, the oil of gladness instead of mourning, the mantle of praise instead of a faint spirit. They will be called oaks of righteousness, the planting of the LORD, to display his glory. They shall build up the ancient ruins, they shall raise up the former devastations; they shall repair the ruined cities, the devastations of many generations.

Isaiah 61:1-4

Compare this verse with Luke 4:16 – 20, and we will find that Jesus proclaimed this very message. As law enforcement officers, we have many occasions to meet the oppressed, brokenhearted, captives and prisoners. This scripture does not say we should totally remove them from their situation, but to speak to them in their situation. To those who feel oppressed, we tell them that Christ may lift them up. To those who feel hurt and pain, we explain to them how Christ can heal them. To those who are held captive, we can show them how they may be freed in Christ. And to prisoners, we may show them the love of Christ, and tell them to go and sin no more. We are not to make judgments about people in these troubles. But we are to minister to them where they are, even if we are taking enforcement action against them. We can do it with the love of God, and help them to see a way to a better life in Christ.

LORD GOD, we ask you to remove all judgment of others from our thoughts. Give us the courage to go into difficult situations and minister to those in trouble. Allow us to be your instruments. Assist us in completing the task that Isaiah and Your Son, Jesus Christ, called us to do. Amen.

JANUARY 18

Then Peter, filled with the Holy Spirit, said to them, "Rulers of the people and elders, if we are questioned today because of a good deed done to someone who was sick and are asked how this man has been healed, let it be known to all of you, and to all the people of Israel, that this man is standing before you in good

health by the name of Jesus Christ of Nazareth, whom you cruci-
fied, whom God raised from the dead. This Jesus is 'the stone that
was rejected by you, the builders; it has become the cornerstone
(the keystone).' There is salvation in no one else, for there is no
other name under heaven given among mortals by which we must
be saved."

Acts 4:8-12

Today, the church celebrates the Confession of Peter. We
each need to make a profession of our faith. We will probably be
rejected for outwardly displaying our faith. In the law enforcement culture, maintaining faith is not at the top of the list. We
may come under ridicule. But remember that the stone that the
builders rejected will become the cornerstone. Don't give in to
the harassment. Just keep the faith.

God, Comfort of Sufferers, send the Holy Spirit that we may
confess our faith in your Son, just as Peter did. May we remain
strong in our faith against the culture, so that we may also
become the cornerstones of your church. Amen.

JANUARY 19

"Simon, Simon, listen! Satan has obtained permission to sift all
of you like wheat, but I (Jesus) have prayed for you that your own
faith may not fail; and you, when once you have turned back,
strengthen your brothers."

Luke 22:31 – 32

Law enforcement has been called and considered a close-knit
group. We work in close quarters with each other. This bond is a
normal development of our social instincts. We have to be in right
relationship with all those with which we work. Our lives depend
on each other. We need to trust our partners. We need to
strengthen each other. Law enforcement is a team sport. We can
only succeed when we work together in a right manner. We are
all brothers and sisters in the body of Christ.

Eternal Father/Mother God, allow us to strengthen each other. We are called together by many common themes. Assist us in helping our partners. Strengthen us that we may repel Satan from our midst. Amen.

JANUARY 20

Above all, clothe yourself with love, which binds everything together in perfect harmony. And let the peace of Christ rule in your hearts, to which indeed you were called in the one body. And be thankful. Let the word of Christ (or of God, or of the Lord) dwell in you richly; teach and admonish one another in all wisdom; and with gratitude in your hearts sing psalms, hymns, and spiritual songs to God (or to the Lord). And whatever you do, in word or deed, do everything in the name of the Lord Jesus, giving thanks to God the Father through him.

Colossians 3:14-17

You need to place love in everything that you do. Love will allow you to get closer to the people around you. Love will enable you to know what people feel despite what they say. God's love is the foundation of creation. Build your foundation on the intended base, love. Be a good citizen by maintaining and upholding the principles of your city, county, state and country. Attempt to break down racial strife, religious differences and class hatred. Remove hate, fanaticism, petty jealousies and unjust ambitions from your being. Continue to walk in love always and everywhere.

Creator of love, allow us to be filled with your love that we may show love to the world. Remove all negativities from us that we may do your work. Preserve us to continue in the path of love in all we do and say. Amen.

JANUARY 21

This was confirmed with an oath; for others who became priests took their office without an oath, but this one became a priest with an oath, because of the one who said to him, "The Lord has sworn and will not change his mind, 'You are a priest forever'"

Hebrews 7:20-21

When we took our jobs, we took an oath of office. We raised our right hands and swore to uphold the law. The wording may be different from jurisdiction to jurisdiction, but the concept is the same. God swore an oath to us that God would not abandon us. We do not believe God breaks promises. We need to strive to fulfill your oath of office to the fullest.

The One to whom our oaths lie, be with us to fulfill our duties. Send the Holy Spirit to assist us in living up to the promises we made on the first day on the job. Be with us as we sustain this promise throughout our career. Amen.

JANUARY 22

God gave Solomon very great wisdom, discernment, and breadth of understanding as vast as the sand on the seashore, so that Solomon's wisdom surpassed the wisdom of all the people of the east, and all the wisdom of Egypt.

I Kings 4:29-30

Law enforcement is full of decision making. Some decisions are easy to make, while others are much more difficult. Some decisions may be made over a period of time after contemplating all the facts, while other decisions must be made in an instant. All of our decisions should be made with as much knowledge and understanding as possible.

Eternal Source of Knowledge, give us the ability to make proper decisions. Fill our hearts with wisdom and understanding. Allow us to make every decision with the best possible outcome in mind. Amen.

JANUARY 23

But each of us was given grace according to the measure of Christ's gift. Therefore it is said, "When he ascended on high he made captivity itself a captive; he gave gifts to his people."

Ephesians 4: 7-8

Each of us has our own God-given gifts. Our gifts lead us to our everyday vocations. God expects us to spread the Gospel through our jobs. Sometimes, it may seem that we are going against the spread of the Gospel. We need to remember that our work is God's work. It was given to us through the Holy Spirit. We were placed here to do a job to further the Kingdom of God.

Generous Provider of all good gifts, we give you thanks for providing us with the gifts to accomplish our jobs. We praise you for guiding us to our proper vocations in your service. Allow us to see ourselves as workers in your Kingdom. Amen.

JANUARY 24

Now the chief priests and the whole council were looking for false testimony against Jesus so that they might put him to death, but they found none, though many false witnesses came forward. At last two came forward and said, " This fellow said, 'I am able to destroy the temple of God and to build it in three days.'"

Matthew 26: 59-61

How many times, in the course of our duty, have people lied to us? It is difficult for us to get to the truth when many come forward in an attempt to deceive us. We see this occurred at the trial of Jesus. We need to make our decisions based on sound evidence. We need to evaluate everything that we hear. Many will come to us to give us false testimony. We need to be agents of the truth.

God of Truth, we ask you to send the Holy Spirit to us that we may be able to know the truth from false testimony. Allow our decision to be based upon the truth. For we know the Way, Truth and the Life. Guide us in walking in the same path. Amen.

JANUARY 25

Saul became increasingly powerful and confounded the Jews who lived in Damascus by proving that (this) Jesus was the Messiah (or the Christ).

Acts 9:22

Today the church celebrates the conversion of Paul. A person who persecuted the early church became one of the greatest evangelists of the first century. Do you remember the day you had your conversion? Even those of us who grow up in the church probably had a time when we experienced our faith in some way. Some of us fall out of the faith and, due to a conversion experience, return. Many of us remember when we came to believe. There are many that we come in contact with that fit into these categories, and many other categories. Never underestimate God's ability to use you for someone else's conversion. Treat each contact with the tenderness that you would want to be treated at your conversion.

God, Companion of the Lonely, remind us of our own personal conversion experience. Send the Holy Spirit that we may be able to assist with the conversion of others, that they may see that you sent your Son into the world for us. Amen.

JANUARY 26

The LORD bless you and keep you; the Lord make his face to shine upon you, and be gracious to you; the LORD lift up his countenance upon you, and give you peace.

Numbers 6:24-26

We sometimes feel after a day's work that we are an outcast to the rest of the world. We believe what we do is apart from everyone. Many times, we seclude our work from our family and friends. We have feelings that no one will understand. But we are never apart from God. Many churches and their worship services

21

end with a benediction. Some may even use the one printed above. As we leave work everyday, we should remember that we are in the hands of the Lord.

God, the guide and inspiration of humanity, leave in us, at the end of the day, your benediction. Bless and keep us, shine upon us and be gracious to us, give us your countenance and peace. Amen.

JANUARY 27

I commend to you our sister, Phoebe, a deacon (minister) of the church at Cenchreae, so that you may welcome her in the Lord as is fitting for the saints, and help her in whatever she may require from you, for she has been a benefactor of many and of myself as well.

Romans 16:1-2

Today, the church remembers three women in the early church, Lydia, Dorcas and Phoebe. Paul baptized Lydia and her household and she permitted Paul and his traveling companions to stay in her home for a while. Dorcas was known for her charitable works, generosity, and skill in making clothing. Phoebe was a deaconess of the church. Paul, in his writings lifts up women as a great help to the church. But, our society still views women as inferior to men in the workplace. This especially occurs in the traditionally male profession of law enforcement. Men and women are equals. People should be evaluated on individual basis, not on their particular gender. We need to lift up the women who work in law enforcement as positive role models for not only women, but for men also.

God, Maker of woman and man in your own likeness, we give you thanks for making all humanity equal. Help us to remove all feelings of gender bias and prejudice. Inspire us to live in a world where the gender of a person does not have to be a disqualifying factor. Amen.

JANUARY 28

"...She will place on your head a fair garland; she will bestow on you a beautiful crown."

Proverbs 4:9

At times, it may seem as if we wear garlands and crowns. We are in charge of our kingdoms. But this is only earthly power. The glory of earthly power and fame is transient. But what kingdom will we rule in the end? We need to not become badge-heavy. We cannot become bigger than our authority allows. We are civil servants. God is the ultimate power. We need to remember to do all that we can for the Higher Power that gives us our authority here on earth.

God of All Power, grant us the ability to know our bounds in asserting authority. May we always remember we are all residents of your Kingdom. Amen.

JANUARY 29

Six days you shall labor and do all your work.

Exodus 20:9

We work about six days a week. Sometimes. We make a little money for our hard work. We should not let our wealth, industry, capital and finance go to our heads. We see officers buy new houses, cars, and all sorts of expensive toys. These are not bad things to have. We have to be careful not to let the pursuit of money become more important than the work we are doing. There will come a time when our riches will not do us any good. We will be paid well for our labors, but let our labors be done properly.

God, Giver of all good gifts, we give you thanks for all that you have given us. We know we will receive fruits for our labors. Sustain us in keeping our labor the important part, not the gaining of money. Guide us in properly maintaining our finances. Help us to give back to you what is already yours. Amen.

JANUARY 30

The Jews were astonished at it, saying, "How does this man have such learning when he has never been taught?"

John 7:15

We go through a lot of formal training: academy, in-service, college; but most of our learning occurs on the streets, actually doing the job. Jesus was the same way. He gained his experience through actually doing it. We can always learn from our experiences. At the end of the day, reflect on what you did, and see if there is anything to learn.

God, Fountain of Wisdom, give us the experiences we need to learn from what we do. Be with us as we work, to be able to gain the knowledge you send us. Amen.

JANUARY 31

You shall not make wrongful use of the name of the LORD your God, for the LORD will not acquit anyone who misuses his name.

Exodus 20:7

We tend to allow our language to deteriorate to the language we encounter on the street. We need to be very careful not to use God's name in inappropriate ways. We need to make sure our language would be acceptable to God.

God, whose name is above all names, guide us to never mention your name but with that reverence which is due from the creature to the Creator. Allow us to use your name to implore your aid in all our undertakings, and to esteem you the source of all good. Amen.

FEBRUARY 1

"Honor your father and mother; also, You shall love your neighbor as yourself."

Matthew 19:19

We are taught to love our neighbor as ourselves. Our neighbor is every person we encounter, especially at work. We are to love everyone we contact. Sometimes, it is tough love. But, everything we do must be out of love, because God loves us.

God, the Giver of Love, inspire us to act with everyone equally, as we would want to be treated. Enhance us to be able to love our neighbor. We give you thanks for loving us. Amen.

FERBRUARY 2

"...And I tell you, you are Peter, and on this rock I will build my church, and the gates of Hades will not prevail against it...."

Matthew 16:18

Remember that gates do not attack. The church should be attacking Hell. And we need to be the rock. We go into Hell everyday. We need to remember that we represent the church. We are called to steer the ship through the troubled waters and to allow others to fulfill their own freedom of responsibility to their own judgement. We need to take the Gospel to the people we encounter and allow them the ability to receive it.

Awesome God, allow us to become rocks to lead your church against the gates of Hell. Give us the strength to persevere. Open the hearts of those we encounter, that they may hear the Gospel. Amen.

FEBRUARY 3

For Zion's sake I will not keep silent, and for Jerusalem's sake I will not rest, until her vindication shines out like the dawn, and her salvation like a burning torch.

Isaiah 62:1

Today the Church remembers Ansgar, Archbishop of Hamburg and missionary to Denmark and Sweden. Ansgar brought the light of Christ to the people of Scandinavia. He was committed to preaching and caring for the poor. Ansgar would wash the feet of the poor and serve them food made from his parish. He loved the poor very much. He had the first church built in Sweden. Ansgar died in 865. How do we care for the poor in our lives? We are also called to bring the light of Christ to the world. There are poor in every community. We see them in our daily activities. When we encounter them, do we attempt to assist them in their situation, or do we just complete our task and move on? We are called to be the light of Christ. Today, look around and see the poor in your community. Try to think of ways that you may be able to help them.

God, Friend of the poor, we give you thanks for providing for us. We ask you to show us how we may help those who are less fortunate than we are. Inspire us to bring the light of Christ to others in the world as your servant Ansgar did for the people in Scandinavia. Amen.

FEBRUARY 4

All scripture is inspired by God and (every scripture) is useful for teaching, for reproof, for correction, and for training in right-eousness.

II Timothy 3:16

We all make mistakes. We are called to make corrections in others as we see them. We are also supposed to accept corrections given to us. Sometimes we are helping those who are less informed. Other times, we are correcting people who have just made a mistake and need to be reminded. Whenever we make a correction, we need to do it in the proper manner, in light of the Gospel.

God of forgiveness and understanding, inspire in us the ability to correct others who make mistakes. Allow us to be open to other who may correct us when we make a mistake. Amen.

FEBRUARY 5

"...so that, with the eyes of your heart enlightened, you may know what is the hope to which he has called you, what are the riches of his glorious inheritance among the saints."

Ephesians 1:18

We are all called to vocations in the service of God. God has called us to law enforcement. We are to live out our Christian lives in this vocation. God has called us to be God's word in the world through this vocation. We should remember that we are servants of God when we do our job. All that we do should be done in service to God.

God, the Heart that inspires us in a vision of justice and love, fill us with the Holy Spirit that we may answer our call from you in this vocation. Allow us to serve you in our jobs. Strengthen us in the tension of justice and love. Amen.

FEBRUARY 6

Do you not know that that you are God's temple and that God's Spirit dwells in you? If anyone destroys God's temple, God will destroy that person. For God's temple is holy, and you are that temple.

I Corinthians 3:16-17

You are God's temple. You need to take care of yourself: mind, body, soul and spirit. God's temple needs to be tended. You are holy. The Holy Spirit dwells within you. Allow that the Holy Spirit strengthen you to be the caretaker of God's temple that resides in you.

God, Almighty Giver of Good, we thank you for allowing the Holy Spirit to dwell in us. Give us strength to take good care of your temple. Watch over our hearts, minds, souls, and spirits. Inspire us to remember that we are holy. Amen.

FEBRUARY 7

Whoever kidnaps a person, whether that person has been sold or is still held in possession, shall be put to death.

Exodus 21:16

Kidnapping has been a serious crime since early biblical days. We handle cases where someone reports someone missing. We need to handle these cases with care. The person calling has an emotional attachment to the missing person, It could be a parent and child, spouse, family member or friend. We need to take them seriously. Whether the person is found in minutes, hours, days or longer, we need to tend to the feelings of all those involved.

God, One who sets the captives free, allow us to tend to all those who are missing and those who are close to them. Inspire us to address the emotions that may come up. Send the Holy Spirit to guide us in finding the missing person. Amen.

FEBRUARY 8

For I am not ashamed of the gospel; it is the power of God for salvation to everyone who has faith, to the Jew first and also to the Greek.

Romans 1:16

We must always remember that we are people of faith. And being people of faith, we live out our lives according to the

Gospel. Everyone who has faith falls under the Gospel. We need to do our job with the Gospel in mind. We still need to enforce the law but the Gospel leads us to treat everyone we contact with the love of sisters and brothers.

God, the Will that gives us Power, allow the Holy Spirit to ignite the Gospel within us. Guide us in loving everyone who we contact. Direct us in leading our lives according to the Gospel. Amen.

FEBRUARY 9

"Ask, and it will be given you; search, and you will find; knock, and the door will be opened for you. For everyone who asks receives, and everyone who searches finds, and for everyone who knocks, the door will be opened...."

Matthew 7:7-8

We tend to believe that we are on our own when doing our job. We believe that we do not need anyone else. But we do. We need our co-workers, family, friends, and the public. We should never be afraid to ask a question. We should always be searching for more. And we should always knock on the doors of opportunity that are presented to us.

God, Answer to All Mysteries, inspire us to realize that we are not in this life alone. Give us the answer to our questions. Allow us to find that for which we search. Open the doors for us that need opened. For all answers come from you. Amen.

FEBRUARY 10

And those who know your name put their trust in you, for you, O LORD, have not forsaken those who seek you.

Psalm 9:10

In whom do you put your trust? We should all put our trust in God. We swore an oath, an oath that we asked God to assist us in fulfilling. We know God's name. We seek God. God will never leave us on our own. Sometimes it may feel that way but continue to trust in God.

God, Source of all Trust, inspire us to trust in you. We know your name and seek you. Encourage us to continue in our jobs, knowing that we are never alone. Amen.

FEBRUARY 11

Wisdom cries out in the streets; in the square she raises her voice.
Proverbs 1:20

We have to make difficult decisions in our jobs. Many times, we are out on the streets, with no ability to stop and take a time out. We have to rely on our God-given wisdom to make proper decisions. We are God's wisdom in the streets and in the squares.

God, Fountain of Wisdom, we ask you to guide us in making proper decisions. Be with us in the streets and in the squares. Amen.

FEBRUARY 12

Then he (Ezra) said to them, "Go your way, eat the fat and drink sweet wine and send portions of them to those for whom nothing is prepared, for this day is holy to our LORD; and do not be grieved, for the joy of the LORD is your strength."
Nehemiah 8:10

We need to be strong in many ways on our job: physically, mentally, emotionally and spiritually. But the strength is not just ours. God gives us the strength to do our job. We need God's strength to support the law in a proper fashion. Rely on God for your strength.

God, Our Refuge and Our Strength, send to us the strength we need to do our difficult jobs. Lift us up physically, mentally, emotionally and spiritually. For your joy is our strength. Amen.

FEBRUARY 13

The head of Ephraim is Samaria, and the head of Samaria is the son of Remaliah. If you do not stand firm in faith, you shall not stand at all.

Isaiah 7:9

Sometimes it seems that we are not making a difference in the world. We come into this job thinking we can change things. After a while, we think it doesn't matter. We need to have faith that we may be making a difference in people's lives. We may never know how. God has faith in you. Have faith in God and in yourself.

Faithful God, we give you thanks for having faith in us. Send the Holy Spirit to us to fan the flame of our faith in you. Strengthen us to realize we can make a difference. Amen.

FEBRUARY 14

Let him kiss me with the kisses of his mouth! For your love is better than wine.

Song of Solomon 1:2

Happy Valentine's Day! Our job sometimes keeps us from spending time with those we love. Take some time out today to send your love to those who are close to you.

Ever Loving God, we give you thanks for the love you give us. Watch over our family and friends while we are away from them. Allow them to know that they are loved by you and by me. Amen.

FEBRUARY 15

Or do you not know that your body is a temple or sanctuary of the Holy Spirit within you, which you have from God, and that you are not your own? For you were bought with a price; therefore glorify God in your body.

I Corinthians 6: 19 – 20

How much do we abuse our bodies as law enforcement officers? First, we do not get the proper amount of sleep. Between shift work, court appearances and training - your body never gets enough time to rest. Second, we do not eat the proper food: we eat while we are driving, we eat a lot of "fast food", and we don't have much time so we eat quickly. Your body isn't getting the proper nourishment. Third, we drive around smoking cigarettes and drinking coffee. How much can our bodies take? And lastly, we do not exercise enough, if at all. We are not in as good as shape as we should be; we don't take care of injuries. When was the last time you told a criminal to wait while you stretched out before a footchase? We need to take better care of our bodies. It is the only one we have. God wants us to take care of it. Start today.

Great Creator, we thank you for giving us life in these bodies. Send Your Holy Spirit to us to guide in taking care of your temple in each of us. Remind us that you work through us in these forms. Keep us from the temptations of laziness. All of this we ask to glorify you. Amen.

FEBRUARY 16

To whom will you liken me and make me equal, and compare me, as though we were alike?

Isaiah 46:5

We have to remember that we are equal with all those that we encounter. The badge we wear does not separate us out as a different class of people. Equality is a necessity of nature, without which we all lead unhappy lives. It is necessary to understand that we all need proper food, shelter and clothing. Many times, we have to obtain them in different manners. If we rob an individual of their equality with all humankind, whom God ordains, we commit a great crime against humanity ourselves. Remember that you may someday soon be in the same position. Equality is a pressing problem that continues to plague us.

Dear God of Nature, give us the wisdom to look upon each other with equal-ness in our hearts. We know that we are all equal brothers and sisters in the name of Your Son, Jesus Christ. Give us counsel that we never forget our equal relations with all humankind. Amen.

FEBRUARY 17

When I was a child, I spoke like a child, I thought like a child, I reasoned like a child; when I became an adult, I put an end to childish ways.

I Corinthians 13: 11

When we begin our law enforcement career, we start out as rookie officers. After time, we move into the status of veteran. Then, as we near the end of our career, we become old-timers. We move through the stages of our job, just as we move through the stages of life. Hopefully, as an old-timer, we are not making rookie mistakes. We are continually looking inside our self for ways to grow. We also need to help those who are in the younger stages of their career. Taking a rookie officer under your wing and giving them some of your adult guidance may help them learn to become a veteran officer.

God of the Beginning and God of the End, give us guidance as we pass through the stages of our career and of life. Allow us to see our mistakes and to learn from them. Strengthen us to help others along the way. Be with us for the whole journey. Amen.

FEBRUARY 18

The he (Jesus) looked up at his disciples and said: "Blessed are you who are poor, for your is the kingdom of God. Blessed are you who are hungry now, for you will be filled. Blessed are you who weep now, for you will laugh. Blessed are you when people hate you, and when they exclude you, revile you, and defame you (or cast out your name as evil) on account of the Son of Man...."

Luke 6:20-22

Today, the church remembers Martin Luther as a renewer of the church. Martin Luther translated the Bible, reformed the liturgy and lifted up literature in the German language. Luther was concerned that religion needed to be understood by the common person. It is in the difficulties of life that when need to hear the Good News of God, sent to us through Christ. We need to take the message to the poor, hungry, mourning, homeless, and oppressed. We encounter these people everyday in our jobs. We need to reach out to them and help them. Maybe we are the instruments that God will use to make them blessed. Maybe we view ourselves in these classes, also. When we have these feelings, we need to remember that we are still the children of God and God will be with us. Today, think of ways that you can make a difference in someone's life, by meeting them where they are in their situation, as Martin Luther did in his time of the first half of the 16th century.

God of much deliverance, we give you thanks for making us blessed. We thank you for sending people like Martin Luther into the world to remind us that we need to reach the people in their situations. Send your Holy Spirit to be with us in times of our difficulties. May the Holy Spirit remain in us as we help those who are in situations where they need to hear the Good News of your son, Jesus Christ. Amen.

FEBRUARY 19

But be doers of the word, and not merely hearers who deceive themselves.

James 1:22

The Bible, the Word of God, is the inestimable gift from God to man. As Christians, we are called to follow the Word. All that we do should be within the bounds of the Word of God. Sometimes we fall short but we continually strive to do what Scripture calls us to do.

God, Giver of the Word, we ask you to strengthen us in following what you have asked us to do, to follow your Word. The

Word you gave us as a gift that we find in the Scriptures. Encourage us to continue on our life journey in accordance to your Word. Amen.

FEBRUARY 20

You shall not take vengeance or bear a grudge against any of your people, but you shall love your neighbor as yourself: I am the LORD.

Leviticus 19:18

Who are our people? Everyone we come into contact with are our people. We are to remember not to hold a grudge against them. We are to love everyone, as we love ourselves. God gives us this command. We are to see the whole human species as one sacred family. We are to love the high and the low, the rich and the poor in the same manner. Being a family, we are to protect each other, support each other, and render aid to each other. We are not to consider the other person's race, age, religion, gender, nationality, or personal opinion on issues, when giving our love. God loves us. We are called to love all those around us.

God, Creative Source of all beings, we thank you for loving us. Assist us in not holding a grudge or seeking vengeance against anyone else. Inspire us to love all those who we encounter in our life. All of this we do for you, the parent of all people. Amen.

FEBRUARY 21

But speaking the truth in love, we must grow up in every way into him who is the head, into Christ.

Ephesians 4:15

"The truth, the whole truth, and nothing but the truth." It always seems that we are in search of the truth. But what slants do we put on the truth. Is it truth against someone, or is it truth in love? Truth is a divine attribute and foundation of every virtue.

We should use truth in love to regulate our conduct. Truth keeps hypocrisy and deceit from among us. Truth in love means dealing with all people with sincerity, promoting their welfare and lifting them up in every situation. Center your truth in love so that we do not add our own slant to the truth.

God, Fountain of Light and Truth, inspire us to be truthful in love with all people. Take away our own beliefs of the truth, and show us what is right. May we love all others as Christ our Head loves us. Amen.

FEBRUARY 22

You shall not pervert the justice due to the poor in their lawsuits.
Exodus 23:6

We are a symbol of justice. Many people look to us to bring justice into their situations. Justice allows us to render to everyone his or her just due, without distinction. Justice holds a society civil and helps us avoid anarchy. We need to be able to do the proper thing without taking into consideration the personal characteristics of the person.

God, arrayed in justice, help us to judge every situation on its merits, and not based on any personal biases. Inspire us to bring justice to all people. Amen.

FEBRUARY 23

Then he (Christ) opened the fifth seal, I (John) saw under the altar the souls of those who had been slaughtered for the word of God and for the testimony they had given; they cried out with a loud voice, "Sovereign Lord, holy and true, how long will it be before you judge and avenge our blood on the inhabitants of the earth?" They were each given a white robe and told to rest a little longer, until the number would be complete both of their fellow servants (slaves) and of their brothers and sisters, who were soon t be killed as they themselves had been killed.
Revelation 6:9-11

Today, the church remembers Polycarp, Bishop of Smyrna. He was burned at the stake in 156CE for refusing to renounce his Christian faith. His name means "many fruits", and he has been regarded by the church to be one of the "first fruits" of the church to die for Christ, as he is believed to be one of the early martyrs for the faith. Because we work for political entities, we are not permitted to actively proclaim our faith during the performance of our job. That does not mean that we must renounce our faith. If someone asks us, we are permitted to answer about our beliefs. Use any conversation you can to talk about your faith, within the confines of the separation of church and state.

God, Sovereign Lord, holy and true, give us the strength to talk about the faith in an environment that attempts to suppress it. Give us the words when opportunities present themselves. We give you thanks for sending people like Polycarp and all the martyrs, who have given their lives in speaking the Good News. Amen.

FEBRUARY 24

Then they (the apostles) prayed and said, "Lord, you know everyone's heart. Show us which one of these two you have chosen to take the place (the share) in this ministry and apostleship from which Judas turned aside to go to his own place." And they cast lots for them, and the lot fell on Matthias; and he was added to the eleven apostles.

Acts 1:24-26

Today, the church remembers St. Matthias. Matthias was the person chosen by God to take the place of Judas among the Twelve. God chose him to take a place that was vacated by someone else. Many times, God chooses us to take the place of someone who has left. We come upon situations where there needs to be a person to say what to do, make a suggestion, or just listen and show compassion. Sometimes, people who have lost the person who has filled that role call us to these places. God places us in these situations to help fill that role. Sometimes it is only for a few moments. A few times, the relationship is a little longer. Remember that God has chosen you. You are called to do the best you can.

God of prophets and apostles, you know what is in our hearts. You have chosen us to fill roles that are left unfilled. Give us the strength to complete are tasks. We pray to you for wisdom and compassion. Amen

FEBRUARY 25

Now about eight days after these sayings, Jesus took with him Peter and John and James, and went up on the mountain to pray. And while he (Jesus) was praying, the appearance of his face changed, and his clothes became dazzling white. Suddenly they saw two men, Moses and Elijah, talking to him. They appeared in glory and were speaking of his departure, which he was about to accomplish in Jerusalem. Now Peter and his companions were weighed down with sleep; but since they had stayed awake, they saw his glory and the two men who stood with him. Just as they were leaving him, Peter said to Jesus, "Master, it is good for us to be here; let us make three dwellings (or tents), one for you, one for Moses and one for Elijah" - not knowing what he said. While he was saying this, a cloud came and overshadowed them; and they were terrified as they entered the cloud. Then from the cloud came a voice that said, "This is my Son, my Chosen; listen to him!" When the voice had spoke, Jesus was found alone. And they kept silent and in those days told no one any of the things they had seen.

Luke 9:28-36

It is during this time of the year that we remember the transfiguration of our Lord Jesus Christ. As he was praying, his face and clothes changed. Peter, John and James saw Moses and Elijah talking with him. They were amazed at what they saw. How many times do we get to see a change in people? We arrive, talk with people, and then we see a transfiguration in them. When we see this change in someone for the good, we need to take a moment and realize the awesomeness of this event. Take a moment and comment to the person that you have observed the change in them. It may start a positive relationship. It may spark a transfiguration in you.

God, Creator of Goodness and Beauty, allow us to have the sight to see the change in people. Inspire us to recognize the significance in the event. Just as you brought the transfiguration of your Son, Jesus, may we be changed in our experiences. Amen.

FEBRUARY 26

Do not be quick to anger, for anger lodges in the bosom of fools.
Ecclesiastes 7:9

How many times do we get angry when we are at work? Anger is not a bad thing. But we are not supposed to immediately become angry. We are to be slow to anger. Don't let your anger take you over so quickly that you lose control and become a fool. Control your anger, express it in appropriate ways, and then let it go. We tend to have such a short fuse that we cause our own problems. Don't allow anger to be lodged in your bosom.

God, Creator of the light, give us the power to be slow to anger. Do not let us have our anger take control of us. We do not want to be fools. Inspire us to deal with our anger in appropriate ways. Amen.

FEBRUARY 27

Cast all your anxieties on him (God), because he cares for you.
I Peter 5:7

We have many anxieties on the job. We have them about what we may encounter. We have them about what will happen to us in the department over our career. We may even have them about the effects of the job on our family and personal life. But we are to cast them upon God. Give them up to God so that we may do our job in the best way possible. By casting them, we totally give them over.

Eternal God, our Answer, take our anxieties from us. Give us the strength to cast them out to you. Inspire us to be less anxious to serve you in a better way. Amen.

FEBRUARY 28

So we are ambassadors for Christ, since God is making his appeal through us; we entreat you on behalf of Christ, be reconciled to God.
II Corinthians 5:20

During this time of the church called Lent, we are to be focused on reflection of what God has done for us in Christ. We should reflect and rededicate ourselves to the service of his church. We are ambassadors for Christ. Everything we do should reflect well on God through Christ.

God, Desire of all nations, we take this time to reflect upon our own lives. Look into our hearts and reveal to us who we truly are, broken sinners. You have given us the light in your son, Jesus Christ. Allow us to be servants for your church. Amen.

FEBRUARY 29

Now faith is the assurance of things hoped for, the conviction of things not seen.
Hebrews 11:1

We go through our lives seeing the worst that humanity has to offer. We may even begin to doubt that God is with us. But we may be assured that God is here, in the midst of humanity. God assures us that we can have faith in things we don't currently have. God assures us that we can believe in things that we have not seen . Faith exists in the things that we cannot see. Be assured that God is with us as we continue in our journey through humanity.

God, Guide of Humanity, may our faith lead us to the assurance of things hoped for in you. Although we may not see these things, we may believe that you are here with us, in the very midst of humanity. Amen.

MARCH 1

But we must always give thanks to God for you, brothers and sisters beloved by the Lord, because God chose you as the first fruits (from the beginning) for salvation through sanctification by the Spirit and through belief in the truth.

II Thessalonians 2:13

We must always give thanks to God. We have been chosen, not only for who we are but also for what we do. We are saved by the sanctification of the Holy Spirit. We also have belief in the truth. It is the truth for which we work. We must bring truth to the people we encounter. It is not our truth, but God's truth.

God, the First and the Last, we continually give you thanks for the saving actions of you, your Son, and the Holy Spirit. May we be inspired to continue to believe in your truth. May our actions live out this truth in the world. Amen.

MARCH 2

Now the word of the LORD came to me (Jeremiah) saying, "Before I formed you in the womb I knew you, and before you were born I consecrated you; I appointed you a prophet to the nations."

Jeremiah 1:4-5

Today the church remembers John and Charles Wesley. They were brothers and priests of the Church of England. Their ministry brought them to become itinerant preachers, hymn writers and social advocates. They performed their ministry on the fringes of the established church. Their spiritual discipline, or method, included frequent communion, fasting and speaking out for social justice. This discipline is how they received the term "Methodists". John had a religious conversion experience that propelled him to become one of the greatest forces in the 18th century revival movement. The Wesleys gave many of the hymns we sing in church today to us. Charles died in 1788 and John died in 1791.

One of the strongest witnesses we may have is speaking out for those who feel they may not have a voice. We are recognized for our positions in the community because of what we do. We see the injustices first hand. If we take the time to speak up for social justice, people may listen. Today, sing your favorite hymn from the Wesleys. Also, think about an area that you see that may burn in your heart. Reflect on how you may bring about a change just by speaking up.

God, Strength of the weak, we give you thanks for all that we have. We thank you for the gift of song. Song is a manner that we may praise your name. We lift up John and Charles Wesley, not only for the magnificent music they have left us, but also as examples of how we may speak up for social justice. Inspire all of us to use our voices to sing your praises and speak out loud. Amen.

MARCH 3

"...So when you are offering your gift at the altar, if you remember that your brother or sister has something against you, leave your gift there before the altar and go; first be reconciled to your brother and sister, and then come and offer your gift..."
Matthew 5:23-24

This job can make you bitter. We see such a lack of reconciliation that we sometimes lose our compassion for those we encounter. We are supposed to fight against bitterness. We are called to be reconciled with our brothers and sisters, even before we offer gifts to God. When you feel a lack of compassion, take a deep breath, focus and go on. If someone has something against you, go to him or her today, and reconcile.

Eternal God our Answer, take away our bitterness. Send compassion into our lives. Allow us to be reconciled to our brothers and sisters, so that we may grow closer to you. Amen.

MARCH 4

"...I will make of you a great nation, and I will bless you, and make your name great, so that you will be a blessing...."

Genesis 12:2

These words come from the call of God to Abram who will have his name changed to Abraham. God has called each one of us. In that call, we receive the blessing of God, to continue in our profession. It is through us that God will make a great nation. God will make our names great in heaven and we will be a blessing for God. Even in our darkest moments, we need to remember that we have a blessing, and we are a blessing.

God, Shield of Abraham, send us your blessing. Allow us to be a great nation. May our names be great in your eyes, and may we be a blessing for you. Amen.

MARCH 5

Wait for the LORD; be strong, and let your heart take courage; wait for the LORD!

Psalm 27:14

There are many times when we must be bold in our position. Many times, people want to argue with us. We need to state our position boldly, so that there is no mistaking where we stand. God also calls us to take a stand, and be bold. We need to wait for the Lord. All things are done in God's name. We are to be strong and have courage in our heart. But in making these stands, we must make sure our stance is for what is right in the sight of God.

God, Eternal Keeper, stand with us when we are bold. Enable us to be strong and fill our hearts with courage. Allow us to wait and see if our actions are right within your sight. Amen.

MARCH 6

Have no dread of them, for the LORD your God, who is present with you, is a great and awesome God.

There are times in any officer's career when fear sets in during a specific time or circumstance. We remember that we go into places that everyone else is leaving. Fear is not necessarily a bad thing. A little fear allows for bravery to take over. Bravery may inspire us to do our job, even in situations where we may feel uneasy. Don't be afraid to think of yourself as brave every once in a while. We are paid to risk our lives. We do these things for a living. But God is great and awesome. We do these things with the knowledge that God is always with us.

God, Eternal One, we give thanks that you are always with us. Turn our fear into bravery, bravery that allows us to walk into dangerous situations. May others see your light in our actions. Amen.

MARCH 7

O LORD, you have searched me and known me. You know when I sit down and when I rise up; you discern my thoughts from far away. You search out my path and my lying down, and are acquainted with all my ways. Even before a word is on my tongue, O LORD, you know it completely. You hem me in, behind and before, and lay your hand upon me.

Psalm 139: 1-5

Our job is to care for others. But who cares for us? God cares for us. God cares for all aspects of our lives. Others may care, but their care may come and go. But God's loving care will always remain. Take some time today to thank God, and to thank all the people that care for you.

Watchful and caring God, we give you thanks for caring for us. Many times it may seem to us that no one cares. May we always know that you are there. Watch over all those who provide care for us, in many ways. Amen.

MARCH 8

"And whenever you fast, do not look dismal, like the hypocrites, for they disfigure their faces so as to show others that they are fasting. Truly I tell you, they have received their reward. But when you fast, put oil on your head and wash your face, so that your fasting may be seen not by others but by your Father who is in secret; and your Father who sees in secret will reward you (openly).

Matthew 6:16-18

We are in the season of Lent. Many people give up something, or fast, for Lent. In Matthew, Jesus tells us that we should not fast in a manner that brings attention to ourselves. Fasting is a way to show devotion to God. Sometimes people choose things to give up that they don't use often anyway. If we choose something to give up, try to choose an item that may be a little more difficult. When you have a desire to have it, maybe that is a time to think about what God gives you, and offer up a prayer of thanksgiving. Don't worry; if you do give in and have some of what you have given up, it is okay. Give thanks to God for providing it for you. God is not necessarily impressed with our piety. God desires to be worshipped. That was the difficulty for Jesus. The people would show how good they were by showing how pious they were. Jesus said that was being a hypocrite. If you choose to give something up for Lent, do it for the right reasons. Don't do it just to show how good you are.

God, Source of all that we have and all that we are, we give you thanks for all you give us. During this period of Lent, inspire us to reflect upon our lives, and grow into a closer relationship with you. Remind us that we are not supposed to be like the hypocrites. Accept us as we are. Amen.

MARCH 9

Do not be conformed to this world (age), but be transformed by the renewing of your minds, so that you may discern what is the will of God - what is good and acceptable and perfect (what is the good and acceptable and perfect will of God).

Romans 12:2

Being a Christian means that we should not think the way the rest of the world thinks. We have to be able to change our mind to what is right in the will of God. We cannot go to places on our job with a pre-conceived notion of what we are going to do. We have to be willing to listen to all the information we have, and then make the proper decision. Many times, we make up our minds, before we even get there. We need to keep our minds open to change.

God of unchangeable power, we know that you do not change. But inspire in us an open mind to be able to change with the information we receive, to do what is your will. May we always keep an open mind, so that we are not conformed to this age but we may remain focused on what is good and acceptable to you. Amen.

MARCH 10

This is my comfort in my distress, that your promise gives me life.

Psalm 119:50

Many times, we arrive in a situation, and the only thing we can do is provide comfort. Our hands may be tied on what we can do as far as the law is concerned. But we may be able to provide some needed comfort to the person. We may be the one that God sends to this person as an assurance that God promises life. Take some time today to thank those who have shown you comfort.

God of comfort, we thank you for sending people in our lives to give us comfort. Use us to provide comfort to others. We do feel distress in our lives but remind us that you promise us life. Amen.

MARCH 11

Be hospitable to one another without complaining.

I Peter 4:9

We work in a complaining environment. People who call the police department are called "Complainants". We arrive and listen to people complain about someone or something. People speak to our supervisor and complain on us. So what do we do? We complain about everything. We are the worst! We need to learn to be hospitable to others. It will be difficult, because it is not in our nature. But when we complain, we just add to the problem. Today, before you say anything, reflect before you speak. If it is a complaint, choose to remain silent. See how it works.

God, Eternal Ruler, hear our confession that we complain too much. Help us to be more hospitable to others by controlling what we say. Bring peace to our lives. And use us sounding boards for others to air their differences. Amen.

MARCH 12

So we can say with confidence, "The Lord is my helper; I will not be afraid. What can anyone do to me?"

Hebrews 13:6

People look to us with confidence. They trust that we will look out for them. We look to the Lord with confidence. We trust that God will help us. As long as we are focused on what God wants, what can anyone do to us? Walk around with an air of confidence that God is your helper. When people ask what makes you confident, tell them.

God, Eternal Spirit of the Universe, thank you for inspiring confidence in us. We walk knowing that you are our helper. Help us to not be afraid. When you are with us, what can anyone do? Amen.

MARCH 13

Not that I am referring to being in need; for I have learned to be
content with whatever I have. I know what it is to have little, and
I know what it is to have plenty. In any and all circumstances I
have learned the secret of being well-fed and of going hungry, of
having plenty and of being in need. I can do all things through
him who strengthens me.

Philippians 4:11-13

We tend to always be wanting. We always want what we
don't have. The other side always looks better. We need to learn
to be content where we are and with what we have. Don't spend
so much time thinking about how things could be different. Enjoy
what you have. Be careful what you wish for, you may just get it.
And it may not be what you wanted after all.

God, Fountain of All Holiness, we thank you for all that you
have given us. You give us what we need. Inspire us to be content with what we have. Help us to learn to live in the today, and
not the yesterday or tomorrow. Amen.

MARCH 14

"... I hereby command you: Be strong and courageous; do not be
frightened or dismayed, for the LORD your God is with you
wherever you go."

Joshua 1:9

There are times on our job when we feel a little tense. We
may be out of our comfort zone. We may even have a little
bit of fear. But, we must go on and do our job. We can be
assured that God is with us in every situation we encounter.
God allows us to be strong and courageous in difficult situations. God helps us to overcome the fears that we do have.
God assists us overcoming our feelings. God is with us wherever we go.

God, Source of all courage and strength, we thank you for being with us wherever we go. Give us strength and courage to survive our daily lives. Help us to overcome our fears and feelings, so that we may do your work in difficult situations. Amen.

MARCH 15

Blessed be the God and Father of our Lord Jesus Christ, the Father of mercies and the God of all consolations, who consoles us in all our affliction, so that we may be able to console those who are in affliction with the consolation with which we ourselves are consoled by God.

II Corinthians 1:3-4

We all have times of crisis in our lives. God brings us mercy and consolation, which helps us get through these situations. We encounter many people in crisis in our daily lives as law enforcement officers. God places us there to provide mercy and consolation to those we encounter. We give to them what God has given to us. We try to help them in the way God has helped us through our times of crisis.

God, Father of all mercies and consolations, we give you thanks for helping us through our own times of crisis. Use us as your instruments in the world to bring your mercy and consolation to others who are in need. Amen.

MARCH 16

For he will hide me in his shelter in the day of trouble; he will conceal me under the cover of his tent; he will set me high on a rock.

Psalm 27:5

There will be trouble and danger in our lives. The amount of danger and trouble increases for us because of the job we do. God does not take trouble and danger away. But, God does provide shelter for us during these times. When things get tough, we can go to God for protection. We are able to continue in the times of danger and trouble, and continue our work.

God, Shelter from the storm, we give you thanks for providing us protection from the storms of our lives. May we always come to you for cover, concealment and shelter. Amen.

MARCH 17

But how are they to call on one in whom they have not believed? And how are they to believe in one of whom they have never heard? And how are they to hear without someone to proclaim him? And how are they to proclaim him unless they are sent? As it is written, "How beautiful are the feet of those who bring good news!"

Romans 10:14-15

Today is St. Patrick's Day. The holiday comes from the Church's commemorations day celebrating Patrick's life as a bishop and missionary to Ireland. Patrick went to Ireland and brought the Good News to the people there. He used the shamrock to teach people about the Trinity. Many people in our neighborhoods have not heard the Good News that we may have to bring. We walk into the mission fields, bringing God through our words and deeds. Remember that others may encounter God for the first time through you. May we look at ourselves as missionaries, being sent out to proclaim the Gospel. Today, as you celebrate St. Patrick, think of someone you know who may not have heard the story. Do as Patrick did, go to them, and tell them what God and Christ have done for them.

God, The Hope of all the ends of the earth, thank you for sending Patrick and many like him to spread your Good News. Send the Holy Spirit to inspire us to take the story of Christ into the mission fields in which we work. Strengthen us as missionaries for the Gospel message. Amen.

MARCH 18

Even though I walk through the darkest valley (or the valley of the shadow of death), I fear no evil; for you are with me; your rod and your staff- they comfort me.

Psalm 23:4

We see death in many different ways on our job. Some die of natural causes after living a long life. Others die young, tragically, with little time spent on this earth. We see these people in their final stages on this earth. You can only see so much death before it begins to get to you. We need to talk about our feelings, even if it is only to God. We can walk through the valley of the shadow of death. We need to be strong, and provide comfort to those we encounter there with us in the valley. But, when death begins to take its toll on us, we need to turn to the one who is our strength.

God, Strength of our life, be with us as we walk around death. Even though we may have fear, we know that you are with us. Send comfort to us and to those we encounter. May we all remember that we have everlasting life in you. Amen.

MARCH 19

Now the birth of Jesus the Messiah (Jesus Christ) took place in this way. When his mother Mary had been engaged to Joseph, but before they lived together, she was found to be with child from the Holy Spirit. Her husband Joseph, being a righteous man and unwilling to expose her to public disgrace, planned to dismiss her quietly. But just when he had resolved to do this, an angel of the Lord appeared to him in a dream and said, "Joseph, son of David, do not be afraid to take Mary as your wife, for the child conceived in her is from the Holy Spirit. She will bear a son, and you are to name him Jesus, for he will save his people from their sins." All this took place to fulfill what had been spoken by the Lord through the prophet: "Look, the virgin shall conceive and bear a son, and they shall name him Emmanuel," which means,

"God is with us." When Joseph awoke from sleep, he did as the angel of the Lord commanded him; he took her as his wife, but had no marital relations with her until she had borne a son (her firstborn son); and he named him Jesus.

Matthew 1:18-25

Today, the church remembers Joseph, husband of Mary and Guardian of our Lord. Joseph was a carpenter who is described in the Bible as an honest and devout man. Joseph listened to the angel of the Lord. He kept Mary as his wife, showed care for her, and took Jesus as his adopted son. Joseph is not mentioned once Jesus becomes an adult. Today, take some time to think about your relationship with your father. Today would be an excellent day to talk to him, whether you have a good relationship or one that is strained. If you are a father, take some time today and spend it with your kids. Tell them how much you love them.

God, Holy Parent, we give you thanks for sending people to this world who are strong in faith, like Joseph. Send to us the Holy Spirit to fill us with love so that we may have right relationships with our parents and with our children. Inspire us to respond to you when you send your angels to us. Amen.

MARCH 20

He heals the brokenhearted and binds up their wounds.

Psalm 147:3

Many of us suffer from some sort of depression. We see many things in our jobs. Many times it takes a toll on us. We turn to many things to deaden the pain but then, depression may set in. We can survive depression. When we are broken, God can heal us. When we suffer from the wounds of depression, God can mend us. We have to be willing to accept these gifts. We can win, with the help of God.

God, Giver of health and salvation, we give you thanks for being with us during our times of depression. Heal our broken hearts and mend our wounds. We realize we cannot overcome these things on our own. Be with us to make us healthier servants for your service. Amen.

MARCH 21

"No one can serve two masters; for a slave will either hate the one and love the other, or be devoted to the one and despise the other. You cannot serve God and wealth...."

Matthew 6:24

People who go into law enforcement tend to be devoted to our jobs. We are definitely not in this job for the money. We want to serve justice and do the right thing. We need to be devoted to our jobs through God. Everything we do should express God's love. Don't be devoted to the money, or the power, or the authority, or the uniform, or the badge and gun. Be devoted to God and do the best job you can do.

God, Fountain of Everlasting Light, we give you thanks for your devotion to us. May we always be devoted to you in everything we do. Remind us when we begin to focus on other masters in our lives. Help us to remove those feelings, so that we may do your work in the world. Amen.

MARCH 22

For the mountains may depart and the hills be removed, but my steadfast love shall not depart from you, and my covenant of peace shall not be removed, says the LORD, who has compassion on you.

Isaiah 54:10

We suffer many disappointments in our lives. We may not get the promotion or the good assignment. Our careers may not move the way we expected. Our personal relationships may not work out the way we wanted. Our lives may not be all we expected them to be. These disappointments will happen to us along the way. But remember that God is always with us. God will be with us in the deepest lows, and when we reach the highest highs. Today, think of a time that God helped you through a disappointing time in your life.

God of all compassion, we give you thanks for being with us during the bad and the good times. Help us to overcome our times of disappointment. Let us see the light of the good you provide in our lives. Amen.

MARCH 23

Why are you cast down, o my soul, and why are you disquieted within me? Hope in God; for I shall again praise him, my help and my God.

Psalm 43:5

How many times have you been discouraged? You can get pretty discouraged doing this job. Sometimes it feels like you are not even making any difference. Nothing ever changes. Even when we are discouraged with what we do, we can always know that God is not discouraged in us. Even in our discouragement, we can have hope in God, praise God, and ask God for help in our life. Today, think of a time you were discouraged, and reflect on how God may have helped you through it.

God, Helper of all persons, we give you thanks and praise for being with us, even in our times our discouragement. We ask for your help to assist us through the difficult times. Amen.

MARCH 24

For on holy mountains, the mountain height of Israel, says the Lord GOD, there all the house of Israel, all of them, shall serve me in the land; there I will accept them, and there I will require your contributions and the choicest of your gifts, with all your sacred things. As a pleasing odor I will accept you, when I bring you out from the peoples, and gather you out of the countries where you have been scattered; and I will manifest my holiness among you in the sight of the nations. You shall know that I am the LORD, when I bring you into the land of Israel, the country that I swore to give to your ancestors.

Ezekiel 20:40-42

Today, the church remembers Oscar Romero, Bishop of El Salvador. He is remembered as an advocate for the poor in El Salvador. After being appointed bishop he preached against the political repression in his country. He, other priests and church workers were considered traitors for their bold stance on justice, especially defending the rights of the poor. Romero received threats on his life for several years. Romero was assassinated while presiding at the Eucharist on March 24, 1980. He is remembered as a martyr who gave his life on behalf of the powerless in his country. Where are the powerless in our society? Our occupation brings us in contact with those who are powerless. Do we serve as their voice in advocating justice, or do we continue the oppression? When we see oppression, do we really believe in the equality of all people created in the image of God, or do we turn our heads and believe that people get what they deserve. Even though we work for the government, we are still able to help those who are more powerless than we. Wearing a badge does give us power and authority. We need to make sure that we are not overstepping our bounds and contributing to the oppression of others.

God of Power and Splendor, we give you thanks for people who stand up for justice, like Bishop Oscar Romero. Inspire us to stand up, and help those who are in positions less favored than our own. Allow us to use our power and authority in appropriate ways in your service. Amen.

MARCH 25

The angel (Gabriel) said to her, "Do not be afraid, Mary, for you have found favor with God. And now, you will conceive in your womb and bear a son, and you will name him Jesus...."

Luke 1:30-31

Today, the church celebrates the Annunciation of our Lord. We remember when the angel Gabriel came to a young, unmarried, Mary, and told her she would bear a son. This would change her life, and history. When has an angel come to you and said that your life would change? We don't always recognize angels when they appear to us. We discredit their message. We tend not to change our lives. Our faith calls us to change our lives when God tells us to through messengers. Today, think of times that angels may have be telling you that your life is going to change.

God, Fountain of light and truth, pour your grace into our hearts. As we remember the announcement of your son by Gabriel, may we see the angels that you send to us. Help us to change our lives in the ways that you ask. Amen.

MARCH 26

"For God so loved the world that he gave his only Son, so that everyone who believes in him may not perish but may have eternal life."

John 3:16

This is probably the most familiar passage in the Bible. But do we really understand it? God loved the world so much, that God would send his only son, to die, so that everyone may have eternal life and live with God forever. Never forget that God loves you that much. At times, it may not seem like it to us, but God does. God sent a son so that we may live with him forever. Our times here on earth may not be the greatest. But we have a future that is great beyond understanding.

God, Giver of life and health, we thank you for loving us. Loving us so much that you sent your son to die for us, so that we may live with you forever. Help us to remember how much you really love us. And may we also share that love with the entire world. Amen.

MARCH 27

For by grace you have been saved through faith, and this is not your own doing; it is a gift of God - not the result of works, so that no one may boast.

Ephesians 2:8-9

God has given us the gift of salvation, through our faith. Our faith is important to us. We need to remember that there is nothing we can do to gain access to heaven. It is through God's gift to us that we may have eternal life. So, do not boast because you are saved, but be humble because you have received the greatest gift there is.

God, Source of salvation, we thank you for giving us the gift of being saved. Help us to remain faithful to your promise. Guide us in our lives that we may not become arrogant and boast of our future. Assist us in remembering it is you, not us that gain us eternal life. Amen.

MARCH 28

But you, O Lord, are a God merciful and gracious, slow to anger and abounding in steadfast love and faithfulness.

Psalm 86:15

God has made promises to us. Even though we may break promises to God, God never breaks them to us. God is always merciful and gracious to us. Times may seem dark and gloomy, but God is still with us. God's love for us abounds, and God is slow to get mad at us. God will be faithful to the promises made to us.

God of steadfastness and encouragement, we thank you for being faithful to us. Forgive us when we may get angry with you. We know you are slow to anger with us. Your love constantly surrounds us. May we be as gracious and merciful to others as you are to us. Amen.

MARCH 29

So Jesus called them (the disciples) and said to them, " You know that among the Gentiles those whom they recognize as their rulers lord it over them, and their great ones are tyrants over them. But it is not so among you; but whoever wishes to become great among you must be your servant, and whoever wishes to be first among you must be slave of all. For the Son of Man came not to be served but to serve, and to give his life a ransom for many."

Mark 10:42-45

Today, the Church remembers Hans Nielsen Hauge. After a mystical experience Hauge began preaching throughout Norway. His writings emphasized a person's vocation as service to God. He urged people to remain faithful with emphasis on private prayer, devotional reading, Bible study, singing and preaching. Do you see working in law enforcement as being God's minister in the world? We are serving God in our profession. We are able to contact so many people in situations where they need to hear the Good News. We should not take a position that we are lording over people because of the authority the government gives us. We should remain servants for all. We can still do our jobs effectively; we just need to keep in mind who we serve. We keep this on our minds by following Hauge's requests. We need to have private prayer everyday. This should contain prayers for others and our confession of our sins. We need to continue to study the Bible. The more we read it, the more we find. We need to set up daily devotion time. Even if it committing to reading this devotional everyday. We need to always be singing and proclaiming the Gospel given to us by God, through Christ with the Holy Spirit. Today, evaluate your busy life. Set aside specific times, so that everyday, there is a time to pray, to read the Bible, to do your devotions, and sing the praises of God.

God of this day, we give you thanks for our jobs that we may serve you in our vocations. Allow us to be servants of all, being your instruments in the world. Fill us with the songs and words to proclaim your Good News. Help us remain faithful by reading your Word, praying, and giving devotion to you. We thank you for sending people like Hans Nielsen Hauge, to remind us how we are to live our lives. Amen.

MARCH 30

And because you are children, God has sent the Spirit of his Son into our hearts, crying, "Abba! Father!" So you are no longer a slave but a child, and if a child then also an heir through God (an heir of God through Christ).

Galatians 4:6-7

We are all God's children. Everyone with whom we come into contact is a child of God. God has sent the Holy Spirit through Christ into our hearts. We need to remember the Spirit in us as we go about our days. We are heirs of God's Kingdom through Christ.

Abba, Father, we thank you for freeing us to be your children. Allow the Holy Spirit to inspire our lives and refresh our hearts as we travel our paths. All of this, we ask through your Son, Jesus Christ. Amen.

MARCH 31

"...do not fear, for I am with you, do not be afraid, for I am your God; I will strengthen you, I will help you, I will uphold you with my victorious right hand."

Isaiah 41:10

There are many times in our job that we have fear. Fear is a human emotion. We have to learn to work through our fears, and continue doing our jobs. God reminds us to not have fear because God is with us. God will help us work through our fears. God will uphold us as we walk through those fearful places. The next time you are fearful, begin a dialogue with God to help calm your fears.

God, Giver of every good and perfect gift, we ask you to be with us during our times of fear. Strengthen and help us overcome our fears to complete our tasks. We give you thanks for upholding us at all times, especially when we are afraid. Amen.

APRIL 1

The fear of the LORD is the beginning of knowledge; fools despise wisdom and instruction.

Proverbs 1:7

How many times have we been called "April Fool"? We play pranks on each other to show how gullible we are. But we can't be called a fool unless we know otherwise. Knowledge brings the ability to become a fool. Fools despise knowing and learning. It is in the knowing and learning that we have a greater chance of being a fool. Trust in the Lord. Follow God's way and you will not be a fool.

God, giver of knowledge, we give you thanks for providing us with the understanding and wisdom needed to accomplish our tasks. Allow us to use this knowledge in ways that glorify you. Send the Holy Spirit to watch over us so that we may not become fools. Amen.

APRIL 2

If we say that we have no sin, we deceive ourselves, and the truth is not in us. If we confess our sins, he who is faithful and just will forgive us ours and cleanse us from all unrighteousness. If we say that we have not sinned, we make him a liar, and his word is not in us.

I John 1:8-10

These are familiar words for many of us. This passage appears in the Confession of Sins portion of many Christian liturgies. We are reminded that we are sinful people. We just need to be honest with God. By confessing sins, we should actually name them. God knows what our sins are but we need to name them for ourselves, that we may remind ourselves what we do that makes us fall short. God is faithful and just. When we tell the truth, God forgives our sins and cleanses us from all wrongdoing. This doesn't mean that we should go on sinning because we know we can confess and be forgiven. But when we do fall short, God makes things right between us. Take time today to make a confession of your sins. You are not telling God anything that God doesn't already know. Make a full confession, naming your sins, and ask for forgiveness.

Most merciful God, we confess that we are sinners in what we think, say and do. We have done things that are wrong, and not done things that that we should have. We are sorry. Have mercy on us and forgive us. Amen.

APRIL 3

There the angel of the LORD appeared to him (Moses) in a flame of fire out of a bush; he looked, and the bush was blazing, yet it was not consumed. Then Moses said, "I must turn aside and look at this great sight, and see why the bush is not burned up." When the LORD saw that he had turned aside to see, God called to him out of the bush, "Moses, Moses!" And he said, "Here I am!" Then He (God) said, "Come no closer! Remove the sandals from your feet, for the place on which you are standing is holy ground."

Exodus 3: 2 – 5

There are times in our profession that we truly see miracles happen. It is at these times that we should probably take off our boots or shoes, because we are on holy ground. Medics bringing someone back from a heart attack. Doctors and nurses in the ER treating someone out of a traffic crash. Going into a house and seeing a teenager taking care of the younger children because the parents are drunk or drugged up. It is during times like these that we need to remember that God is able to work through individuals. We never know when we will arrive at the scene of a "burning bush".

Dear Lord, You called Moses to take off his sandals on holy ground, and to lead his people out of bondage. You call us to take off our shoes and lead your people to safety. Allow us to have reverence for the work you do through others. And allow us to do your work. Amen.

APRIL 4

For no one can lay any foundation other than the one that has been laid; that foundation is Jesus Christ.

1 Corinthians 3:11

Today, the church remembers Benedict the African, a confessor of his faith. Benedict was born a slave on the island of Sicily. After he was freed, he joined a community of hermits. After leading the group, he chose to return to his former position in the community as cook. Benedict proclaims his faith in Jesus Christ well. Many visitors came to hear the voice of this humble cook. He is also known as Benedict the Moor. He is remembered for his patience and understanding when confronted with racial prejudice. Benedict died in 1589. We still see racial prejudice today. We encounter many people who act out their prejudices. We need to remember not to encounter hate with hate. When you encounter prejudice, return to your firm foundation, which is Christ. Remember that Christ died for all of us. Try to find an understanding with people who speak with prejudice. Explain to them that we are all equal and the same in the eyes of God. Today, reflect upon your own feelings, and attempt to resolve any prejudices you might hold.

God, the Mind that unifies all creation, we give you thanks for inspiring those who speak out against racial prejudice. Allow us all to remove prejudice from our hearts. Send the Holy Spirit upon us that we may be filled with a firm foundation, which is Jesus Christ. Amen.

APRIL 5

To do righteousness and justice is more acceptable to the LORD than sacrifice.

Proverbs 21:3

Sometimes we lose sight of what we are to do in our jobs. We become renegades doing whatever we want. Then, we reconcile ourselves by going to church and saying we'll change. But we don't. We need to remember that God accepts people doing justice, when it is oriented in the proper direction. What we do for a living is righteous, if we do it with God in our heart. God would rather we do our jobs properly, than being outside the scope and making promises we may or may not keep.

Dear LORD, help me to remember what I am here to do. Allow me to be righteous in your sight by doing justice in your name. Even though I make promises to change, many times I do not. Give me the sight to see your will. Amen.

APRIL 6

In that day the LORD of hosts will be a garland of glory, and a diadem of beauty, to the remnant of his people;

Isaiah 28:5

Today the church remembers Albrecht Durer and Michelangelo Buonarroti. Durer was a Catholic engraver and painter whose work is a close examination of the beauty of creation. He presented this splendor in the human body, animals, grass and flowers. Michelangelo is probably the most famous Renaissance artist. He was known as a painter, sculptor, architect, and poet. His art embodied the human dignity. It was believed that both of the artists were divinely inspired in their works. Durer died in 1528 and Michelangelo in 1564. How many images do we see each day that do not seem inspired by God? We need to remember to turn our sight to the beauty of creation that God has given us. It is too easy to look at the images that we should not see. Today, concentrate on removing the images that may be offensive, whether they are on television, print, or in the world at large.

God, Source of creation, we give you thanks for providing us with the beauty of the world. You provide us with artists that enable us to see you in your creative work. Help us to turn our sight to what is beautiful to you. Amen.

APRIL 7

It is better to be of a lowly spirit among the poor than to divide the spoil with the proud.

Proverbs 16:19

We need to remember that the badge that we wear every day does not give us special privileges. We do not have the right to think we deserve better than others. We need to remain humble, even in the most difficult of circumstances. There are many times we could show our authority for the sake of acting proud. "I have the badge!" is what we tell people. Humility in all situations should be our starting point.

All Powerful God, help us to remain humble in your service. Remind us that we should be comfortable with the poor and not spoiled by the proud. It is difficult to remain humble when everyone knows what we do. Amen.

APRIL 8

"...Keep awake therefore, for you do not know on what day (or at what hour) your Lord is coming...."

Matthew 24:42

We all think about the future. How will things be tomorrow, in a month, a year, and at retirement? But that thinking leads us to put too many things off. We always think that we have more time. Jesus tells us that we do not know when he will return. We should live every day like it is the last, even though there may be a tomorrow. We need to tell others the things we need to say. We need to complete the tasks that need to be done. We need to make confession and ask for forgiveness for our sins. We need to make ourselves right with God, our neighbors, and ourselves every day, because we never know when it will be our last. Today, take some time and do all the tasks that you have been putting off. Talk to the people that should hear from you. Tell God everything you have to say.

God of all times and places; we do not know when you will send your son to return. We give you thanks for the time you have given us. We put off too many things in our lives. Send the Holy Spirit to inspire and help us complete all that we have to say and do. Aid us in living every day as our last, looking for the return of your son, our Savior and Lord, Jesus Christ. Amen.

APRIL 9

"...As you (God) have sent me (Jesus) into the world, so I have sent them (the disciples) into the world. And for their sakes I sanctify myself, so that they also may be sanctified in truth. I ask not only on behalf of these, but also on behalf of those who will believe in me through their word, that they may be one. As you, Father, are in me and I am in you, may they also be (one) in us, so that the world may believe that you have sent me. The glory that you have given me I have given them, so that they may be one, as we are one, I in them and you in me, that they may become completely one, so that the world may know that you have sent me and have loved them even as you have loved me...."
John 17:18-23

Today, the church remembers Dietrich Bonhoeffer. Bonhoeffer was a German theologian who resisted the Nazis and was linked to a failed assassination plot against Hitler. Bonhoeffer was one of the founders of the Confessing Church, which spoke out against the Nazis. He was arrest in 1943 for his antiwar activities and was taken to a concentration camp, and then to prison. Bonhoeffer wrote many books during his life that discuss the importance of remaining true to the faith. Bonhoeffer patiently walked to the gallows on this day in 1945 where he was executed. As he was being hanged, the guns of the allied forces could be heard in the distance. They would arrive days later to liberate the prison. Bonhoeffer's courageous life and death is a strong witness to the life, death and resurrection of Jesus Christ. We too, should be God's agents of truth in the world. We need to stand up for what is right in God's eyes. As we are in this Easter season, let us reflect on what God has done for us, through Christ and allow the Holy Spirit to move us to stand up for truth and justice.

Almighty God, your Holy Spirit gives the word of wisdom, the word of knowledge and the word of faith. We give you thanks for imparting those gifts to us. We see your grace in the world by your sending servants like Dietrich Bonhoeffer. We pray that by his teachings, we can be brought to a fuller understanding of truth, which can only be seen through your Son, Jesus Christ. Inspire us to be your agents of truth. Amen.

APRIL 10

Trust in the LORD with all your heart, and do not rely on your own insight. In all your ways acknowledge him, and he will make straight your paths.

Proverbs 3:5-6

We are a very non-trusting group. We don't trust many people at all. We trust our family, our partners, and ourselves. We do what we think is best. But do we always know what is best? We branch out on our own, trusting no one but ourselves, not even God. We should trust in God. God knows what is best in each situation. In everything we do, we need to acknowledge God's presence in it. We need to open ourselves up to the will of God to work through us. Not making a situation where the will of God has to work despite us. If we can't trust anybody, sometimes not even ourselves, we can always trust in God. Today, stop for just a moment and pray for God's will in each decision you make.

God of all being, we give you thanks for knowing how we may best serve your will. Send the Holy Spirit to us so that we may trust in you, to do what you know is the best, and to give you praise. Amen.

APRIL 11

If any of you is lacking in wisdom, ask God, who gives to all generously and ungrudgingly, and it will be given you.

James 1:5

We look in many places for guidance. We ask family members, friends, sometimes even strangers, to give us guidance in certain matters. But how often do we ask God for guidance? God knows what is best for us. We need to be open to the wisdom that God gives to us. And when we receive this guidance from God, we should use it. Sometimes, we ask God to answer specifics. We gain an understanding on the specific item through prayer. But is it what we wanted to hear, or what God was telling us. We tend to take the understanding we have through prayer, and decide in favor of other directions. In essence, we tell God that God doesn't understand what is going on. Today, ask God to give you guidance in all your decisions, either large or small. And when you receive the guidance, use it.

God, Guide of humanity, we thank you for knowing what is best for us. Help us when we ask you for guidance. Inspire us to follow your direction for you give generously when we ask for understanding. Amen.

APRIL 12

For this perishable body must put on imperishability, and this mortal body must put on immortality.

I Corinthians 15:53

We believe that we have to put mortality out of our minds to do our job. If we think about mortality, it may cause us to hesitate and someone may get hurt. This is a natural happening. We need to remember that God is what will provide us with immortality. We will someday leave these bodies but we rest on the promise of God that we will have eternal life.

Ever living God, Give us the strength to do our jobs in the face of mortality. Assist us in removing doubt from our minds and assure us that you promise everlasting life. Amen.

APRIL 13

Then I acknowledge my sin to you, and I did not hide my iniquity; I said, "I will confess my transgressions to the LORD," and you forgave the guilt of my sin.

Psalm 32:5

Many of us confess our sins, but we still carry around the guilt that we have for committing them. We may do something wrong, make it right, and make confession; but we still feel guilty. When we confess our sins, God not only forgives us, but God also takes away the guilt that is associated with it. It is not the sin itself that eats away at us, but it is carrying around the guilt. Today, confess your sins, and then allow yourself to be forgiven and to have the guilt taken away.

God of grace and glory, we offer our confessions up to you. We ask that you forgive us our sins and take away our guilt. We want to be right with you and be a whole person that you created. We give you thanks for your forgiveness and cleansing acts. Amen.

APRIL 14

So we do not lose heart. Even though our outer nature is wasting away, our inner nature is being renewed day by day.

2 Corinthians 4:16

This job takes a toll on our physical bodies. The nature of what we do affects our bodies in negative ways. We may, or may not try to stay in shape. We should strive to be in the best possible condition we can be. But as age and wear takes over, we can remember that although our outside may be wasting away, our inner self can be renewed every day through God. We need to work just as hard to maintain our inner spiritual nature as much as we do our outer physical one. The outside will waste away, but God always refreshes our inner being.

God of all flesh, we give you thanks for providing us with bodies to do your will. Strengthen us to accomplish our jobs in your service. As our bodies wither, refresh our spirit everyday, so that we may be renewed in you. Amen.

APRIL 14

"... he will wipe every tear from their eyes. Death will be no more; mourning and crying and pain will be no more, for the first things have passed away."

Revelation 21:4

At work, we see quite a lot of the "first things". We see the hurt, pain and suffering. Many times, we even experience them ourselves. We cannot escape these feelings here on earth. We work through them. But, there will be a time when all these feelings will not exist. God will wipe our face, and welcome us into living in heaven, forever.

God of Eternal Might, we ask you to be with us as we try to struggle through the difficult times of our lives. Give us the strength to work through all our sufferings. We look forward to living with you in eternity and we give you thanks for providing us with a heaven that will never pass away. Amen.

APRIL 15

"And To the angel of the church in Laodicea write: The words of the Amen, the faithful and true witness, the origin (or beginning) of God's creation:..."

Revelation 3:14

We use "Amen" to conclude prayer. We may even use it as a way to show agreement. It may also be a symbol of completion and establishment of the full realization of all that God has created. We may see evidence of God's creation at work. Maybe we should take a moment when we encounter God's creation, to verbally say, "Amen."

God, Creator of All, open our eyes to see all the forms of your great creation. Inspire in us the awe to feel emotion from that which you knew from the very beginning of creation. Move us to say, Amen.

APRIL 16

When they were approaching Jerusalem, at Bethphage and Bethany, near the Mount of Olives, he (Jesus) sent two of his disciples and said to them, "Go into the village ahead of you, and immediately as you enter it, you will find tied there a colt that has never been ridden; untie it and bring it. If anyone says to you, "Why are you doing this? Just say this, 'The Lord needs it and will send it back here immediately.'" They went away and found a colt tied neat a door, outside in the street. As they were untying it, some of the bystanders said to them, "What are you doing, untying the colt?" They told them what Jesus had said; and they allowed them to take it. Then they brought the colt to Jesus and threw their cloaks on it; and he sat on it. Many people spread their cloaks on the road, and others spread leafy branches that they had cut in the fields. Then those who went ahead and those who followed were shouting, "Hosanna! Blessed is the one who comes in the name of the Lord! Blessed is the coming kingdom of our ancestor David! Hosanna in the highest heaven!" Then he entered Jerusalem and went into the temple; and when he had looked around at everything, as it was already late, he went out to Bethany with the twelve.

Mark 11:1-11

During this Easter season, we remember Jesus' triumphal entry into Jerusalem. We call it Palm Sunday. Think back and see if you can remember when Jesus rode into your life. He rode into your life at baptism, but can you remember when you realized Jesus was in your life? Today, take some time and think about all the times that Jesus has ridden into your life.

Almighty God, we give you thanks for sending your son, Jesus Christ, to ride into Jerusalem, and to ride into each one of our lives. Strengthen us so that we may be servants in Jesus' Church. Inspire us with the Holy Spirit that we may provide an avenue for Jesus to ride into the lives of others. Amen.

APRIL 17

"Come to me, all you that are weary and are carrying heavy burdens, and I will give you rest...."

Matthew 11:28

Being a Christian doesn't mean that we don't have hurts and pains in our lives. The very course of living assures us that we will have difficulties. But, Jesus tells us that when we can't take it anymore, that he will bear our burdens. When we come to Christ with our problems, Jesus will lift them from us. That doesn't mean that is the end of problems. It means, for a time, we may have rest. Today, take some time to give your hurts and pains to Christ, so that you may get some rest.

God of Compassion, we give you thanks, for sending your son to us, to take our burdens upon him and give us rest. Be with us in our times of hurt. Send your Holy Spirit upon us to work through our pains. And when we can't take it anymore, may we be directed to you through your son, by the power of the Holy Spirit. Amen.

APRIL 18

Rejoice in hope, be patient in suffering, persevere in prayer.

Romans 12:12

Many times, we look at the situations we encounter and believe there is no hope for change. We respond to the same addresses, on the same calls, dealing with the same people over and over again. We do not have hope for change. Scripture calls us to have hope. Never give up hope for anything. It may take awhile, but change may occur. Even though there is suffering, try to be patient. It does not say you don't experience suffering. It says that we will suffer, but be patient. And also, continue to pray.

God of Hope and Joy, we ask you to instill hope in us, even in difficult situations. Inspire us to be patient in our suffering. And as we pray now, guide us in bringing everything to you in prayer. Amen.

APRIL 19

In the fear of the LORD one has strong confidence, and one's children will have a refuge.

Proverbs 14:26

There are many times that we have insecurities. We feel insecure at work, we feel insecure in our personal life, we may even feel insecure in our relationship with God. But even in our insecurities, we have a place to go to be safe. Although we may not be as sure about our relationship with God, God is secure in the relationship with us. God provides us with a place to go, when we believe there is nowhere else. God has a strong confidence in us, and we are God's children. Today, when you begin to feel a little insecure about something, take some time to talk to God about those feelings. God will provide a safe place to talk.

God our Companion, we give you thanks for having confidence in us. Send your Holy Spirit to us so that we may have a safe place when we feel insecure. Allow us to continue our service even when we are not sure about ourselves. Amen.

APRIL 20

For I (Paul) received from the Lord what I also handed on to you, that the Lord Jesus on the night when he was betrayed took a loaf of bread, and when he had given thanks, he broke it and said, "This is my body that is for (or is broken for) you. Do this in remembrance of me." In the same way he took the cup also, after supper, saying, "This cup is the new covenant in my blood. Do this, as often as you drink it in remembrance of me." For as often as you eat this bread and drink the cup, you proclaim the Lord's death until he comes.

1 Corinthians 11:23-26

These are familiar words. It is what Jesus said to his disciples at the Last Supper, which is where we have received the practice of Communion. We commemorate the Last Supper on Maundy Thursday. But here we quote from Paul. This is the only place in Paul's letters where he talks about Jesus before his death. Even Paul viewed this event as very important for the church. The taking of Communion is important for us. Many of us work during hours of the day and days of the week that most people do not. Sometimes, we skip going to church and receiving Communion so that we may do other things. Try to find a way to make going to church and taking Communion a regular part of your life, even if you are only able to go once a month.

Lord God, your son left us a wonderful sacrament in memorial of his suffering and death for us. May Christ's body and blood in Communion work in us so that we may live a life where we proclaim the forgiveness of sins through him. Amen.

APRIL 21

What then are we to say about these things? If God is for us, who is against us?

Romans 8:31

Sometimes we feel that we are alone in our position. We believe that no one else is on our side. But, we find that God is on side. God supports what we are doing. As long as we are within bounds that are set down for us, we may have faith that we receive the blessings of God in what we do.

God, Creator and Preserver of all humankind, we thank you for being on our side. We give you praise for sending your Son for us. We ask that you guide us in all that we do, that all may see that we are doing your will. Amen.

APRIL 22

Jesus, knowing that the Father had given all things into his hands, and that he had come from God and was going to God, got up from the table (from supper), took off his outer robe, and tied a towel around himself. Then he poured water into a basin and began to wash the disciples' feet and to wipe them with the towel that was tied around him. He came to Simon Peter, who said to him, "Lord, are you going to wash my feet?" Jesus answered, "You do not know now what I am doing, but later you will understand." Peter said to him, "You will never wash my feet." Jesus answered, "Unless I wash you, you have no share with me." Simon Peter said to him, "Lord, not my feet only but also my hands and my head!" Jesus said to him, "One who has bathed does not need to wash, except for the feet, but is entirely clean. And you are clean, though not all of you." For he knew who was to betray him; for this reason he said, "Not all of you are clean." After he had washed their feet, had put on his robe, and had returned to the table, he said to them, "Do you know what I have done to you? You call me Teacher and Lord - and you are right, for that is what I am. So if I, your Lord and Teacher have washed your feet, you also ought to wash one another's feet. For I have set you an example, that you also should do as I have done to you. Very truly, I tell you, servants (or slaves) are not greater than their master, nor are messengers greater than the one who sent them. If you know these things, you are blessed if you do them...."

John 13:3-17

John's Gospel records this account of Jesus' Last Supper with his disciples. Jesus humbled himself by washing their feet. Jesus reminded his disciples that they are to serve others. We are servants of the public. We are not above those whom we serve. We may think at times that we are far better, but in reality, we are there to serve them. We need to accomplish our tasks with humility, not power and authority. We should, in good conscience, be able to wash the feet of anyone we encounter. We are called to live out our Christian life in this vocation. Being in law enforcement allows us to get into places and meet people that may not have any relationship with God. We are God's messengers; we are also the servants of the people. We need to always remember our place, as Christ did.

God, our Lord and Teacher, thank you for sending your son, Jesus, to show us examples of how we are to live. Send the Holy Spirit to us, that we may always remember our place. We are your messengers, and we are the servants of all. Amen.

APRIL 23

Let love be genuine; hate what is evil, hold fast to what is good; love one another with mutual affection; outdo one another in showing honor.

Romans 12:9-10

Today the church remembers Toyohiko Kagawa. Kagawa's family disavowed him when he became a Christian. During his time in seminary, he became aware of his Christian responsibilities in the face of all that was wrong in the world. He worked on behalf of those who lived in slums, labor unions, governmental relief agencies, and religious social welfare organizations. He was arrested for his efforts to reconcile Japan and China after the Japanese attack in 1940. Kagawa died in 1960. Our job takes us into some of the very same places that Kagawa worked. Do we stand up for the rights of those who have less than we do? Can we love one another with mutual affection? Even if the other person doesn't appear to be showing love to us, we should let our love be genuine and love them anyway. Take some time today and reflect on how you may be able to help the poor and oppressed.

God, Guide of the meek, we give you thanks for all that you have given us. We lift up Toyohiko Kagawa and all those who witness to your word by assisting those who are less fortunate. Inspire us to walk in those same areas. May we show the genuine love to all, that you show to us. Amen.

APRIL 24

"Blessed are those who mourn, for they will be comforted."
Matthew 5:4

We see a lot of death in our jobs. We are around people who are suffering from grief. We need to handle the bereaved with a sense of added care. We should not just go on with our business in a stiff manner. We should take time and comfort those who are suffering a loss. We may be the ones that God has sent to comfort those who mourn.

God of all comfort, we ask you to be with all those who grieve the loss of one type or another. Allow us to be a calming presence to help them in their time of bereavement. Amen.

APRIL 25

The beginning of the good news (gospel) of Jesus Christ, the Son of God.

Mark 1:1

This is the first verse of Mark's Gospel. Today, the church remembers St. Mark the Evangelist. Although Mark was not an apostle, he was probably a member of one of the earliest Christian communities. The Gospel that is attributed to Mark is brief and direct. Mark's Gospel is believed by many to be the first Gospel written. Its emphasis is on the suffering of Jesus. The Gospel of Mark challenges the reader to share in Jesus' sufferings. Mark was martyred in Alexandria. His symbol is the winged lion. Where is the beginning of the Gospel for you? When did you first hear the Good News of Jesus Christ? Today, reflect on how the good news of Jesus has affected your life. Think of opportunities that you may be able to share that good news with someone else.

God of all ages past, present and future, you have enriched your church with Mark's proclamation of the Gospel. Give us grace to believe firmly in the good news of salvation and walk daily according to it. Remind us of how the good news of your Son has worked in our lives. Inspire us to spread the good news to others. Amen.

APRIL 26

Anxiety weighs down the human heart, but a good word cheers it up.

Proverbs 12:25

How many times has an act of kindness lifted up your spirit? When we are in times of anxiety, we need a kind word or an act of kindness to calm us down. God works through each of us. We work in an environment that can be chaotic; chaotic for us, and also for those that we encounter. When we show a little kindness in our work, the situation may calm down. Even if we are performing tasks that may have a negative impact on the other person, if we perform them with kindness, it may go a little easier. Today, try to do everything with kindness. God has shown us kindness. Let us show kindness to each other.

God of all goodness, we give you thanks for all the kindness you have shown to us. Inspire us to be kind in all our actions. Allow us to provide some calm in times of anxiousness. Amen.

APRIL 27

My God, my God, why have you forsaken me? Why are you so far from helping me, from the words of my groaning?

Psalm 22:1

We might be able to see ourselves saying these words, but it may be difficult for us to remember that Jesus said those words from his cross, on the day we remember as Good Friday. We are reminded that Christ went to the cross to die for our sins. When we may cry out, Jesus speaks to us, that he has already made it possible for us to have eternal life. Today, make confession of all your sins. Go somewhere by yourself and name them out loud, if you want but confess your sins to God. God already knows them, but you need to name them.

Almighty God, we ask you to look upon us sinners with mercy. We give you thanks that you sent your son, Jesus Christ, to die on a cross. Lord Jesus, you carried our sins with you on Calvary. Holy Spirit, wash us clean of all our sin that we may live in new life. Amen.

APRIL 28

When you pass through the waters, I will be with you; and through the rivers, they shall not overwhelm you; when you walk through fire you shall not be burned, and the flame shall not consume you.

Isaiah 43:2

We see the catastrophes that occur in the human experience. We are the ones that need to keep a level head through these times of trial. We step forward and take care of others, denying our own safety. This is our job. But we also know that God is with us during these times. God gives us the strength to do our jobs in these difficult situations. God allows us to be the calm in the storm.

God, Eternal Source of Peace, be with us during times of catastrophe. Allow us to help those who need our assistance. Give us the strength to carry on when even we show fear. Amen.

APRIL 29

When the sabbath was over, Mary Magdalene, and Mary the mother of James, and Salome bought spices, so that they might go and anoint him (Jesus). And very early on the first day of the week, when the sun had risen, they went to the tomb. They had been saying to one another, "Who will roll away the stone for us from the entrance to the tomb?" When they looked up, they saw that the stone, which was very large, had already been rolled back. As they entered the tomb, they saw a young man, dressed in a white robe, sitting on the right side; and they were alarmed. But he said to them, "Do not be alarmed; you are looking for Jesus of Nazareth, who was crucified. He has been raised; he is not here. Look, there is the place they laid him. But go, tell his disciples and Peter that he is going ahead of you to Galilee; there you will see him, just as he told you."

Mark 16:1-6

He is risen! He is risen indeed! Alleluia! This is the mystery of our faith; Christ has died, Christ has risen, Christ will come again. This is the Good News. We celebrate the resurrection of Christ as the highpoint of our faith. This is the story that we have to tell to everyone. Today, tell everyone you encounter the story of Christ; he has died, he has risen, he will come again. Alleluia!

God, who art perfect love, we thank you for the gift you gave us in your son, Jesus Christ. We celebrate his life, death and resurrection. Send the Holy Spirit to us, until that time, that Christ will come again. A time when we will all experience your perfect love. Amen.

APRIL 30

O Lord, all my longing is known to you; my sighing is not hidden from you.

Psalm 38:9

We all have longings. We look at what we want or what we have had in the past, and long to have it. We long for changes in our lives. We long for things to get better. God knows that we long for things. Desire for something isn't bad in and of itself. We are not supposed to let those longings dominate our lives. It is all right to long, desire, want; we just need to do it in proper perspective. God also hears us when we sigh because we do not get what we long for. To have longings is human nature. Don't let them dominate your life. Turn them over to God, who already knows what you want. Today, make a list of everything that you long for. Take some time in prayerful consideration, why you long for these things. Then turn it all over to God.

God, Life of all that is seen, we give you thanks for all that you have given to us. Even during those times when we want more. Hear our sighs when we don't get what we want. You know what we desire. Open our eyes to see what we really need, and what we already have. Amen.

MAY 1

Philip said to him, "Lord, show us the Father, and we will be sat-
isfied." Jesus said to him, "have I been with you all this time,
Philip, and you still do not know me? Whoever has seen me has
seen the Father. How can you say, 'Show us the Father'? Do you
not believe that I am in the Father and the Father is in me? The
words I say to you I do not speak on my own; but the Father who
dwells in me does his works. Believe me that I am in the Father
and the Father is in me; but if you do not, then believe me
because of the works themselves. Very truly, I tell you, the one
who believes in me will also do the works that I do and, in fact,
will do greater works than these, because I am going to the
Father. I will do whatever you ask in my name, so that the Father
may be glorified in the Son."

John 14:8-13

Today, the church remembers the apostles Philip and James.
Philip was one of the first disciples. James, the son of Alphaeus,
is called "the less" to distinguish him from another apostle named
James. Philip asks Jesus to show him God. Jesus tells Philip that
if he sees him, he sees God. Wouldn't it be nice to see God? Then
faith would be easy. But, can we see God when we do God's
work? When we are on patrol, and go out of our way to help
someone, is it possible that person sees God in our actions? I am
sure it is possible. Not that the good works we do make us any
better, or get us closer to God. But people can feel the good news
in our actions. Who have you encountered that allowed you to see
God through them?

Almighty God to know you is to have eternal life. Grant us
to know your Son, as the apostles Philip and James did. In knowing your Son, we begin to know you. We thank you for sending
people like Philip and James, who were able to show you to others through their actions. Amen.

MAY 2

For this reason I (Paul) bow my knees before the Father (of our Lord Jesus Christ), from whom every family in heaven and on earth takes its name. I pray that, according to the riches of his glory he may grant that you may be strengthened in your inner being with power through his Spirit, and that Christ may dwell in your hearts through faith, as you are being rooted and grounded in love. I pray that you may have the power to comprehend, with all the saints, what is the breadth and length and height and depth, and to know the love of Christ that surpasses knowledge, so that you may be filled with all the fullness of God. Now to him by the power at work within us is able to accomplish abundantly far more than all we can ask or imagine, to him be glory in the church and in Christ Jesus to all generations, forever and ever. Amen.

Ephesians 3:14-21

Today the church remembers Athanasius, Bishop of Alexandria. Athanasius attended the Council of Nicea in 325, where he defended the divinity of Christ. From then on, he was a defender of the Christian faith against heresies. He was bishop of Alexandria for 45 years. Because he was a defender of the faith, the church named a creed after him. Although he did not write it, it contains many of his ideas. Athanasius died in 373. The Athanasian Creed states what we believe the Trinity to be. We need to remember that each of the persons of the Trinity plays a part in our daily lives. Today, find a copy of the Athanasian Creed and read it. Then reflect on the role the Trinity plays in your life.

Heavenly Father, shepherd of your people, we give you thanks for sending servants like Athanasius, who were faithful in caring and nurturing your flock. We lift Athanasius up as an example of how we may grow in our faith. We realize that each person of the Trinity is active in our lives today. In the name of the Creator, Redeemer and Sustainer, we pray. Amen.

MAY 3

...the LORD appeared to me (Jeremiah) from far away (to him long ago). I have loved you with an everlasting love; therefore I have continued my faithfulness to you.

Jeremiah 31:3

We all know that God loves us. But do we realize that God loves us all the time. When we have our highs and when we are in our lows, God loves us. When we are doing right and when we are going wrong, God still loves us. When we love God, and even when we feel as if we don't, God will still love us. God's love for us is everlasting. God is faithful to us when He loves us. And since God's love is forever, God will be faithful to us forever. Today, think of all the ways God's love for you is displayed.

God of Holy Love, we give you thanks for loving us and being faithful to us. Inspire us to share your love with others. Amen.

MAY 4

The human mind plans the way, but the LORD directs the steps.

Proverbs 16:9

We make many decisions in our life. Some of them are small, some are very large. We try to take control of our own decisions. We want to do what is best for us. We will even pray to God to give us a specific outcome to a decision. Then we are very upset when God's answer is, "NO!" We make the decisions, but we need to allow God to direct our decision-making process. We need to be open to the larger picture. When we pray, we should pray for guidance, not outcomes. Today, allow God to direct a decision you make.

God, Gracious Giver of Knowledge, we pray that you direct all of our decisions. We thank you for looking out for us and desiring what is best for us. Inspire us to look to you when we need to make choices in our lives. Amen.

MAY 5

"Blessed are the merciful, for they will receive mercy."

Matthew 5:7

This comes from Jesus' Sermon on the Mount. How many times have you been asked to give someone a break, a warning, to go lightly? Is that showing mercy? We are required to enforce the law. But we are allowed discretion in our enforcement actions. Sometimes we are required to take a certain course of action. But many times, it is up to us how we handle a situation. We need to enforce the law, protect people, and possibly modify behavior. That doesn't mean that we come down hard on someone that doesn't deserve it. We need to show mercy in our actions. If someone needs a harsh punishment, then so be it. If someone can respond to a lesser punishment, then give it a try. Maybe going easy on someone that you think needs to be hammered would show a little mercy. Remember, God always shows us mercy, no matter if we need a light talking to or a hammering. When you show mercy, God will bless the person through you, and will also bless you.

God, Source of Mercy, we give you thanks for being merciful upon us. Inspire us to show your mercy throughout the world. Bless those who need mercy in their lives. Amen.

MAY 6

No one who conceals transgressions will prosper, but one who confesses and forsakes them will obtain mercy.

Proverbs 28:13

We all make mistakes. But when we make mistakes, we need to be accountable for our actions. We need to stand up and say that we were wrong, even if it means suffering the consequences. Citizens call in and come in and file complaints on us. Sometimes, they are not telling the truth. Many times, it is just a difference in perception. But sometimes, we do things that are wrong. The best thing to do is admit we were wrong. Don't try and cover it up. This is true in all aspects of our life: home, family, and friends. If we make a mistake, just admit it. It is with admittance that we may obtain mercy. Hiding it only makes things worse. Today, take some time and make confession of all the mistakes you have made recently. Try and reconcile with the people who are affected. You may be surprised how much mercy you receive.

God, Upholder of the Falling, we give you thanks for showing us mercy. We make mistakes and fall short. Give us the strength to make confession to you and to those affected. And remind us to be as merciful when people confess doing wrong to us. Amen.

MAY 7

Then he (Jesus) said to Thomas, "Put your finger here and see my hands. Reach out your hand and put it in my side. Do not doubt but believe." Thomas answered him, "My Lord and my God!" Jesus said to him, "Have you believed because you have seen me? Blessed are those who have not seen and yet have come to believe."

John 20:27-29

Thomas, one of the twelve disciples doubted that Jesus had been resurrected. Jesus stands before Thomas to convince him he is alive. Jesus doesn't say that we shouldn't have doubt. Jesus said we should try to work through the doubt, and believe before we are able to see the result. How many doubts do we have in our lives? Having doubts is human nature. We need to work through those doubts. You don't have to see it before you believe it. Think of the doubts you have today. Pray for guidance, and then let go and release your doubts.

God, Fountain of Life, thank you for being with us during our times of doubt. Help us to live the example your son provided for us. Guide us to remove the doubt from our minds. Amen.

MAY 8

And he (Jesus) said to them, "Take care! Be on your guard against all kinds of greed; for one's life does not consist in the abundance of possessions.'

Luke 12:15

We won't get rich in this job. We don't get into law enforcement for the money. But we still need to be careful about greed. New police officers usually go out and buy new cars, new houses, and new toys. Things get a little tight financially, so we start looking for overtime, or special duty assignments. Our life starts to go down hill because we have to work so much. We need to provide for our families and ourselves. Just remember that we don't want to fall into the trap of greed. We can have all these new things, but just weigh the possessions against the toll all the work takes on you, your family and your friends.

God of Heavenly Powers, we give you thanks for all that we have. We are able to provide for our family and ourselves. Remind us of why we do this job. Remove the lust for possessions from us. Inspire us to be on our guard against greed. Amen.

May 9

"...I give you a new commandment, that you love one another. Just as I have loved you, you also should love one another."

John 13:34

We work in a very highly emotional environment, whether we want to admit it or not. We get close to one another because our very lives depend on each other. There may even be times when we fall in love with people that we work with. We need to be careful to truly love each other, without crossing boundaries that may cause difficulty. Bringing a personal relationship into the workplace may be dangerous. It can even be more dangerous if one or both parties are married. We are commanded to love one another. We should be honest with our feelings. But we also need to be careful that boundaries are not crossed.

God of the loving heart, we are commanded to love one another. Fill us with love that shows your love for us. Help us guard against situations that may be harmful and inspire us to the fulfillment of this commandment. Amen.

MAY 10

The LORD is near to the brokenhearted, and saves the crushed in spirit.

Psalm 34:18

Having faith in God does not mean that we will never suffer. Even the faithful will have times of mourning. In our jobs, we encounter people in various stages of mourning. Mourning does not have to be just a death, but any type of loss. It may be the end of a relationship, a child running away, loss of a belief. We come upon people who need to know that in their mourning, there is love to be found. God is near to those who suffer and is with those who feel they have been crushed. God may work through us to bring love and understanding to others. When we encounter people in states of brokenness, we need to remember that we are in the presence of God, who is always with people who mourn.

God, Holiness of those who mourn, we give you thanks for being with us, even in our most broken times. Send your Holy Spirit to those who mourn, that they may know that you are near. Inspire us to be your hand in a broken world. Amen.

MAY 11

Train children in the right way, and when old, they will not stray.
Proverbs 22:6

How we treat our children affects how they will be in their adult life. Many times, our jobs get in the way of being good parents. We miss school events, sports, or just spending time together. We need to specifically set aside time to be with our children. They aren't children for very long. We don't want to waste the small amount of time we have with them. If you have children, tell them that you love them and spend some significant time with them today.

God of all generations, we thank you for the miracles that are our children. Watch over them with protection and guidance. Be with them during the times that we cannot. Send your Holy Spirit to them so that they may not stray. Remind us to take the time to be with our children when we think we have important tasks to complete. Amen.

MAY 12

We are afflicted in every way, but not crushed; perplexed, but not driven to despair; persecuted, but not forsaken; struck down, but not destroyed;
II Corinthians 4:8-9

There are many times that we may feel overwhelmed in life. We have the pressures of a stressful job. We want to spend time with our spouse and our children. We have friends, school, and we need to have time to ourselves. We try to juggle all of this, and it feels overwhelming. It feels as if we are not a good person because we can't do it all. St. Paul reminds us that it is human to be afflicted, perplexed, persecuted, struck down, overwhelmed. But we know that we have not gone over the edge. We do not have to be crushed, we don't have to be in despair, we are not forsaken, and we are not destroyed. The troubled times will be there. We need to know that God loves us for our humanness. We don't have to be perfect and get everything done. There will be times when we feel overwhelmed, but God is still with us. God may also use us to display hope to others who have these same qualities.

God of peace, we give you thanks for being with us when we are overwhelmed. Allow us to see through the troubles and work through them. Do not let us feel crushed and in utter despair. Remind us that in you, we are not forsaken, and we are not destroyed. Use us as your instruments, to communicate your presence with others who feel struck down. Amen.

MAY 13

"Blessed are the poor in spirit, for theirs is the kingdom of heaven."

Matthew 5:3

The "poor in spirit" are those people we encounter who have no reason for hope. Our jobs take us to many places where we find people who feel utterly hopeless in their lives. We find people who don't believe their lives will ever get any better. And many times, the sad truth is, their lives don't get any better. Why does Jesus call these people blessed? It is for people who have no reason to hope, that the kingdom of heaven is Good News. The fact that they will reside with God someday, may be the only Good News they have in their life. And it is for them, the poor in spirit, the hopeless, that the Gospel provides a blessing. We are called to try to bring hope to those who feel hopeless. Maybe someday, when it is one of us who feels hopeless, someone like you will come.

Great God our Hope, we give you thanks for providing reasons to have hope in our lives. Strengthen that hope that we may be able to impart it to others that are poor in spirit. Be with us as we spread the Good News of the Kingdom of Heaven, among those who need to hear it the most. Amen.

MAY 14

...and (the priest) shall say to them: "Hear, O Israel! Today you are drawing near to do battle against your enemies. Do not lose heart, or be afraid, or panic, or be in dread of them;..."

Deuteronomy 20:3

How many times have we pulled up on a call and it looks like absolute panic. Everyone is running around, screaming, pointing, and grabbing at you, asking you to bring peace to the situation. We are the ones who are called to go into the chaos. But we cannot become part of the panic. If we loose our sense of calmness, we will not be able to bring peace. We know that God walks with us in the chaos. God is with us so that we do not lose heart, become afraid, panic, or become paralyzed. God brings us a sense of calm that allows us to run into situation when everyone else is running out. When you feel panic start to creep in, stop, take a deep breath, say a prayer, and allow the Holy Spirit to be with you.

God, Source of Peace, we give you thanks for being with us in times of chaos. Fill us with the Holy Spirit so that we may bring peace to a situation in turmoil. Inspire us to not lose heart, be afraid, or panic. May we, along with your son, Jesus Christ, be instruments of your peace. Amen.

MAY 15

A friend loves at all times, and kinsfolk are born to share adversity.

Proverbs 17:17

Law enforcement officers are social beings. That's part of what draws us to the job. Because of what we do, we can usually count our friends on one hand. Many of our friends are cops, also. We need to have people we can talk to that will understand us. But many times, we don't give others the chance. A real friend will be able to help, even if they do not understand the situation exactly. We have to learn to trust that our friends won't let us down. And even when they do let us down, we are always able to talk to God in prayer.

Best friend of all, send to us people who will listen to us. May we have many friends who can guide us through difficult situations. Give us the strength to trust our friends with our inner feelings. Thank you for being our best friend, loving us and sharing even the bad times with us. Amen.

MAY 16

And we urge you, Beloved, (brothers and sisters) to admonish the idlers, encourage the fainthearted, help the weak, be patient with all of them.

1 Thessalonians 5:14

We find ourselves in situations where we may become frustrated. We try to instruct those who are not living right on how to live a better life. We try to cheer up and encourage those who are discouraged, that they may see the potential they have. We try to help those who are not able to help themselves. But all of this may not be easy. We may have difficulty explaining to others how they may better care for themselves. We are called to raise these issues up to people. Many times, it is like we are banging our heads against a wall. We are also called to be patient with everyone we encounter. Sometimes, we may need to step back a little, gather our thoughts and try again. The most calming thing we can give others is to be a non-anxious presence with them. We shouldn't add to another's stress. Today, whenever you find yourself becoming frustrated, step back, take a breath, gather your thoughts, and be patient with all those you encounter. Remember, God is very patient with us.

God of all patience, we give you thanks for showing patience with us as we try to follow your will. Be with us as we lift up to others how they may change their lives, through your son Jesus Christ. Send the Holy Spirit to us, that we may be filled with patience as we live out our call. Amen.

MAY 17

"Blessed are the meek, for they will inherit the earth."

Matthew 5:5

As we go through daily routines, do we really see those who are lowly and insignificant? The meek are the invisible population. Society discounts the meek, to the point that we just block them out of our sight. Jesus saw them. The Kingdom of heaven being at hand is Good News for the meek, because now they will be seen. Their voices will be heard. They will make a difference. Our jobs take us to places where we encounter the meek. We are called to help them, to give them a voice. We should lift up their concerns, so that society actually looks into their faces. This will be hard. Leaders will want you to sweep these issues under the rug. "We don't have a homeless problem here. We don't have people living well below the poverty level here. We don't have marginalized citizens here. We don't have illegal aliens, just trying to get work to support their families here. I don't know why you are bringing up these issues here." But we see it firsthand, if our eyes are not blinded by society's beliefs. Today, look around, see the meek in your community. Open your eyes, hearts and minds to them and their concerns. Remember, the meek are blessed, and they will inherit the earth.

Gracious God, blessed are those who are considered lowly and insignificant. Be with us as we provide for them, and take up their issues. Send the Holy Spirit to strengthen us when times become difficult. As your son, Jesus Christ reminded us, we walk among the blessed and they will inherit the earth. Amen.

MAY 18

May the LORD give strength to his people! May the LORD bless his people with peace!

Psalm 29:11

Many of us are called peace officers. We are called to bring peace to a particular geographic area. Many times we say we are here to keep the peace. But there are times when we arrive and peace does not abound. We just add fuel to the fire. We get caught up in the situation and add to the chaos. We are called to bring peace. God will give us the strength to address the situation properly. God will also give us peace, so that we do not add to the problem. We need to be receptive to these gifts. We tend to close our minds and do what we feel is right. But when we place our trust in the Lord, our foundation is sure.

God, Lover of Peace, we give you thanks for the strength and peace you give to us. Allow us to use these gifts that we may bring peace into the lives of others. May the feeling of your peace give them the strength they need to carry on with their lives. Amen.

MAY 19

Happy are those who do not follow the advice of the wicked, or take the path that sinners tread, or sit in the seat of scoffers.
Psalm 1:1

Law enforcement is a very close-knit sub-culture. We take care of each other. Our lives depend on each other. We tolerate our partners saying and doing things that may be out of bounds, because they are our partners, and that means everything. We need to be careful that if we make the choice that we are not going to turn someone in for a minor theft at an open business; or going out of district to spend time with a boyfriend or girlfriend; or some other violation, that we don't get pressured into committing the offenses ourselves. It is so easy for peer pressure to set in, and before you know it, you are doing the very same things. It is difficult to turn our partners in. But one way we can be an example to them, is when they ask us to participate, we say no, and explain why we believe it is wrong. No value judgments, no accusations, just saying it is wrong for us.

We will be happy when we don't give in to peer pressure. Not only because we are trying to do the right thing, but we may also be ministering to our partners by showing them a reflection of themselves against what is right and wrong.

God of all righteousness, we give you thanks for sending us people who we can place our own lives in their hands. Give us strength to do what is right. Inspire us to not give into peer pressure. And forgive us when we do. Allow us to be a mirror of will to others. Amen.

MAY 20

May the God of hope fill you will all joy and peace in believing, so that you may abound in hope by the power of the Holy Spirit.
Romans 15:13

We are always hoping for something. We hope for changes, we hope for additions and we hope for subtractions in our lives. Many times we think we can bring these changes about by ourselves, or by the work of someone else. But God is the source of all hope. Through hope that God will work everything in our lives, we are able to have a sense of peace. The Holy Spirit will fill us with hope to carry us through the day.

God, source of all hope, fill us with the Holy Spirit that we may abound in joy in peace through you. Remove the uncertainty of our lives. Allow us to see that all change may come through you. Amen.

MAY 21

"Blessed are those who hunger and thirst for righteousness, for they will be filled."
Matthew 5:6

How many times have we heard it said by people that there is no justice? In this beatitude, Jesus is talking about those who receive absolutely no justice in this life. They hunger and thirst to be treated properly, but they never are. The arrival of the kingdom of God is Good News to these, because finally, they will receive justice. We encounter people who truly believe they receive no justice. Maybe just once in their lives, we can provide them with that for which they hunger and thirst. As we come upon people who say there is no justice, remember, Jesus says these people are blessed.

God, Proclaimer of justice, we give you thanks for bringing justice to the world. We ask that the Holy Spirit may bring righteousness and justice to all. Use us as instruments of justice, for those who your son, Jesus Christ, said are blessed because they believe there is no justice. Amen.

MAY 22

"Blessed are those who are persecuted for righteousness' sake, for theirs is the kingdom of heaven."

Matthew 5:10

Do we have religious persecution in this country? Well, as governmental workers, we are not permitted do display and talk about our faith openly in our work setting. There is a supposed separation of church and state. But how about when we speak up, or speak out about a wrongdoing? We may not invoke the name of God, but we may be standing up for the righteousness of God. But the world really doesn't want to hear what we have to say. We may do our best to lead righteous lives, but we may be looked at as outcasts for not conforming to society's views. Jesus said that those who are persecuted for the sake of righteousness would be blessed. The Good News that the kingdom of heaven is at hand sounds good, because the persecution will stop. Those who are persecuted for righteousness sake will live in the kingdom of heaven, where right living is the norm of society. Don't be afraid to stand up for what is right, even if it goes against the grain of what society believes.

God of life and death, we give you thanks for giving us the strength to try to live righteous lives. Send your Holy Spirit to us, that we may continue on in the face of persecution for doing your will. Inspire us by knowing your Son, Jesus Christ said that we are blessed, and will receive Your Kingdom. Amen.

MAY 23

I have fought the good fight, I have finished the race, I have kept the faith.

2 Timothy 4:7

We are never promised that being a Christian will be easy. We do not hear that we will get the good things in life. In fact, it is the very opposite. We hear, even from Jesus, that our path will be difficult, and many people will probably hate us because we call on the name of Christ. We hear images about the good fight, and the race. What we have to learn is how to persevere, even when things are difficult. God is the source of our perseverance. We can always rely on God to keep us going when we feel we have reached our end. Our reward will come. So fight the good fight, finish the race, and keep the faith.

Inexhaustible God, we give you thanks for keeping us going when we have nothing left. Keep us in the faith, so that we may fight the fight and run the race. Inspire us when we feel like giving up. Amen.

MAY 24

Let the heavens be glad. And let the earth rejoice; let the sea roar, and all that fills it; let the field exult, and everything in it. Then shall all the trees of the forest sing for joy before the LORD; for he is coming, for he is coming to judge the earth. He will judge the world with righteousness, and the peoples with his truth.

Psalm 96:11-13

We live in a world that is exploding with scientific discoveries. We work in a profession where the application of science is always growing. Today, the church remembers Nicolaus Copernicus and Leonhard Euler, teachers and scientists. Scientists such as these two, inspire us to think about the mysteries of the universe and the magnificent creation of God. Copernicus' thirst for knowledge led him to shake the world when he said the earth is not the center of the universe, but revolves around the sun. Euler is known as one of the founders of the science of math and made contributions to mechanics, hydrodynamics, astronomy, optics and acoustics. Copernicus died in 1543 and Euler in 1783. As we struggle with finding a balance between science and religion, remember that God has created everything, even science. We lift up these two scientists to give some religious understanding to science. As you apply science today, remember that God is the creator of all, and that science helps us to understand more about creation. Help others to understand how we see God in creation, through science.

Almighty God, beautiful in majesty and majestic in holiness, we give you thanks for sending scientists into the world like Copernicus and Euler, to help us understand your great creation. You have shown us the splendor of your creative work through these servants. Inspire us to help others see you in your creation, through the application of science. Amen.

MAY 25

Then I (Jeremiah) said, "Ah, Lord GOD! Truly I do not know how to speak, for I am only a boy." But the LORD said to me, "Do not say, 'I am only a boy'; for you shall go to all to whom I send you, and you shall speak whatever I command you. Do not be afraid of them, for I am with you to deliver you, says the LORD."

Jeremiah 1:6-8

How many times do we feel intimidated on our job? Some of the people we work with use intimidation to gain control of a situation. Some people and situations intimidate us. The job itself, and its affect on our lives, may be a little intimidating. We can over come this intimidation we feel by realizing that God will help us along the way. We do not have to do it all ourselves. God will help us find the right words or the proper actions to complete the task. We do not have to be afraid of not knowing or not having enough experience or just being overwhelmed. Today, during times when you feel a little intimidated; stop, and offer your words and actions to God, and see if you are able to work through that fear.

God, Source of all Strength, be with us in times when we may feel intimidated by what life brings to us. Thank you for providing us with the words and deeds to work through the fear. Allow us to continue in our service to you, even when we feel that we are not adequate. Amen.

MAY 26

Pray in the Spirit at all times in every prayer and supplication. To that end keep alert and always persevere in supplication for all the saints.

Ephesians 6:18

Many times, we wonder to ourselves, "what can we do here?" The answer is, "Pray!" Prayer gives us guidance in difficult situations. At any time, we can take a moment and pray. Pray for knowledge, strength, support, or pray for those who you are dealing with. Lift anything to God in prayer. God knows what we need. God knows what others need. Pray opens the avenues of communication. And then, always be ready for an answer to come.

God, Answer to all prayers, we give you thanks for knowing what we need even before we ask. Send your Holy Spirit to us so we may have the answers for which we search. All things we ask of you through son, our savior, Jesus Christ. Amen.

MAY 27

Therefore we will not fear, though the earth should change, though the mountains shake in the heart of the sea; though its waters roar and foam, though the mountains tremble with its tumult. Selah

Psalm 46:2-3

Today, the church remembers John Calvin. Calvin was a French reformer and theologian. Calvin had a conversion experience in which he embraces the views of the Protestant Reformation. Calvin formulated his theological ideas in the "Institutes of the Christian Religion". He organized the reform in Geneva with rigid discipline. John Calvin is considered the founding father of the Reformed tradition churches. Our times are quickly changing. We need to be willing to embrace and lead change when we know that it is right. We need to be willing to stand up for our beliefs, even when it seems somewhat radical. Through history, many have led change to bring us to where we are. If they hadn't, we would be living in a much different world. Take some time today to evaluate and see if there is a cause to embrace change. It doesn't have to be large. If the change is for the right reasons, support it.

Almighty God, we praise you for the people you have sent to call the Church to its tasks and renew its life. We lift up John Calvin, and all who have served your purpose. Raise up in our own time, people inspired by the Spirit, whose voices will give strength to your Church and proclaim the reality of your kingdom. Inspire us to embrace change. Amen.

MAY 28

"Blessed are the pure in heart, for they will see God."

Matthew 5:8

We need to strive to be pure in heart. Being pure in heart means, being one of those whose innocence is not merely outward but derives from their innermost self. This is not something that we can fake. We need to cleanse ourselves from the inside out. This process allows us to see God. When we stop clouding of minds, our eyes are opened to God and what God provides.

God, Inspiration to Goodness, we thank you for allowing us to see you. We strive to cleanse ourselves, so that we may be pure in heart. Send the Holy Spirit to us that we may be able to change from the inside out. All of this we do, because your son, Jesus Christ, did it for us. And he told us we should do the same. Amen.

MAY 29

God is our refuge and strength, a very present (or well proved) help in trouble.

Psalm 46:1

Being a Christians does not mean that we won't have problems. We have our fair share of problems. In fact, Jesus tells us that people will cause problems for us just because we are Christians. What we need to remember is that God will hold us up during those times of troubles. The Scripture doesn't say God takes away our problems, it says that God will provide help and strength for us to get through them. Whenever we are having any type of problem, small or large, we should take a moment and pray to God to be our strength and help during this time. Even if we do not ask, God will still be there for us.

God, Guardian of our lives, we give you thanks for always being present with us. Give us strength and help during our times of troubles. Forgive us when we do not rely on you. And remind us that you are always with us. Amen.

MAY 30

But when the goodness and loving kindness of God our Savior appeared, he saved us, not because of any works of righteousness that we had done, but according to his mercy, through the water (washing) of rebirth and renewal by the Holy Spirit.

Titus 3:4-5

Today, think about the ways that God has shown goodness and kindness in your life. Maybe it is the big decision that God has helped with, maybe it was the little things that just made life a little easier. Even when we are not kind and good to others, God shows us love. We should always strive to be kind to others as God is kind to us. For the rest of the day, try to show kindness to everyone you encounter. Maybe they will see God's kindness in their lives, through you.

God of goodness and loving kindness, we give you thanks for all that you have given to us. We are reborn and renewed through the power of the Holy Spirit. We realize this gift is not because of anything that we have done. But because of the love you have for us. Inspire us to show the kindness and goodness to others that you give to us. Amen.

MAY 31

"Blessed are the pure in heart, for they will see God."

Matthew 5:8

Jesus calls us to be pure in heart. We are to be a person whose innocence is not merely something that we do for show. Our innocence should come from the inside, from the inner core of our being. We must first work on our insides being faithful to God. When we are pure in heart, we can't help but to do and say the right things. This is the state of being that we should strive to attain. As we move to being pure in heart, we are able to live out our faith in a stronger manner.

God, Pure and Upright One, we give you thanks for dwelling in our hearts. Help us to follow your son's direction to us, to be pure in heart. Send the Holy Spirit to us, to make our hearts purer, so that we may see you. Amen.

JUNE 1

Then he (Jesus) led them out as far as Bethany, and lifting up his hands, he blessed them. While he was still blessing them, he withdrew from them and was carried up into heaven. And they worshipped him, and returned to Jerusalem with great joy; and they were continually in the temple blessing God. Amen.

Luke 24:50-53

Jesus has ascended to live with God. Even though we are not able to see him, he is still with us. We believe that he will come again. Jesus has ascended to that place and time where God's Kingdom has been fulfilled. The risen Lord enters the invisible presence of God in order to be present in all times and places. We now receive the Holy Spirit to guide us, until that time that Jesus returns, and God's Kingdom is realized for all. Today, where will you find the risen Lord?

God of wonders, you took up your only Son into heaven where he now acts on our behalf. We pray that we may someday be taken up into your Kingdom. Help us to live our lives in a manner that glorifies you, in the name of our risen and ascended Lord, Jesus Christ.

JUNE 2

He (God) reached down from on high, he took me; he drew me out of mighty waters.

Psalm 18:16

There are times in our lives that we need relief. We will have times when things get a little difficult. God is the one who reaches down and pulls us out of our distress. We shouldn't fight it when God does this for us. Sometimes, we fight to stay in our distress, even though God sends relief. We encounter people many times, in our jobs, who need relief. They may need physical, mental, and/or emotional relief. They are just like us. God may be using you, to provide relief for someone else. Never push away God's relief that is sent to you. And never underestimate the relief you may be able to provide to someone else.

God our Helper, we give you thanks for sending us relief in our times of distress. Open our eyes to your work in our lives. Inspire us to do your work in providing relief to others, as you have provided for us. Amen.

JUNE 3

"Blessed are the peacemakers, for they shall be called children of God."

Matthew 5:9

We are called peace officers. That is who we are. By the very nature of our job, we are called to actively work for peace. Our job is to bring and provide peace in our area. People need peace from many issues. People are looking to us to provide that peace. We are to walk into the most difficult of situations, and bring peace to all. It is up to us to decide how that peace may come. We need to open ourselves up to God's work. It is not always what we think is best. We need to look at the whole situation, so that we may determine the most peaceful solution for the entire situation. Jesus said that peacemakers are blessed, and shall be called children of God. Today, try and bring peace to every situation you encounter. Allow everyone you meet, to see your Father through you.

God, Sovereign of Peace, we give you thanks for bringing peace to our lives. Send the Holy Spirit to us, that we may become peacemakers. Allow us to fulfill the words of Christ, so that we may be blessed, and be called children of God, for the furtherance of your Kingdom. Amen.

JUNE 4

I will both lie down and sleep in peace; for you alone, O LORD, make me lie down in safety.

Psalm 4:8

We all need time to rest. No matter how good we think we are, we need to let our bodies recover. We lead difficult lives. We work different shifts and have different days off than others. We have other time we have to be at work. We also try to live as if we are like everyone else. We need to take time to rest. God not only wants us to rest, but God makes us rest. So today, take some time and just rest.

God, Maker of rest, we give you thanks for caring for us. You know our needs better than we do. Inspire us to take time and enjoy the safe rest that you provide for us. Allow us to be refreshed, so that we may continue in your service. Amen.

JUNE 5

"...For those who want to save their life will lose it, and those who lose their life for my sake will find it."

Matthew 16:25

We are paid to take risks. It is our job to do the things people are afraid to do. It is our duty to go into places, that everyone else is running out. We train to not take unnecessary risks. We don't do things just for the thrill of it. There is a reason for what we do. Jesus asked his disciples to take risks. Jesus asks even to risk one's life. We are called to take risks in our service and ministry. Those risks should not be taken unnecessarily, or by making uninformed decisions. But, we are called to lay it out on the line. We are called to take the Good News of Jesus Christ to the most dangerous places in the world. The same place that we work every day.

God, surrounded by glory, we give you thanks for keeping us safe. The way of the cross is difficult, and takes us to dangerous places. Send the Holy Spirit to us, so that we may be able to take risks for your service. As Jesus asked his disciples to take risks, we understand that Jesus also asks us to put it all on the line. Amen.

JUNE 6

"... And remember, I am with you always, to the end of the age. (Amen)"

Matthew 28:20b

Being in law enforcement can be a lonely job. Many times we work by ourselves. It is only us in the cruiser, or walking the beat, or riding the bike, or guarding a cellblock. There is only ourselves to talk to. We feel alone. We drive around on holidays watching families celebrate together. Whether our lives are going good, or going really bad, we don't have anyone to share our feeling with. We think we only have ourselves. We fear talking to others at work about the reality in our lives. Somehow we believe that it presents a soft image it we talk about feelings. So we keep it inside ourselves. We believe that no one can really understand us. We become lonely and depressed. But, there is one that is always with us. Jesus told his disciples that he would always be with them. Jesus is always with us, willing to listen. When you need to talk, just talk, Jesus will hear you. Words don't have to be in the form of a particular prayer for God to hear them. Prayer is a conversion between you and God. Today, when you begin to feel lonely and by yourself, just start talking. You will be heard. Maybe you will gain answers.

God of the entire world, we give you thanks for always being with us. We thank you for sending your son, that we may never be alone. Hear our prayers, even when we are just talking out loud. Be with us so that we may never feel as if we are alone. Amen.

JUNE 7

But you do see! Indeed you note trouble and grief, that you may
take it into your hands; the helpless commit themselves to you;
you have been the helper of the orphan.

Psalm 10:14

Many times we wonder if God knows that we are sad. We are
assured that God sees our sadness. As law enforcement officers,
we believe we have to suppress our feelings and emotions. God
created us to be emotional beings. When we are able to feel sadness, we may be able to enjoy our happiness. We need to learn to
work through sadness in our lives. Working through sadness does
not mean that we must forget what has made us sad. We need to
remember the situation in a healthy way. God takes note of our
sadness. God is able to help us through those times when we are
sad about situations in our lives. Today, lift up in prayer everything that has sadness on your heart. Ask God to help you work
through those situations.

Great God, we ask you for help in our sadness. Help us to see
the path through these difficult times. We know that you see our
emotions. We offer ourselves to you, so that you may take us in
your hands. Amen.

JUNE 8

"Are not five sparrows sold for two pennies? Yet not one of them is
forgotten in God's sight. But even the hairs of your head are counted.
Do not be afraid; you are of more value then many sparrows.

Luke 12:6-7

We work in unstable environments. We wonder if anyone else is
out there, covering our backsides. Sometimes, we may even feel that
we are so insignificant, that if something happened to us, no one
would notice. Jesus tells us that God even cares for the inexpensive
sparrows. God knows us to the point God knows the number of hairs

on our heads. We are not insignificant. We can feel safe in knowing that God does care about us. We can feel safe in knowing that we are significant to God. We are not left out there on our own.

Great God of Power, we give you thanks for watching over us and keeping us safe. As powerful as you are, you are able to know each one of us individually. Watch over us as we walk in our unstable places. Continue to remind us of the words of your son, Jesus Christ. Through the power of the Holy Spirit, we need not be afraid. Amen.

JUNE 9

Of course, there is great gain in godliness combined with contentment;

I Timothy 6:6

We are always looking for more. We always want more. The sad fact is we will never attain everything. God provides us with everything that we need. We need to learn to be satisfied with what we have. When God gives us more, we accept it. When we are in periods where we have less, we can be content with what we have. Look around you today, and take an inventory of all that you have. Realize all the God has provided for you, and feel content in where you are.

God, Provider of all, we give you thanks for all that you have given to us. Allow us to see what we have and not want more than we need. May we learn to be content with what we have at all times. Amen.

JUNE 10

In my Father's house there are many dwelling places. If it were not so, would I have told you that I go to prepare a place for you? And if I go and prepare a place for you, I will come again and will take you to myself. So that where I am, there you will be also.

John 14:2-3

Part of our faith is that we believe Christ will come again. At Christ's second coming, we will be able to enjoy paradise with Christ, the Holy Spirit, and God. Christ told his disciples that we went to his Father's house to prepare a place for them. Christ also went to his Father's house to prepare a place for us. When Christ comes again, we will have a place reserved for us.

God, Great Ruler of the world, we give you thanks for sending your son to us, that we may have eternal life. We wait for Christ's second coming, so that we may be with you, and Christ, and the Holy Spirit. Amen.

JUNE 11

News of this came to the ears of the church in Jerusalem, and they sent Barnabas to Antioch. When he came and saw the grace of God, he rejoiced, and he exhorted them all to remain faithful to the Lord with steadfast devotion; for he was a good man, full of the Holy Spirit and of faith. And a great many people were brought to the Lord.
Acts of the Apostles 11:22-24

Today, the church remembers Barnabas the Apostle. Barnabas was not actually one of the twelve apostles, but the book of Acts gives him the title of apostle. Barnabas was originally called Joseph, and with Paul organized the first missionary trip. At the Council of Jerusalem, Barnabas defended the claims of Gentile Christians in relation to the Mosaic Law. As people of faith, we need to help and remind others of faith to remain steadfast. We are sent out into the world not only to spread the news to those who haven't heard, but also to assist others who already believe. Today, when you run into conflict and disagreement, what kind of wisdom can you provide, through the Holy Spirit, to help resolve the issue?

God, High and Holy One, grant that we may follow the example of your faithful servant Barnabas, who sought the well being of your church. Allow us to spread the Gospel of Jesus Christ as he did. And fill us with the Holy Spirit, so that we may assist others of the faith to remain steadfast in their devotion to you. Amen.

JUNE 12

The LORD is my rock, my fortress, and my deliverer, my God, my rock in whom I take refuge, my shield, and the horn of my salvation, my stronghold.

Psalm 18:2

Many people look to us, as law enforcement, as their source of security. But whom do we look to for security? God provides us with security, even when we perform the most dangerous of tasks that we do. God may also work through us, to provide security for others. Today, think of all the ways that God is your refuge, shield, fortress and rock.

God, Source of all security, we give you thanks for being there for us. We need a rock to rely on. Even in times that we feel that we have no one, remind us that you are there. Send the Holy Spirit to us, that you may use us to provide security to others. Amen.

JUNE 13

When the day of Pentecost had come, they were all together in one place. And suddenly from heaven there came a sound like the rush of a violent wind, and it filled the entire house where they were sitting. Divided tongues, as of fire, appeared among them, and a tongue rested on each of them. All of them were filled with the Holy Spirit and began to speak in other languages, as the Spirit gave them ability.

Acts of the Apostles 2:1-4

On the fiftieth day of Easter, we celebrate Pentecost. On Pentecost, we remember how the Holy Spirit descended like tongues of fire upon the believers. They were filled with the Holy Spirit and began to speak in other languages. The spoke in other languages so they could tell the Gospel to more people in languages they could understand. Do you remember the first time you were filled with the Holy Spirit, and was able to do something that you didn't think was possible? What were your thoughts and feelings immediately after? We are filled with the Holy Spirit to accomplish many things. God sends the Holy Spirit to fill us. We are able to speak the Gospel in ways that other people are able to understand. It may not be another language, but it may be the language of compassion, sincerity, love and caring. We are constantly filled with the Holy Spirit to do God's work. Allow the Spirit to fill you so that you may speak in other languages.

God, Sender of the Holy Spirit, as you send the Spirit to the disciples, allow us to be filled with the Holy Spirit, that we may feel the Spirit's power and speak in a variety of languages. May the tongues of fire of the Spirit constantly kindle our love for you. May that love strengthen our faith in you, so that we may live our lives in service of your kingdom. All of this we ask through Jesus Christ. Amen.

JUNE 14

Render service with enthusiasm, as to the Lord and not to men and women,

Ephesians 6:7

We are civil servants. We are hired to serve the people. We should always remember our place as a servant. We are here to serve. But ultimately, we are serving the will of God. We should serve with enthusiasm, because we are doing God's work. Jesus reminded his disciples that he came to be a servant, and so they should be servants. As you work today, with each encounter you have, remember that you are a servant, and you are doing God's work.

God, we give you thanks for sending your son, Jesus Christ, to the world, so that we may see the greatest example of a servant. Send the Holy Spirit to us, to keep us enthusiastic in our service to your work. Amen.

JUNE 15

Wash me thoroughly from my iniquity, and cleanse me from my sin. For I know my transgressions, and my sin is ever before me. Against you, you alone, have I sinned, and done what is evil in your sight, so that you are justified in your sentence and blameless when you pass judgment. Indeed, I was born guilty, a sinner when my mother conceived me. You desire truth in the inward being; therefore teach me wisdom in my secret heart. Purge me with hyssop, and I shall be clean; wash me, and I shall be whiter than snow.

Psalm 51:2-7

We struggle with issues of shame in ourselves. We hide our shame behind a badge and a gun. We have participated in shaming others. Was this because we are not able to work through our own? God already knows what we have done. So why do we try to hide it from God? The easiest way to relieve shame is to make a full confession of what we have done. The shame comes from hiding our actions. Today, take some time and make full confession of the actions that you hide. Name them, specifically and out loud to God. Ask for forgiveness and to have your shame removed. You may find that God washes you, relieves you of your shame, and makes you clean.

God, Judge of all humankind, you look upon us and see sinners, deserving of your punishment. We confess the sins that are already known to you. We no longer want to walk with shame in our hearts. We ask you to cleanse us, wash us, forgive us, and make us well. Amen.

JUNE 16

For who is greater, the one who is at the table or the one who serves? Is it not the one at the table? But I am among you as one who serves.

Luke 22:27

We are public servants. Many times, we forget this fact, and think that we are the bosses. In every situation, we need to remember that we are actually serving the people that we encounter. Even when we stand in positions of authority, we are still servants. Sometimes, we feel people throw this fact in our face by saying, "I pay your salary!" or "You work for me!" These statements tend to stir our emotions. But those facts are correct. Remember, Jesus came among humans as a servant. We are servants of God's Kingdom. Today, in every situation, remember that you are a servant.

God, Helper of the weak, we thank you for sending your son to us. We remember that Jesus came as a servant. Send the Holy Spirit to us, to assist us in remembering that we, too, are servants of your kingdom. May our work help the weak in our midst, as you help us. Amen.

JUNE 17

The LORD is my light and my salvation; whom shall I fear? The LORD is the stronghold (or refuge) of my life; of whom shall I be afraid?

Psalm 27:1

Many people see law enforcement officers as a sign of power. Many officers believe that they are the ultimate power. How many times have you heard, "I have the gun and the badge, and I make the rules!" We don't make the rules, we just enforce then. We also answer to others, who have power over our work. And ultimately, God is the greatest power. And all our power comes from God. When we rely on God, we don't have to worry about people exerting power over us, because we do not have to be afraid of them. We may have to follow their direction, but our power lies in God.

God, Power that Shields, we give you thanks for watching over us. We turn to you as our ultimate authority and source of all power. We realize we cannot accomplish everything ourselves, but we need your power, so that we may have no fear. Amen.

JUNE 18

Therefore, since it is by God's mercy that we are engaged in this ministry, we do not lose heart. We have renounced the shameful things that one hides; we refuse to practice cunning or to falsify God's word; but by the open statement of the truth we commend ourselves to the conscience of everyone in the sight of God.

II Corinthians 4:1-2

We live in a world where shame is a large emotion that we feel. Many people are ashamed when we arrive at a situation. We carry our own shame along with us. Sometimes, the things that we do to others are motivated by our own shame. Shame occurs when we hide things. Shame can be overcome when the facts are in the open. Part of our job is to get the facts in the open. We are trained to get to the truth. But in doing so, we need to assist the person in their emotional needs. This is also our ministerial vocation. We are to provide ministry to others, by helping them when they are in need. We should not be making their situation worse out of our own shame. We need to start with ourselves. Today, make confession to God everything that you need to get out in the open. Remember, God already knows. This confession is for you. Renounce the actions that cause you to feel shame. We should stop talking behind the backs of others, so as not to bring shame to them. Be open with the truth and do everything in light of the community. When we are purged of our shame, we are able to help other through theirs. And lastly, God is merciful. God forgives us our sins. God already knows what causes us to feel shame, and is working with us now.

God, Keeper of our souls, we make confession to you of all that needs to be brought to light. Forgive us of our sins. Purge us of our shame. And help us to minister to others in their shamefulness. Amen.

JUNE 19

A tranquil mind gives life to the flesh, but jealousy makes the bones rot.

Proverbs 14:30

We don't get into law enforcement for the money. We encounter many people in higher economic classes than we hold. Even in our own profession, we see others achieving more than we do. We should not be jealous of what others have. Whether it is money, or material things, or positions or status, we should remain content with what we have at the moment. We add to our own stress when we begin to worry why we don't have what others have. There will always be people who have more than we have. Be tranquil in what we have, so that we may have life. God provides us with everything that we need, and not necessarily what we want. Today, think of how others may look at you and be jealous of you for what you have.

God, giver of health and salvation, we give you thanks for all that you have provided us. When jealousy creeps into our bones, remove it from us. Remind us you provide all that we may need. Amen.

JUNE 20

The prayer of faith will save the sick, and the Lord will raise them up; and anyone who has committed sins will be forgiven.

James 5:15

People in law enforcement tend to be some of the sickest people. We work long hours. We work irregular shifts. We don't eat properly. We don't exercise enough. We come into contact with a variety of diseases. And we have this belief that we are tough enough that we don't have to properly take care of ourselves. By the nature of our profession, we are going to contract illness and sickness easier. We need to take care of ourselves. When we are sick, we should pray to God for healing. And then do what God says, by taking our medication, seeing the doctor, and so on. We need to constantly taking care of our bodies. We should get on a proper diet. We should get on an exercise program. God has given us this body. We should use is to its fullest potential. Today, evaluate how you care better your physical well-being. Then, begin the steps to recovery.

117

God, Power that brings healing to the sick, we pray to you to bring us healing. Help us to bring ourselves to better health. Inspire us to use our bodies for all that you have created us to do. When we are sick, heal us. When we are healthy, encourage us. Help us to do your work in the world. Amen.

JUNE 21

Then Jesus told his disciples, "If any want to become my followers, let them deny themselves and take up their cross and follow me."

Matthew 16:24

We live in a selfish world. We want everything our way, when we want it, how we want it. But we work in a profession that tells people, "No, you can't have it your way." But we also need to remember that we are not there to make things our way. We are called to deny ourselves. We must make sure that things are done Christ's way. We need to try and center ourselves on Christ, pick up our cross, and follow him. We cannot be selfish, especially in spreading the Gospel. Take a moment today, and see if you are being selfish in any areas.

Infinite God, we give you thanks for all that you have given us. Send the Holy Spirit to us so that we may not become selfish. Assist us when we deny ourselves, pick up our cross, and follow your son, Jesus. Amen.

JUNE 22

For you did not receive a spirit of slavery to fall back into fear, but you have received a spirit of adoption. When we cry, "Abba! Father!" it is that very Spirit bearing witness with our spirit that we are children of God, and joint heirs with Christ - if, in fact, we suffer with him so that we may also be glorified with him.

Romans 8:15-17

The first Sunday after Pentecost, we usually celebrate Holy Trinity Sunday. This festival celebrates the mystery of God is we find it in the Triune God. The full understanding of the Trinity is beyond our rational explanation. Christians are born of water and of the Spirit. We make the sign of the cross to remember our baptism in the name of the Father, and of the Son and of the Holy Spirit. We are God's children. It is our belief in the trinity that separates us from all the other religions. Today, whenever you feel difficulties, make the sign of the cross over yourself, and remember your baptism, and that you are a child of God.

Triune God, you have given us grace, by our belief in the eternal Trinity. Allow us to continue in the true faith, to worship you in the unity of the Three-In-One. May we always remember our baptism and that we are your children. Amen.

JUNE 23

For everything there is a season, and a time for every matter under heaven: a time to be born, and a time to die; a time to plant and a time to pluck up what is planted; a time to kill, and a time to heal; a time to break down, and a time to build up; a time to weep, and a time to laugh; a time to mourn, and a time to dance; a time to throw away stones, and a time to gather stones together; a time to embrace, and a time to refrain from embracing; a time to seek, and a time to lose; a time to keep, and a time to throw away; a time to tear, and a time to sew; a time to keep silent, and a time to speak; a time to love, and a time to hate; a time for war, and a time for peace.

Ecclesiastes 3:1-8

As law enforcement officers, we need to know when to be hard and when to be soft, the balance of the hammer of justice with the arm of compassion. We use our discretion in many decisions that we make. This comes from experience. We need to weigh the evidence in from of us, and make the proper decisions.

We cannot always come in and be a heavy. We also cannot always soft and left people off the hook. We need to use our discretion, and have the proper response to the situation. This decision can be very difficult. We should not always react in a way that we believe is appropriate, but react in a way that God would believe is appropriate. We know that God allows for each end of the spectrum, and all the response in between. We just have to know that right time to use each of the responses. Allow God to influence your reactions to situations. Sometimes these decisions need to be made in a split second, other times, we can weigh our options. We can also change the direction during an encounter. If the time dictates a change, raise or lower the level accordingly. We just need to know what time it is.

God, Provider of all times, we give you thanks for allowing us to experience the wide range of emotions. Help us to react to situations in the proper manner. May we always know what time it is. Amen.

JUNE 24

Now the time had come for Elizabeth to give birth, and she bore a son. Her neighbors and relatives heard that the Lord had shown his great mercy on her, and they rejoiced with her. On the eighth day they came to circumcise the child, and they were going to name him Zechariah after his father. But his mother said, "No; he is to be called John." They said to her, "None of your relatives has this name." Then they began motioning to his father to find out what name he wanted to give him. He asked for a writing tablet and wrote, "His name is John." And all of them were amazed. Immediately his mouth was opened and his tongue freed, and he began to speak, praising God. Fear came over all the neighbors, and all these things were talked about throughout the entire hill country of Judea. All who heard them pondered them and said, "What then will this child become?" For, indeed, the hand of the Lord was with him.

Luke 1:57-66

Today, the church remembers the birth of John the Baptist. It is celebrated six months before Christmas Eve. John stated that he must decrease as Jesus increases. John knew his place in the way his ministry would work out. Do we decrease as Jesus increases in our lives? We tend to believe that we are the most important, that we are number one. We work in jobs where we tend to be on our own, with no one else to watch over us. This autonomous feeling leads us to believe that we are greater than anyone or anything. Sometimes, we may even believe that we are bigger than the system, or even the law. We get into difficult situations when we believe that nothing can stop us. We need to be more like John the Baptist. We should remember that there is always someone greater than us. We do answer to a higher calling. We should be working to better God's world, not making tit ours. John realized his place; we should try to realize ours.

Almighty God, you called John the Baptist to witness to your Son. Grant us the wisdom to know your purpose in our work. Send the Holy Spirit to us, so that we may decrease as Christ increases in our lives. May we be witnesses to your kingdom. Amen.

JUNE 25

I will exult and rejoice in your steadfast love, because you have seen my affliction; you have taken heed of my adversities,
                                                          Psalm 31:7

We see the worst the humanity does to humanity. We cannot help to feel sorrow, not only for what we see, but also what we experience in our own lives. We feel the pain of others as we perform our duties. We suffer pain in our own lives by being human. We understand that being children of God does not relinquish from the emotion of sorrow. But God reacts to our sorrow. God sends ways for us to work through our emotions. God walks with us as we experience our affliction. God helps us work through the difficulties. God may also use us as the means to help others through their sorrow. We may be the answer to people's prayer as we do our jobs as law enforcement professionals. God's love is always there for us, even during the difficult times. Today, lift up your concerns that bring sorrow to your life.

God, Knower of our sorrows, we thank you for seeing our afflictions and walking with us as we heal from our pain. Be with us through our difficulties and adversities. Send your Holy Spirit to us and use us as answers to the sorrowful prayers of others. Amen.

JUNE 26

I am confident of this, that the one who began a good work among you will bring it to a completion by the day of Jesus Christ.

Philippians 1:6

God has begun a good work in you. As we walk through our daily journey as a law enforcement officer, we come upon many trials. We encounter many situations that cause us to rely on a faith in God to get us through. This good work is a process of spiritual growth inside us. Our accomplishments and our failures help our spirituality grow. We need to walk in faith throughout our lives. We should always be growing in our faith. Our spiritual growth may help others come to know God. Today, reflect on your spiritual growth. What do you need to change to help you grow in relationship with God?

God, Source of all spiritual growth, we thank you for allowing us to be part of your good work. May we continually grow in our relationship with you. Use us to bring others to know you. Amen.

JUNE 27

He gives power to the faint, and strengthens the powerless. Even youths will faint and be weary, and the young will fall exhausted;

but those who wait for the LORD shall renew their strength, and they shall mount up with wings of eagles, they shall run and not be weary, they shall walk and not be faint.

Isaiah 40:29-31

Many of us work out to stay physically strong. We want to be able to accomplish whatever task is placed in front of us; whether that be wrestling with a suspect, running after someone, or pushing a car out of the street. We want to be as strong as we can be. But no matter how much we work out, there will come a time when we feel exhausted, when we can't go on, when we feel powerless, and when we feel faint. It is during times like these that we are able to use our real strength. Our strength comes from and is God. God provides us with the strength to accomplish everything. God even provides us with the bodies we have and keep strong. God promises to strengthen us for the tasks that God wants us to accomplish.

God, Strength of those who labor, we thank you for strengthening our minds, bodies, and spirits, so that we may accomplish everything in your name. As Jesus knew you where his strength through all his difficulties, may we receive your Holy Spirit to provide us strength to work through all of our difficulties. Amen.

JUNE 28

"... You shall eat not only one day, or two days, or five days, or ten days, or twenty days, but for a whole month - until it comes out of your nostrils and becomes loathsome to you - because you rejected the LORD who is among you, and have wailed before him, saying, 'Why did we ever leave Egypt?'"

Numbers 11:19-20

Moses knew, through God, that the Hebrew people needed to leave Egypt. They were afraid to leave, and after they had, they complained about going back. Our job as law enforcement officers may be our Egypt. There will come a time when God tells us to leave. Many of us are afraid to leave the job that we know.

How many people have you seen stay too long in law enforcement? When God tells us it is time to go, we need to get out. God will provide for us once we are gone. We do not want to be one of those people who hang on too long. We also need to think about leaving our job, and start preparing for it. Even if you are a rookie and just started, start planning for retirement. Today, look at where you are, and begin the planning to retire. Whether that retirement is in one year or thirty years, it will be easier to go when God tells us to, if we have a plan.

Mighty God, we thank you for being with us in our jobs as law enforcement professionals. We know that you care for us, and communicate to us the best for our lives. May we hear you when you tell us it is time to leave this profession. Be with us in this difficult decision, as we move beyond this job, into another avenue of service for you. Amen.

JUNE 29

So let no one boast about human leaders. For all things are yours, whether Paul or Apollos or Cephas (Peter) or the world or life or death or the present or the future - all belongs to you, and you belong to Christ, and Christ belongs to God.

I Corinthians 3:21-23

Since 258CE, the church has remembered St. Peter and St. Paul on this day. We remember these two great apostles as two of the most important leaders in the early church. Both apostles preached and witnessed to the Gospel. They realized that they were not the most important, but Christ who was more important, who was sent by God, the most important. Both Peter and Paul came from other professions. But both of them had to bring the Good News to others. As we live our lives being law enforcement officers, may we also proclaim the Good News and witness to Christ in what we say and do. May we center ourselves on the Gospel, like Peter and Paul. May we realize that we are not to boast about human leaders, but about the real leaders: God, Christ and the Holy Spirit.

Almighty God, we thank you for sending apostles like Peter and Paul who glorified you in their preaching and witness. May we be inspired by their teaching and example, to proclaim the Good News. Through the Holy Spirit, may we witness to the church, which is the body of your son, Jesus Christ. Amen.

JUNE 30

Be gracious to me, O LORD, for I am in distress; my eye wastes away from grief, my soul and body also.

Psalm 31:9

We have a very stressful job. We go through periods of boredom, immediately into fearful situations. Our lives are full of stress. We feel like being this way is the only way to live. We use various things to try to take the edge off; alcohol, drugs, sex, etc. We fall into moods of depression when none of those work. We need to realize that stress is a natural part of what we do. We need to find healthy ways to minimize our stress. We can't go around, taking it out on the people we encounter, our family, our friends, or even ourselves. God understands our stress. When we give the stresses up to God, we receive answers on how to realize the stress we feel. Today, lift all of the stresses in your life to God in prayer. See if God doesn't give you answers on how to deal with the stresses. God will be with us, even where we are in distress.

All-knowing God, we give you thanks for walking with us through this difficult life. We ask you to be gracious to us in our times of distress. Send relief to our bodies and our souls, so that we may carry out your ministry with ease. Watch over us as we walk through our difficult times. Amen.

JULY 1

As God's chosen ones, holy and beloved, clothe yourselves with compassion, kindness, humility, meekness, and patience. Bear with one another and if, anyone has a complaint against another, forgive each other; just as the Lord (or as Christ) has forgiven you, so you also must forgive.

Colossians 3:12-13

We carry a lot of strife inside of us. Many times, when we are upset with someone, we hold it in. But, it comes out in ways that are we are not able to control. We are called to work things out with each other. We are to live with compassion. If we take the time to work things out, it will pay out larger in the long run. The Lord has forgiven us when we do wrong against him. So should we forgive when someone wrongs us. This is difficult many times. Today, think of all the people who you have something against. Try to go to them to bring peace to your relationship. Now, think of the people you may have wronged. Try and go to them to ask forgiveness. All you can do is your part.

God, Teacher of peace, we thank you for forgiving us when we offend you. Help us to forgive those who may have offended us. Inspire us to go to those that we may have offended. May your children live in peace, kindness, humility and patience. Amen.

JULY 2

For God did not despise or abhor the affliction of the afflicted; he did not hide his face from me, but heard when I cried to him.

Psalm 22:24

We can be afflicted with many sufferings: physical, mental, emotional, spiritual. Many times, we think we are alone in these sufferings. We feel as if no one understands our pain. We cry out, and we believe that God may not hear us. But, the Psalmist reassures us that God does hear us. God knows our afflictions whether we acknowledge them to God or not. When it seems everyone else has left us, God walks with us through our suffering. God will never turn his face from us, nor will God not hear us when we cry.

God, Hearer of all suffering, we give you thanks for never turning your face from us, and always hearing our cries. Walk with us through these times of our sufferings. Remind us that we are not alone, and that with you, we may see our way through them. Amen.

JULY 3

Because he (Jesus) himself was tested by what he suffered, he is able to help those who are being tested.

Hebrews 2:18

How easy it is for those of us in law enforcement to fall into temptation. We are constantly placed in situations that tempt us; we are placed in circumstances that tempt us. After awhile, we may feel that we are above the law. We don't have to follow the rules, because we enforce them. Who will stop us? The temptations run the whole gambit, from the smallest to the largest. We have seen many of our partners and friends fall into temptation. We, ourselves, may have even given in to temptation. But, we cannot live our lives in a bubble. To live the lives that we do, we have to walk through the temptations. And honestly, there may be times when we give it. But, Jesus will be with us, to help us work through our temptations. No matter how bad things may look, Jesus can help us. We may have to pay the penalty for our actions. We may have to suffer the consequences for our behavior. But we are not alone. God is with us during the times of trial. Are whether we win against a specific temptation, or we fall victim, remember, Jesus is with you. Today, spend some time in prayer, lifting up all the temptations in you life right now. Ask God to help you through them. Allow Jesus to walk along side you through them.

Forgiving God, we give you thanks for sending your son, Jesus Christ, to the world, so that we may be forgiven. As Jesus was tempted, so are we tempted. Help us through our temptations. Send the Holy Spirit to guide us away from the temptations of our life. Forgive us when we fall. Walk with us as we struggle. Amen.

JULY 4

But our citizenship (or commonwealth) is in heaven, and it is from there that we are expecting a Savior, the Lord Jesus Christ.
Philippians 3:20

Today, we here in the United States of America, celebrate our independence. As law enforcement officers, we take an oath of office that says we will uphold the beliefs that we know are true. We live in a world of freedom. And we are the thin blue line that defends that freedom. We need to take our duty to this country seriously. But we also know that there is a higher truth. There is One who has a final say. While we defend our country, we also do the ministry of Christ that we are called to do. On this national holiday, we should give thanks for our freedom. We should also give thank to God for creating us free.

God, Lord of all nations, guide the people of this country by your Holy Spirit, to go forward in justice and freedom. Above all things, give us faith in you, that our nation may bring glory to your name and blessings to all people. Amen.

JULY 5

From that time on (after Peter's confession), Jesus began to show his disciples that he must go to Jerusalem and undergo great suffering at the hands of the elders and chief priests and scribes, and be killed, and on the third day be raised. And Peter took him aside and began to rebuke him, saying, "God forbid it, Lord! This must never happen to you." But he turned and said to Peter, "Get behind me, Satan! You are a stumbling block to me; for you are setting your mind not on divine things but on human things."

Matthew 16:21-23

Just when you thought you were doing well, you went to your supervisor and gave advice on how things should be. Your supervisor probably told you to get back in line. That is what Jesus says to Peter in this passage. Peter tries to tell Jesus how things should be. Peter doesn't see the big picture. Many times, we don't see the big picture. We see our own little part. But because we are closest to the action, we think we know best. We are told to get back in line. God tells us to get back in line when we stray from our Christian path. Jesus doesn't tell Peter to leave, just to straighten up and get things in the right perspective. God doesn't tell us to get out, God just tells us to straighten up and see things through the proper view. Take some time today and reflect on how you can get back in line with your Christian walk. Set a plan for doing it. Remember, Peter was still the rock, and you are still God's child.

Forgiving God, we give you thanks for guiding us through this life. We confess that there are times that we stray. We ask you to tell us to get back in line when we drift. May we hear you, as Peter heard your son, Jesus. Send the Holy Spirit to us so that we may make the necessary corrections. Amen.

JULY 6

I will give to the LORD the thanks due to his righteousness, and sing praise to the name of the LORD, the Most High.

Psalm 7:17

We need to take time to give God thanks. All that we have, we receive through God. We should to the time to say, "Thank you." Set aside some time every day, to say "thank you" to God for everything that you have received.

God, Life of all who live, we give you thanks for all you have given us. We may not always to the time to tell you "thanks", but know that we are truly thankful. Amen.

JULY 7

The LORD is good, a stronghold in a day of trouble; he protects those who take refuge in him, even in a rushing flood. He will make a full end of his adversaries (or of her place), and will pursue his enemies into darkness.

Nahum 1:7-8

When people are in trouble, they call people like us. Law enforcement officers arrive to help make the trouble go away. But we have trouble in our lives, also. And some times, it is trouble that law enforcement cannot help with. We get into the midst of things that seem like a flood. Who do we call in times of trouble? The prophet Nahum reminds us that God is always there to call on in times of trouble. God is a stronghold, something to hold on to, in difficult times. It is during those times that we need to be in prayer. No matter how bad the trouble may be, God will always be there for us. Today, spend some time looking at the troubles in your life. Lift them up in prayer, and ask God to strengthen you during those times. And remember, you may be God's answer to someone else's prayer for strength during trouble.

God, our Stronghold, we give you thanks for being strong for us during our times of trouble. Strengthen us so that we may overcome our difficult times. Use us as your instruments, to bring strength to others. Amen.

JULY 8

A false balance is an abomination to the LORD, but an accurate weight is his delight.

Proverbs 11:1

We live in an unfair world. The system for justice is Lady Liberty holding the scales of justice. We see situations, even in the justice system, where there is a false balance. We see how there is not a balance in how people are treated. We see the unfairness of our society. We represent justice, fairness and balance. When we arrive, people expect fairness. We have to weight the scales of justice with the facts that we have, and make decisions based on the facts. We cannot use our authority to tip the balance according to our feeling and beliefs. We have to remove our own emotions, and treat everyone with the same fairness. God desires fairness. God uses us as instruments of balance. People look to us as the representative of justice.

God, Source of all fairness, we give you thanks for the balance your desire in your creation. Help us to bring balance to our own lives. Use us as your instruments to show justice in the world. May we continue to defeat the falseness of oppression, and help to bring this world into a place where everything is weighed accurately. Amen.

JULY 9

Owe no one anything, except to love one another' for the one who loves another has fulfilled the law. The commandments, "You shall not commit adultery; You shall not murder; You shall not steal; You shall not covert"; and any other commandment, are summed up in this word, "Love your neighbor as yourself." Love does not wrong to a neighbor; therefore, love is the fulfilling of the law.

Romans 13:8-10

As law enforcement officers, we know all about keeping the law. We are the ones that enforce the rules. What the rules do is keep each other in line. God's laws keep us in right relationships; with our neighbors, with God, and with ourselves. If we love our neighbors, our God, and ourselves, then we remain in right relationships. By loving, we are keeping the laws. We don't do away with them; we keep them as a result of our love.

God of love, we thank you for loving us. Help us to stay in right relationships so that we may love all those around us, love ourselves, and most important, love you. Amen.

JULY 10

But thanks be to God, who gives us the victory through our Lord Jesus Christ.

1 Corinthians 15:57

We always strive to win. We feel as if we have fallen short when we don't gain the victory. We strive to win in life. But we fall short in our sinful nature. We feel as if we can never win. But God has provided us with the victory. Our Lord Jesus Christ has already defeated sin for us. Christ has given us the victory. We are to live continuing to strive, but we have the knowledge that we have already won. Today, give thanks to God the Father, God the Son, and God the Holy Spirit for giving you the victory.

God, Source of all victory, we give you thanks that you sent your son, our Lord Jesus Christ, to defeat sin so that we may have the victory. Send the Holy Spirit to us, so that we may continue in our battle. A battle that we know has already been won. Amen.

JULY 11

...but he (the Lord) said to me, "My grace is sufficient for you, for power (or my power) is made perfect in weakness." So, I will boast all the more gladly of my weaknesses, so that the power of Christ may dwell in me. Therefore I am content with weaknesses,

insults, hardships, persecutions, and calamities for the sake of Christ; for whenever I am weak, then I am strong.

2 Corinthians 12:9-10

As law enforcement officers, we believe that we cannot be weak. If we are weak, we cannot effectively do our job. Many times, we believe that as Christians, we will not have times of weakness. Truth is, we do feel weak. We do have times when we believe that we are not strong enough to accomplish a task, or even do our job. God knows that we will feel weak at times. God walks through those times of weakness with us. Through Christ, God gives us the power and strength to accomplish what we have set out to do. There will be times when we have hardships. But we know that we can gain strength from the ultimate source of power.

God, Source of all power, we give you thanks for walking with us in our hardships. Give us the strength to overcome our weaknesses. Remind us, that through your Son, Jesus Christ, we may gain the strength to carry on. Send your Holy Spirit to us when we suffer persecutions, insults hardships, and calamities. Even when we are weak, you make us strong, to accomplish the tasks you place before us. Amen.

JULY 12

I pray that the God of our Lord Jesus Christ, the Father of glory, may give you a spirit of wisdom and revelation as you come to know him,

Ephesians 1:17

We make many decisions at work. Some we have to make in a spilt-second. Some, we have the ability to stop and evaluate all the information we know at the time. These decisions may be minor, and may have life and death implications. We rely on a number of attributes to make these decisions. God gives you the ability to have the necessary wisdom to make the proper decision.

God will allow you to see what the proper course of action is in a situation. Whenever you need to make a decision, pray that God gives you the wisdom to decide.

God, Source of all wisdom, we give you thanks for being with us in all our decisions. Send the Holy Spirit to us, to bring us the wisdom we need to make proper choices. May we always rely on you as our source of revelation. May we continue to follow your Son, our Lord Jesus Christ, in making the right decisions. Amen.

JULY 13

When God saw what they did, how they turned from their evil ways, God changed his mind about the calamity that he had said he would bring upon them; and he did not do it. But this was very displeasing to Jonah, and he became angry. He prayed to the LORD and said, "O LORD! Is not this what I said while I was still in my own country? That is why I fled to Tarshish at the beginning; for I knew that you are a gracious God and merciful, slow to anger, and abounding in steadfast love, and ready to relent from punishing. And now, O LORD, please take my life from me, for it is better for me to die than to live." And the LORD said, "Is it right for you to be angry?" Then Jonah went out of the city and sat down east of the city, and made a booth for himself there. He sat under it in the shade, waiting to see what would become of the city. The LORD God appointed a bush, and made it come up over Jonah, to give shade over his head, to save him from his discomfort; so Jonah was very happy about the bush. But when dawn came up the next day, God appointed a worm that attacked the bush, so that it withered. When the sun rose, God prepared a sultry east wind, and the sun beat down on the head of Jonah so that he was faint and asked that he might die. He said, "It is better for me to die than to live." But God said to Jonah, "Is it right for you to be angry about the bush?" And he said, "Yes, angry enough to die." Then the LORD said, "You are concerned about the bush, for which you did not labor and which you did not grow; it came into being in a night and perished in a night. And should I not be concerned about Nineveh, that great city, in which there are more than a hundred and twenty thousand persons who do not know their right hand from their left, and also many animals?"

Jonah 3:10-4:11

We encounter a variety of people in our profession. Sometimes, we have prejudices about people. Jonah didn't want the Ninevites to be saved because he didn't like them. When they were saved, because of how God used him, Jonah whined and pouted. Do we pout when God asks us to minister to people we don't like? Many times we do. We pout when we show no partiality at work. Justice means justice for everyone, whether we like him or her or not. And remember, God will use you, even when you don't like it, just like Jonah.

God, Judge Eternal, we give you thanks for listening to us pout and whine. We have difficulties working through our prejudices. Help us to minister to those that are different from us. Use us to further your kingdom, even when we pout and whine. Amen.

JULY 14

"So do not worry about tomorrow, for tomorrow will bring worries of its own. Today's trouble is enough for today."

Matthew 6:34

How often do we worry? We worry about everything. We worry about many things that we cannot control. We spend our lives worrying about the worst-case scenario. Some times it is good to plan alternatives. But it is not good to spend a lot of time worrying about things that may never come to pass, or things that are not of concern. We have enough concerns to think about everyday. Today, what you start to worry about something, think to yourself if you really need to worry so mush. If not, let the issue go. If it is a concern, it will come back again.

God, Refuge of those who put their trust in you, we thank you for being there for us. We need to learn to put our trust in you. We should spend less time worrying about issues that are not of a great concern. We know that you will provide for us. Help us to remove the worry from our lives. Amen.

JULY 15

Do not remember the sins of my youth or my transgressions; according to your steadfast love remember me, for your goodness' sake, O LORD!

Psalm 25:7

Can you think of all the wrongs you have committed? We do things purposefully, and sometimes, we commit wrongs by accident. The best thing we can do is make amends and go on. We should learn from our mistakes. God doesn't remember our sins. Once we make confession, God puts them in the past. God remembers us in love. God never stops loving us, even when we have a sinful past. Today, take time to put all your wrongs in the past. Ask God to forgive you, and remember God's steadfast love for you.

Redeeming God, we give you thanks for remembering us in your steadfast love. We ask that you forget all the sins we have confessed that are in our past. Help us to move ahead in the service of your kingdom. Amen.

JULY 16

When he (Jesus) entered the temple, the chief priests and the elders of the people came to him as he was teaching, and said, "By what authority are you doing these things, and who gave you this authority?" Jesus said to them, "I will also ask you one question; if you tell me the answer, then I will tell you by what authority I do these things. Did the baptism of John come from heaven, or was it of human origin?" And they argued with one another, "If we say, 'From heaven,' he will say to us, 'Why then did you not believe him?' But if we say, 'Of human origin,' we are afraid of the crowd; for all regard John as a prophet." So they answered Jesus, "We do not know." And he said to them, "Neither will I tell you by what authority I am doing these things. What do you think? A man had two sons; he went to the first and said, 'Son, go and work in the vineyard today.' He answered, 'I will not'; but later he changed his mind and went. The father went to the second and said the same; and he answered, 'I go, sir'; but he did not go. Which of the two did the will of the father?" They said, "The first." Jesus said to them, "Truly I tell you, the tax collectors and the prostitutes are going into the kingdom of God ahead of you. For John came to you in the way of righteousness and you did not believe him, but the tax collectors and prostitutes believed him; and even after you saw it, you did not change your minds and believe him."

Matthew 21:23-32

"I am the one with the gun and the badge, so I am in charge!" How many times you have said that? We are placed in a position of authority. But do we always asset our authority in the proper manner. Authority is something that is given to us; we do not take it for ourselves. We should always use our authority in the proper manner. God also gives us authority, authority to go into the world and spread the Good News of Jesus Christ. Do we overstep our authority as Christians, also? God is the ultimate and final authority. When we realize we have acted improperly, we need to change our mind, and submit to the proper authority, just like the first son in the parable. Today, reflect upon all the times you may have abused your authority, or not submitted to proper authority. Take some time to have a change of mind, submit to the One authority, and continue spreading the Gospel.

God, Keeper of the covenants, we give you thanks for providing us with the authority to do our jobs, and the authority to proclaim the Good News. We ask you to forgive us when we overstep our authority, or we when we do not submit to proper authority. Fill our hearts with understanding, so that we may carry out our vocation in the ministry of your Kingdom. Amen.

JULY 17

So if anyone is in Christ, there is a new creation: everything old has passed away; see, everything has become new! All this is from God, who reconciled us to himself through Christ, and has given us the ministry of reconciliation; that is, in Christ God was reconciling the world to himself, not counting their trespasses against them, and entrusting the message of reconciliation to us.
2 Corinthians 5:17-19

The world that we work in is still a broken place. The Gospel doesn't allow us to conform to the ways of the world. We are restless with the brokenness and violence we encounter. We are called to struggle against these evils. The church is a new creation from God. But we are still part of this broken world. We are a community of saints, righteous before God on account of what Jesus self-giving love. But we are still a community of sinners. We live under the cross, in repentance and forgiveness, hoping for the coming of the full reign of God. When we see the brokenness, we should work in ways that brings reconciliation. Today, look around for ways that you can assist with reconciliation.

God, Life of the universe, we give you thanks for reconciling us to you, through the love of Jesus. We struggle in this broken world. Be with us in this struggle. May we be instruments of your reign, by providing possibilities for reconciliation. Amen.

JULY 18

When they had brought them (the apostles), they had them stand before the council. The high priest questioned them, saying, "We gave you strict orders not to teach in this name, yet here you have filled Jerusalem with your teaching and you are determined to bring this man's blood on us." But Peter and the apostles answered, "We must obey God rather than any human authority. The God of our ancestors raised up Jesus, whom you had killed by hanging him on a tree. God exalted him at his right hand as Leader and Savior that he might give repentance to Israel and forgiveness of sins. And we are witnesses to these things, and so is the Holy Spirit whom God has given to those who obey him."

Acts 5: 27-32

We can see both sides of this story. We are agents of human authority, in the course and nature of our employment. But, we are also agents of this highest authority. We are members of a believing community that strives to pioneer new ways of addressing emerging social problems. As believers, we have a responsibility to mediate conflict, and to advocate just and peaceful solutions to the world's divisions. We should support institutions and policies that serve the common good, and work and learn from others. As a prophetic presence, this church has the obligation to name and denounce the idols which people bow, to identify the power of sin, and to advocate in hope with poor and powerless people. When structures, ideologies or authorities claim to be absolute, we, as members of the body of Christ must stand up and say that we must obey God. This is what Peter and the apostles had to do; this is what many of the martyrs had to do; this is what we are to do. We need to remember who the highest authority is.

God, Ruler of the universe, we give you thanks for being the highest authority in the world. Help us to remain faithful to your authority. May we continue to follow your instructions of how we are to be in this world. Help us support those who need us to speak up. Amen.

JULY 19

What then are we to say? Should we continue in sin in order that grace may abound? By no means! How can we who died to sin go on living in it? Do you not know that all of us who have been baptized into Christ Jesus were baptized into his death? Therefore we have been buried with him by baptism into death, so that, just as Christ was raised from the dead by the glory of the Father, so we too might walk in newness of life.

Romans 6:1-4

One of the ways the church participates in society is through its members. In dying to sin and rising with Jesus Christ in baptism, Christians are called to "walk in newness of life". They fulfill their baptismal vacation in ordinary life as family members, citizens, workers, and all other aspects of life. Since daily life is the primary setting for the exercise of the Christian calling, it is in that setting that Christians are to serve God and neighbor. You are called to serve God in your roles in the family, as a friend and as a law enforcement officer. God will use you in everything that you do. Remember that everyone you encounter sees God through you. And everywhere you go, you do the work of God.

God, Lover of souls, we give you thanks for bringing us to a newness of life through Christ. Help us to live out our baptismal calling wherever we may be. May you always use us as representatives of your kingdom to the world. Amen.

JULY 20

Once more Jesus spoke to them in parables, saying: "The kingdom of heaven may be compared to a king who gave a wedding banquet for his son. He sent his slaves to call those who had been invited to the wedding banquet, but they would not come. Again he sent other slaves, saying, 'Tell those who have been invited: Look, I have prepared my dinner, my oxen and my fat calves have been slaughtered, and everything is ready; come to the wedding banquet.' But they made light of it and went away, one to his farm, another to his business, while the rest seized his slaves, mistreated them, and killed them. The king was enraged. He sent his troops, destroyed those murderers, and burned their city. Then he said to his slaves, 'The wedding is ready, but those invited were not worthy. Go therefore into the main streets, and invite everyone you find to the wedding banquet.' Those slaves went into the streets and gathered all whom they found, both good and bad; so the wedding hall was filled with guests.

Matthew 22:1-10

It was the custom to invite guest to a wedding twice in that time: first, to announce the banquet; then second, to tell them that the banquet was ready. In this parable, the king goes even farther, and invites them a third time. God invites us to the royal wedding feast over and over again. God calls everyone to enjoy the feast of the kingdom of heaven. God will continue to invite us. You are invited to that wonderful feast, as a guest. You are also the servants who go out offering the invitation for the king. Our lives take us to many places. Our words and our actions should be an invitation from God, to the kingdom of heaven, for all who we encounter. Today, think of the ways and people you can invite to meet God. And give thanks for the many invitations that God has given you.

God, life of the world, we give you thanks for continually offering us an invitation to your kingdom. Use us as your servants, to announce the invitation to your banquet. May all who hear us, answer the call. Amen.

JULY 21

But we have this treasure in clay jars, so that it may be made clear that this extraordinary power belongs to god and does not come from us.

2 Corinthians 4:7

We have the treasure of the Gospel in clay jars to show that the transcendent power belongs to God and not to us. We set forth our words and deeds with the prayer that they may be clay jars of the witness to the power of the cross. We care for and serve the earth, our neighbor, and our society with the joyful confidence that God's faithfulness alone sustains us. May God renew our faith, hope and love. May our witness be a response to God's faithful love that we receive in Word and Sacrament. The bread and the wine, the body and the blood of Christ are a gift of love. As love and support are given to us, may we in turn render love and support to the entire world. Today, think of the ways that you may be a witness to the body of Christ.

God, light of the faithful, we give you thanks as the power the alone rules the world. May we be your clay jars in our words and actions. May we serve as a witness to the life-giving love of Christ. And may the Holy Spirit continue to provide us with faith, hope and love. Amen.

JULY 22

But Mary (Magdalene) stood weeping outside the tomb. As she wept, she bet over to look into the tomb; and she saw two angels in white, sitting where the body of Jesus had been lying, one at the head and the other at the feet. They said to her, "Woman, why are you weeping?" She said to them, "They have taken away my Lord, and I do not know where they have laid him." When she had said this, she turned around and saw Jesus standing there, but she did not know that it was Jesus. Jesus said to her, "Woman, why are you weeping? Whom are you looking for?" Supposing him to be the gardener, she said to him, "Sir, if you have carried him away, tell me where you have laid him, and I will take him away." Jesus said to her, "Mary!" She turned and said to him in Hebrew (or Aramaic), "Rabbouni!" (which means Teacher). Jesus said to her, "Do not hold on to me, because I have not yet ascended to the Father. But go to my brothers and say to them, 'I am ascending to my Father and your Father, to my God and your God.'" Mary Magdalene went and announced to the disciples, "I have seen the Lord"; and she told them that he had said these things to her.

John 20:11-18

Today, the church remembers Mary Magdalene. She was one of the first people to find the tomb empty, and was a primary witness to the resurrection. Mary was healed by Jesus, and became one of his followers. She followed him throughout the rest of his journeys. Her devotion to Jesus was confirmed when she stood at the foot of the cross, when the rest of the disciples abandoned him. We should strive to be more like Mary Magdalene. Even when others abandon the faith, we should remain to proclaim the truth. We are to be like Mary, by proclaiming the story of Jesus' resurrection to as many people as we can tell.

Almighty God, your Son, Jesus, healed Mary Magdalene in body and in mind. Jesus called her to be a witness to his resurrection. Heal us in mind and body, so that we may be witnesses to Jesus' resurrection. Call on us to serve you, through the power of the Holy Spirit. Amen.

JULY 23

Keep your lives free from the love of money, and be content with what you have; for he has said, "I will never leave you or forsake you."

Hebrews 13:5

We did not get into law enforcement for the money. But, money does control some of what we do. The Bible says more about money, than just about any other topic. We need to remember that God owns everything. So therefore, we don't have to fear losing it, we don't have to have conflict in the family over it, and we don't have to have guilt about it. Our love of money puts us in debt. To free ourselves, we have to get out of debt. We start by not putting ourselves farther in debt. We should determine exactly how much we owe, develop a plan to pay it all off, and then follow it. We need to be committed to this. But, the pressure is taken off because God owns all of it. And God has said that He will not leave us or forsake us. So today, take some time and seriously come up with a plan to relieve yourself of the bondage of money.

God, Owner of all things, we give you thanks for all that you have given us. Help us to break the chains that money has over us. Assist us in proper stewardship of what you have given us. For we know that you will never leave us, nor forsake us. Amen.

JULY 24

(Jesus Said) "This is my commandment, that you love one another as I have loved you. No one has greater love than this, to lay down one's life for one's friends.

John 15:12-13

Law enforcement can be a lonely job. Many times, we are sent out on our own. But we are not sent out on our own in life. We have friends to share all our joys and sorrows. We are not supposed to lead isolated lives. Our friends are there for us, during our ups and our downs. We are to love one another as Christ loved us, to give everything. You have friends who are willing to do that for you, just as you are willing to do it for your friends. And even when it may seem that you are alone, Christ is always with you. Christ loves you. Christ has already laid down his life for you. Today, think of the friends that you have, and ask them to support you and be with you through the ups and downs of life.

God, Steadfast and Loving One, we give you thanks for loving us so much that you sent your Son to lay down his life for us. Send the Holy Spirit to us, to inspire us to be there for others, as they are there for me. Remove us from our isolated worlds. Help us to live and love one another, as Christ commanded us. Amen.

JULY 25

About that time King Herod laid violent hands upon some who belonged to the church. He had James, the brother of John, killed with the sword.

Acts of the Apostles 12:1-2

Today, the church remembers the apostle, James the Elder. James, the son of Zebedee and brother of John, is the only apostle whose martyrdom is recorded in Scripture. James is often pictured with a shell, a reminder that he was a fisherman and that he later baptized new Christians. Of the two men named James who became apostles, this James is called the elder, or the greater, because we know more about him. James was called as fisherman to minister in Christ's Church. You are also called as law enforcement officers to minister to the people you come into contact, in their situation. Some may have seen James as an ordinary fisherman. Some may see you as an ordinary law enforcement officer. But you can still make a huge difference for the Kingdom of God.

O Gracious God, toady we remember your servant and apostle James, first among the Twelve to suffer martyrdom for the name of Christ. Pour out upon the people of your Church that spirit of self-denying service which is the true mark of authority among your people. Amen.

JULY 26

Have nothing to do with profane myths and old wives' tales. Train yourself in godliness, for, while physical training is of some value, godliness is valuable in every way, holding promise for both the present life and the life to come.

1 Timothy 4:7-8

As law enforcement officers, we train in the gym and others places to remain physically fit. Our job requires us to be able to accomplish physical tasks. But do we train to be spiritually fit? Our spirituality is just as important. We need to learn to spend as much time, training to be godly people, as we spend trying to be strong. Catching a glimpse of God's glory is the ultimate. It will cause us to want to be more like God. And this means reflecting God in our daily life. This type of training is just as much a workout as the weights. Today, take some time to find ways to train-up your spirituality on a daily basis.

God, Maker of all things, we give you thanks for giving us strong bodies. Help us to train ourselves spiritually be more like you. Amen.

JULY 27

"... Do not work for the food that perishes, but for the food that endures for eternal life, which the Son of Man will give you. For it is on him that God the Father has set his seal."

John 6:27

We need to constantly be modeling Christ while we are at work. There is a difference in the experience, performance and behavior of a Christian in the workplace, as opposed to a non-Christian. We work with a sense of being called by God to our vocation. We display character in the workplace. We deliver skills that are gifts from God. And we model serving. Anyone we encounter at work should be able to see that we are Godly law enforcement officers.

God, Maker of heaven and earth, we give you thanks for sending our skills to us, calling us to our professions, and walking with us in our workplace. May all that we do glorify you. Amen.

JULY 28

Do not get drunk with wine, for that is debauchery; but be filled with the Spirit, as you sing psalms and hymns and spiritual songs among yourselves, singing and making melody to the Lord in your hearts, giving thanks to God the Father at all times and for everything in the name of our Lord Jesus Christ.

Ephesians 5:18-20

Today, the church remembers Johann Sebastian Bach, Heinrich Schutz, and George Frederick Handel. These musicians used their gifts of composition to enrich worship and devotional lives of Christians from their time until today. Schutz died in

1672, Bach died in 1750, and Handel died in 1759. These three musicians used their God-given gifts, in their own field to further the Kingdom of God. We too, as law enforcement officers, are able to use our own God-given gifts and talents, in our own situations to proclaim the Good News of Jesus Christ. Today, reflect on areas of your life that are gifts from god, that you may use in everyday life to further the Gospel.

Almighty God, beautiful in majesty, you have shown us the wonders of your creation through the works of Johann Sebastian Bach, Heinrich, Schutz, and George Frederick Handel. Teach how to use our gifts like these men to further your kingdom. Amen.

JULY 29

Now a certain man was ill, Lazarus of Bethany, the village of Mary and her sister Martha. Mary was the one who anointed the Lord with perfume and wiped his feet with her hair; her brother Lazarus was ill. So the sisters sent a message to Jesus, "Lord, he whom you love is ill." But when Jesus heard it, he said, "This illness does not lead to death; rather it is for God's glory, so that the Son of God may be glorified through it." Accordingly, though Jesus loved Martha and her sister and Lazarus, after having heard that Lazarus was ill, he stayed two days longer in the place where he was.

John 11:1-6

Today, the church commemorates Mary, Martha and Lazarus of Bethany. They are remembered for their hospitality and refreshment they offered Jesus in their home. We have the opportunity to offer hospitality and refreshment to many people. One of the nicest acts of love is to offer hospitality. Hospitality causes you to open yourself to others. Today, reflect on the role of hospitality in your life. Ask how you may provide refreshment to others.

Mighty and Forever God, we give you thanks for sending your Son to us, as an act of hospitality and refreshment. May we be places that others may be able to be refreshed. We lift up people like Mary, Martha and Lazarus as examples of hospitality. Amen.

JULY 30

For David, after he had served the purpose of God in his own gen-
eration, died (or fell asleep), was laid beside his ancestors, and
experienced corruption; but he whom God raised up experienced
no corruption. Let it be known to you therefore, my brothers, that
through this man forgiveness of sins is proclaimed to you; by this
Jesus everyone who believes is set free from all those sins from
which you could not be freed by the law of Moses.

Acts of the Apostles 13:36-39

There is a difference between you and other Christians you
work with, and those law enforcement officers who are not
Christian. Your experience, performance and behavior as a
Christian should lead others to see Christ through your work.
People should be able to see what Christ has done for you. A
Christian should evidence a sense of calling in your profession.
Your job is you ministry. A Christian should display character in
your workplace. Others should be able to Christ working through
you. A Christian delivers skill. You should be the best you can be,
to give glory to God. A Christian models serving. You are out
there to serve the community in which you work. How you carry
yourself, and carry out your work sets you apart as a person who
has Christ in their life. Others may come to know Christ, by seeing Christ in you.

God, Maker of Light, we give you thanks for giving us the
Light of Christ in our lives. May we carry the Light with us in our
work. May others see the Light by our actions. Like David, you
have called us to a purpose in our own generation. Strengthen us
to accomplish the tasks you set before us. Amen.

JULY 31

For through the law I died to the law, so that I might live to God.
I have been crucified with Christ; and it is no longer I who live,
but it is Christ who lives in me. And the life I now live in the flesh

I live by faith in the Son of God (or by the faith of the Son of God), who loved me and gave himself for me.

Galatians 2:19-20

Being a person of God means that we no longer live our own life, but the life God desires us to live. It is now Christ who lives in us, and allows us to do the will of God. Even though we still live in the flesh of this life, we live by the faith Christ has given to us by his death on the cross. Christ, who gave himself for us, now influences us. We are now servants of the Kingdom of God. But, we can still be leaders, showing others how to be servants of God. Reflect today on the parts of your life that still hold you back from becoming a servant of God. Offer these areas of your life up to Christ. Place your love in Christ, not in the things of this world.

God, Mighty Redeemer, we give you thanks for sending your Son so that, through Him, we die to the law and live through you. Send your Holy Spirit to us, so that we may no longer rely on the things of this world. Inspire to be servants of your Kingdom. Amen.

AUGUST 1

"... For what will it profit them if they gain the whole world but forfeit their life? Or what will they give in return for their life?"

Matthew 16:26

Following Christ means that our lives take a radical change. God calls us to let go of the whole world. We make mistakes, but we need to move on from them. The influence of the Holy Spirit allows us to bury the past and let go. We continue moving forward with God. Reflect today about the areas in your life that you need to bury and let go. Offer them to God, so that you will profit.

One and Eternal God of time and space, we want to profit in your. Help us to let go of the past mistakes in our lives, and to bury them in our past. Send your Holy Spirit to assist us in refraining from forfeiting our life. We desire to be disciples of your Son, Jesus Christ. Amen.

AUGUST 2

Am I now seeking human approval, or God's approval? Or am I trying to please people? It I were still pleasing people, I would not be a servant (or slave) of Christ.

Galatians 1:10

Whose approval do we seek? Who is ultimately the one we worship? Many times, we worship what we have, who we are, or ourselves. We do everything in our lives to please and look good for others. By turning to God, we need to learn to give those things up. We need to give up the future aspirations, climbing the rank and promotion ladder, to prove who we are. God will provide for our future. God will reveal the plan for us. We need to give up trying to maintain our reputation, how people see us. God will provide our reputation as a child of God. We need to give up the pursuit of money; worshiping the dollar, working overtime or special duty, measuring ourselves by how much we have. God provides us with the means to take care of ourselves. We need to give up our possessions, keeping up with everyone else. God will provide us with the necessities of life. We need to give up our time to God. Too often, we neglect our spiritual life and doing the work of the Kingdom. We need to give up our worrying about our bodies. We worship how we look. God will heal us and keep us whole. To be a servant of Christ means that we need to give up these things every day. Today, reflect on what you need to give up.

God, Mind of the universe, we give you thanks for providing for us. Send your Holy Spirit to us so that we may give up the trappings of this world. Assist us in being servants of your Son, Jesus Christ. Amen.

AUGUST 3

"Teacher, which commandment in the law is the greatest?" He (Jesus) said to him, " 'You shall love the Lord your God with all your heart, and with all your soul, and with all your mind.' This is the greatest and first commandment. And a second is like it: 'You shall love your neighbor as yourself.' On these two commandments hang all the law and the prophets."

Matthew 22:36-40

Christianity is easy, love God with everything and love your neighbor as yourself. Living out our faith becomes very difficult. We build up so many different walls that we stop ourselves from fulfilling God's commands. We need to spend more time breaking down these walls that we place before ourselves. As law enforcement officers, we tend to have a we/them mentality about everything. This is against the words Jesus gave us. We need to move toward reconciliation, so that we can love our neighbors. Embracing reconciliation means that we have to live out the Great Commandment. Offer everything up to God. And then, love everyone as you would love yourself. Today, reflect on ways that you can move closer to reconciliation with people that are separated by walls.

God, Only One, we struggle to live out the commandments that you have given us. Help us to love you with everything that we are. Assist us in following the commandments of Jesus, loving our neighbors as ourselves. Send you Holy Spirit to us so that we may be reconciled with all your children. Amen.

AUGUST 4

Therefore, since we are surrounded by so great a cloud of witnesses, let us also lay aside every weight and the sin that clings so closely (or the sin that easily distracts), and let us run with perseverance the race that is set before us, looking to Jesus the pioneer and perfecter of our faith, who for the sake of (or who instead of) the joy that was set before him endured the cross, disregarding its shame, and has taken his seat at the right hand of the throne of God.

Hebrews 12:1-2

You don't have to work too many years in our profession, before you may begin to think that there is no hope for us. We encounter situation after situation that appears hopeless. But, being a godly person, means that we are to have faith for our times. We are to lay aside the weight that we bear in this life. Jesus has endured the cross for us. We are not ones who believe that our faith will make everything all right. We have to persevere. We will still have weight, and sin, and shame. But Christ is our pioneer and the perfection of our faith. Christ has made it possible to have hope. Even through the difficult times, we should have hope for our time and that Christ will work through us.

God, Source of all deliverance and help, be with us as we persevere on the race set before us. Help us to work through the difficult times. We know that Christ has given us hope. Amen.

AUGUST 5

Happy is everyone who fears the LORD, who walks in his ways.
You shall eat the fruit of the labor of your hands; you shall be
happy, and it shall go well with you. Your wife will be like a fruit-
ful vine within your house; your children will be like olive shoots
around your table. Thus shall the man be blessed who fears the
LORD. The LORD bless you from Zion. May you see the pros-
perity of Jerusalem all the days of your life. May you see your
children's children. Peace be upon Israel!

Psalm 128:1-6

Knowing that there is hope for our time, even when it may appear that there is not, calls us to action. We are to be the ones who are agents of revival. We are to be the ones that proclaim the hope we have in God. We are to be agents of revival in many areas. We should be agents of revival for ourselves. We are to be happy in the Lord. God has hope for our lives. We are to be agents of revival for our family. No matter how difficult times may become in our family life, there is hope. God wants us to be happy in our family lives. We are to be agents of revival for our church. As Christians, we disagree a lot. But God wants us to be united in Christ, so that we may bring hope to others. God has hope for our churches. We are to be agents of revival in our workplace. As law enforcement officers, we encounter people who believe there is no hope. God places us in those situations, say that we may bring a word of hope to them. We are to be agents of revival in our communities. Society appears to be taking quite a downslide. We are to provide our communities with a sense that God wants us to be blessed. Our times are difficult. But God works through our lives, to give us hope. With this hope, we are to be agents of revival in a distressed world.

God, Our Creator and Our Teacher, we give you thanks for having hope in us. You are our peace in a troubled world. Send your Holy Spirit to us so that we may find the happiness you desire for us. And help us to be agents of revival, in the name of your Son, our risen Savior and Lord, Jesus Christ. Amen.

AUGUST 6

When I shut up the heavens so that there is no rain, or command the locust to devour the land, or send pestilence among my people, if my people who are called by my name humble themselves, pray, seek my face, and turn from their wicked ways, then I will hear from heaven, and will forgive their sin and heal their land.

II Chronicles 7:13-14

God spoke these words to Solomon. God speaks these words to us. We live in a sinful world. Our profession places us where we are able to see what humanity does to humanity. Many times, we get caught up in the sinfulness ourselves. We need to hear these words from the Lord. We need to remind others that we should humble ourselves, pray, seek God and turn from our wicked ways. God has said that our sins will be forgiven. Today, reflect on places in your life where you need to pray, humble yourself, and seek God's face for forgiveness.

God, Our Source and End, we give you thanks for sparing us. We are people who call on your name. Be with us as we humble ourselves before you. We pray that we may have our sins forgiven by you. Help us to turn from our wicked ways. Amen.

AUGUST 7

Blow the trumpet in Zion; sanctify a fast; call a solemn assembly; gather the people. Sanctify the congregation; assemble the aged; gather the children, even infants at the breast. Let the bridegroom leave his room, and the bride her company.

Joel 2:15-16

We live in a world that focuses on the individual. We work in a profession where we are isolated. There are many times that we have no one to talk to about things on our minds. We are called to be with other people. Christianity is not a religion that is practiced alone. We need to find a community of faith to worship with on at least a weekly basis. We also need to find one person who can be the one we go to with difficult issues. Even the Pope has a Confessor. The prophet Joel reminds us that the gathered assembly is a sacred place, where we offer glory to God. Today, if you do not have a church where you regularly worship, find one. If you do not have one person in your life that can listen to you, give you direction, and act as a confessor, find one. Our faith is lived out in community.

God, Power that saves, we give you thanks for saving us. Help us to find a worshipping community and a person to be our confident friend. We know that our faith is lived out with others. Assist us in being more like your ultimate community, the Holy Trinity, Father, Son, and Holy Spirit. Amen.

AUGUST 8

A leper came to him (Jesus) begging him, and kneeling he said to him, "If you choose, you can make me clean." Moved with pity, Jesus stretched out his hand and touched him, and said to him, "I do choose. Be made clean!" Immediately the leprosy left him, and he was made clean. After sternly warning him he sent him away at once, saying to him, "See that you say nothing to anyone; but go, show yourself to the priest, and offer for your cleansing what Moses commanded, as a testimony to them." But he went out and began to proclaim it freely, and to spread the word, so that Jesus could not longer go into a town openly, but stayed out in the country; and people came to him from every quarter.

Mark 1:40-45

We work in a profession where people are outcasts, and people cast others out. The leper is an outcast in this story. He has been cast out from the community. When have you been the outcast? Many times, we are the outcasts in society, because of the uniform or our job. People would just as soon kill us as call us by name. When have you been the one to cast someone else out? We are the enforcers of the law. We remove people from places, people, and situations. Sometimes, we even cast people out by helping send them to jail or prison. But what can we learn from Jesus in this story. Jesus was more interested in restoring the leper back to the community. Jesus stepped over the law to accomplish this task. Jesus could have been considered an outcast for even speaking to the leper, let alone touching him, which was against the law. When we evaluate situations, both at work and in our personal lives, we need to weigh the law against the value of showing compassion for the person. It is living in this gray area of tension that is our Christian life. Each time you make a decision, if you are able, weigh the law and the Good News of Christ, and come up with the best answer.

God, Source of truth and law, we give you thanks for sending your Son to us so that we who are outcasts may be restored to your family. We also thank you for sending Jesus as an example of loving one another, and at times, stepping over the law to accomplish this commandment. Be with us in times when we are the outcast and when we may cast someone out. Send us the wisdom, through the Holy Spirit, to make the proper decision involving all your children. Amen.

AUGUST 9

His divine power has given us everything needed for life and godliness, through the knowledge of him who called us by (or through) his own glory and goodness. Thus he has given us, through these things, his precious and very great promises, so that through them you may escape from the corruption that is in the world because of lust, and may become participants of the divine nature.

II Peter 1:3-4

We live in a corrupt world. We work in a profession that tries to rid the world of corruption. But, even we are subject to becoming corrupt. How do we overcome these difficult times? God has made promises to us. We must keep an ongoing process of striving to be godly. This is not an once-in-a-lifetime event, but a life-long journey. We must understand that it is through God's power that we are able to stay on the course. If it were up to us, we would fall into corruption. Live in God's promises, and continually renew your promises to God.

God, Radiance of faithful souls, we give you thanks for the precious promises you have made and kept with us. Forgive when we have fallen into corruption and not upheld our promises to you. Strengthen us, by your power, to escape from the corruption of this world. Amen.

AUGUST 10

When he (Jesus) returned to Capernaum after some days, it was reported that he was at home. So many gathered around that there was no longer room for them, not even in front of the door; and he was speaking the word to them. Then some people came, bringing to him a paralyzed man, carried by four of them. And when they could not bring him to Jesus because of the crowd, they removed the roof above him; and after having dug through it, they let down the mat on which the paralytic lay. When Jesus saw their faith, he said to the paralytic, "Son, your sins are forgiven." Now some of the scribes were sitting there, questioning in their hearts, "Why does this fellow speak in this way? It is blasphemy! Who can forgive sins but God alone?" At once Jesus perceived in his spirit that they were discussing these questions among themselves; and he said to them, "Why do you raise such questions in your hearts? Which is easier, to say to the paralytic, 'Your sins are forgiven,' or to say, 'Stand up and take your mat and walk'? But so that you may know the Son of Man has authority on earth to forgive sins" – he said to the paralytic – "I say to you, stand up, take your mat and go to your home." And he stood up, and immediately took the mat and went out before all of them; so that they were all amazed and glorified God, saying, "We have never seen anything like this!"

Mark 2:1-12

How easy is it for us to forgive? Jesus asks the question, "Which is easier?" But we have a difficult time with forgiveness. We don't forgive ourselves, we don't forgive others, and sometimes we don't forgive God. In the Lord's Prayer, the petition is, "Forgive us our sins, as we forgive those who sins against us." Do we really want God to forgive us the same way we forgive others? Probably not, because we are better at sinning than we are at forgiving. Today, take some time to think about situations that need forgiveness. Forgive yourself, forgive others with whom you have issues, and offer up to God your confessions and forgiveness.

God, Source of all freedom, we give you thanks for offering forgiveness to us. We know that Christ has the authority to forgive sins. We know we should forgive, but it is difficult for us. Send the Holy Spirit to us, to assist us in forgiving others as you have forgiven us. May we all be restored to wholeness and reconciled to you, through Jesus Christ. Amen.

AUGUST 11

"You are the salt of the earth; but if salt has lost its taste, how can its saltiness be restored? It is no longer good for anything, but is thrown out and trampled under foot. You are the light of the world. A city built on a hill cannot be hid. No one after lighting a lamp puts it under the bushel basket, but on a lamp stand, and it gives light to all in the house...."

Matthew 5:13-14

We work in a profession where there is a distinct separation of church and state. We are not able to openly proclaim our faith to others. But Jesus tells us that we are the salt of the earth and the light of the world. The salt preserves the meat. The light illumines the house. We are to be the preservatives and the illumination. Our actions, our words, our character speaks to who we are. Even though we cannot openly proclaim Christ, people can tell that we are in Christ by who we are. We can still work for the betterment of the world. We are not to lose our saltiness and light. We must continue, in a variety of different ways. Today, think of different ways that you may be salt and light to the communities you serve.

Radiant and glorious God, we give you thanks for sending your son to this world. Through the Holy Spirit, may we continue to be the salt and the light, helping to preserve and illumine your creation. Amen.

AUGUST 12

One of the scribes came near and heard them disputing with one another, and seeing that he answered them well, he asked him, "Which commandment is the first of all?" Jesus answered, "The first is, 'Hear, O Israel: the Lord our God, the Lord is one; you shall love the Lord your God with all your heart, and with all your soul, and with all your mind, and with all your strength.' The second is this, 'You shall love your neighbor as yourself.' There is no other commandment greater than these."

Mark 12:28-31

In our profession, we enforce a lot of laws. Some laws have superiority over others. Jesus is asked which is the greatest law. He says to love God with everything you have, and to love your neighbor as yourself. We are called to enforce these laws as the greatest. We have to have these laws in mind when we are enforcing any of the others. The way we influence and change the world is through our obedience to the Great Commandment.

God, Redeemer and Deliverer, we give you thanks for sending us your Son, so that we may hear the truth. Send your Holy Spirit to us so that we may continue to love you above all else and love our neighbors as ourselves. Through these actions of yours, may we do your work of influencing the world. Amen.

AUGUST 13

They (saints) sing a new song: "You are worthy to take the scroll and to open its seals, for you were slaughtered and by your blood you ransomed for God saints from every tribe and language and people and nation; you have made them to be a kingdom and priests serving our God, and they will reign on earth." Then I looked, and I heard the voice of many angels surrounding the throne and the living creatures and the elders; they numbered myriads of myriads and thousands of thousands, singing with full voice, "Worthy is the Lamb that was slaughtered to receive power and wealth and wisdom and might and honor and glory and blessing!" Then I heard every creature in heaven and on earth and under the earth and in the sea, and all that is in them, singing, "To the one seated on the throne and to the Lamb be blessing and honor and glory and might forever and ever!" And the four living creatures said, "Amen!" And the elders fell down and worshipped.

Revelation 5:9-14

We run into a wide variety of people in our profession. Everyone that we encounter are sisters and brothers in Christ. Christ is the Lamb who was slain. Christianity is a reconciling religion. The goal of reconciling activity is to draw out of the earth people from every nation, race, and language. We will join together in worshipping and glorifying him in a new heaven and a new earth. We can only fully accomplish this when Christ returns, but it is his will for the church to work toward and to model this eternal reality in this world, until he returns.

God, refuge of those who put their trust in you, we give you thanks for sending your son, to be the Lamb of the world. We await his return so that we may live in the new heaven and new earth. Send your Holy Spirit to us, so that we may be one with all nations and races, glorifying and worshipping you. Amen.

AUGUST 14

"If you love me (Jesus), you will keep my commandments. And I will ask the Father, and he will give you another Advocate (or Helper), to be with you forever. This is the Spirit of truth, whom the world cannot receive, because it neither sees him nor knows him. You know him, because he abides with you, and he will be in (or among) you."

John 14:15-17

We work in an environment where we have to depend on our partner. We place our lives in our partner's hands. Jesus has a partner with him in being with us. God sends the Holy Spirit; the Advocate, the Helper, the Spirit of Truth to be with us. The Holy Spirit becomes our partner in accomplishing the task of keeping Jesus' commandments. We are never alone. If we are truly to become disciples who not only profess Jesus Christ as our Savior, but who also love and obey him as our Lord and Master, we must understand he calls us to obey his commandments. Even in our struggles, and times we fall short of keeping Jesus' commandments, we still have our Helper. Today, spend some time thinking about the times the Holy Spirit has worked in your life.

Righteous God, we thank you for sending the Holy Spirit to us, so that we may work towards keeping Jesus commandments. Forgive us when we fall short. Help us to continue being your children. Amen.

AUGUST 15

And Mary said, "My soul magnifies the Lord, and my spirit rejoices in God my Savior, for he has looked with favor on the lowliness of his servant. Surely, form now on all generations will call me blessed; for the Mighty One has done great things for me, and holy is his name. His mercy is for those who fear him from generation to generation. He has shown strength with his arm; he has scattered the proud in the thoughts of their hearts. He has brought down the pow-

erful from their thrones, and lifted up the lowly; he has filled the hungry with good things, and sent the rich away empty. He has helped his servant Israel, in remembrance of his mercy, according to the promise he made to our ancestors, to Abraham and to his descendants forever." And Mary remained with her (Elizabeth) about three months and then returned to her home.

Luke 1:46-56

Today, the church remembers Mary, the Mother of Our Lord. Martin Luther referred to Mary as the "God-bearer", the bearer of the Word. Mary is often seen as the model of devoted motherhood. But, her life also reveals that God is present among the humble and the poor. This passage in Luke is called the Magnificat, or Mary's Song. The Magnificat speaks of the reversals in the reign of God. Sometimes we think that God has abandoned the humble and poor in our society. Our profession takes us into places where we see the lowly. But, we need to remember that God exists among the humble, lowly, poor and broken. In fact, Mary's son, Jesus, lifts these classes of people up as the examples of godly living.

Almighty God, you chose the Virgin Mary to be the mother of Our Lord. Grant that we, who have been redeemed by his blood, may share with Mary in the glory of your eternal kingdom. Help us to look highly upon the humble, poor, and broken in our world. May we all realize that we need to come to you as lowly children and humble servants. Amen.

AUGUST 16

"...God is not a human being, that he should lie, or a mortal, that he should change his mind. Has he promised, and will he not fulfill it? Has he spoken, and will he not fulfill it..."

Numbers 23:19

God has been making promises to humanity since creation. God has reaffirmed those promises to humanity throughout history. God has made promises to us, through his Son, Jesus Christ, by the power of the Holy Spirit. God keeps promises. God is not like humanity, who has difficulty keeping promises. God has spoken, and will fulfill the promises given to us. Today, reflect on the promises you have made; to family, friends, work, and God. Knowing that God will keep the promises made with you, strive to keep the promises you have made. God's promises to us, shape who we are and the ministry we provide to those we love. This also raises the standard for what it means to live godly lives. We are meant to be guided to the life of Christ, so that Christ may transform us from the inside out. This transformation will help in keep the promises we have made.

Righteous God, we give you thanks for making promises with all creation. We also give you thanks for keeping those promises. Send your Holy Spirit to us, to help us keep the promises we have made. May we all be transformed into the life of your Son, Jesus Christ. Amen.

AUGUST 17

For the message about the cross is foolishness to those who are perishing, but to us who are being saved it is the power of God. For it is written, "I will destroy the wisdom of the wise, and the discernment of the discerning I will thwart." Where is the one who is wise? Where is the scribe? Where is the debater of this age? Has not God made foolish the wisdom of the world? For since, in the wisdom of God, the world did not know God through wisdom, God decided, through the foolishness of our proclamation, to save those who believe. For Jews demand signs and Greeks desire wisdom, but we proclaim Christ crucified, a stumbling block to Jews and foolishness to Gentiles, but to those who are called, both Jews and Greeks, Christ the power of God and the wisdom of God. For God's foolishness is wiser than human wisdom, and God's weakness is stronger than human strength.

1 Corinthians 1:18-25

We see the results of many power struggles in our profession. Many criminal acts are the assertion of power and control of one over another. We even have power struggles in our own ranks. People try to take a variety of attributes, and turn them into their own power position. But, God is the ultimate power. Christ is the ultimate power and wisdom of God. When we do not surrender our own belief in power and wisdom, we are not able to fully sense what God has given to us. We become foolish. Our mission is to bring people to realize the God has the power and the wisdom. God sent power and wisdom to us in Christ. By the Holy Spirit, we are able to live with God's structure of power and wisdom. Today, reflect on how the power of God, revealed in the life of Jesus, was different than the power we see in most human power struggles.

God, righteous one of all generations, we give you thanks for sending us your power and wisdom in Jesus. Help us to overcome the temptation to gain power over others. Send us your Holy Spirit that we may come to know all you have given us. Amen.

AUGUST 18

For Christ also suffered (or died) for sins once for all, the righteous for the unrighteous, in order to bring you (or us) to God. He was put to death in the flesh, but alive in the spirit, in which also he went and made a proclamation to the spirits in prison, who in former times did not obey, when God waited patiently in the days of Noah, during the building of the ark, in which a few, that is, eight persons, were saved through water. And baptism, which this prefigured, now saves you – not as a removal of dirt from the body, but as an appeal to God for (or a pledge to God from) a good conscience, through the resurrection of Jesus Christ, who has gone into heaven and is at the right hand of God, with angels, authorities, and powers made subject to him.

1 Peter 3:18-22

We live in a world of "in-between". We work in a world "in-between". We are baptized children of God; our sins of a fallen humanity have been washed away. We live at the foot of the cross, forgiveness of sins for eternal life. But we live in the "in-between" of the font and the cross, between baptism and eternal life. We struggle in the wilderness of sin. We are tempted, and sometimes give in. We work in a world where people are struggling with their "in-between" time. We need to remember that in baptism and through the cross, Christ walks with us in the "in-between" wilderness of our lives. We are not alone. This is the message we can give to others. ; that we struggle as they struggle. But there is someone who walks with us in our struggle. The one who sits at the right hand of God, and will be God's counsel for us. The one who is your Savior.

God, rock of all creation, we struggle in the wilderness of our lives. We are people who live in between our baptisms and our eternal life with you. We thank you for sending your Son to us. Through the Holy Spirit, we are able to walk upright, even during our struggles. Amen.

AUGUST 19

The he (Jesus) began to teach them that the Son of Man must undergo great suffering, and be rejected by the elders, the chief priests, and the scribes, and be killed, and after three days rise again. He said all this quite openly. And Peter took him aside and began to rebuke him. But turning and looking at his disciples, he rebuked Peter and said, "Get behind me, Satan!" For you are setting you mind not on divine things but on human things."

Mark 8:31-33

Have you ever been in a briefing where the big plan was laid out, and you didn't like the way it looked for you: maybe a plan for a raid, or a tactical plan, or a plan on how we would handle certain situations if they arise. You see the big picture, and you don't like the way it looks. That may be how Peter felt in this passage. This is the first time, in Mark's Gospel, where Jesus predicts his own passion, and tells the whole story of what is going to happen. Peter takes Jesus aside and tries to convince him that may not be the way to do it. We may have the same feelings. We may not want to accomplish the tasks we are assigned at work. We may also not want to do all the things the Jesus asks us to do in our journey. We raise questions. Jesus told Peter to get back in line, to take his proper position. Jesus didn't tell Peter to leave him. Jesus used Peter, even though he knew Peter didn't see the whole plan. Jesus uses us, even when we don't see the whole plan. Jesus tells us to get back in line. Today, look at the areas of your life that may not be consistent with where you should be. Then, move yourself closer to being back in line.

God, Rock of Jacob, we give you thanks for sending your Son, Jesus, to us, so that we may better understand your bigger picture for us. Forgive us when we question, when we do not follow through, when we disagree with where we should be. Send your Holy Spirit to us, so that we may be able to follow Christ in our lives. Amen.

AUGUST 20

When they had finished breakfast, Jesus said to Simon Peter, "Simon son of John, do you love me more than these?" He said to him, "Yes, Lord; you know that I love you." Jesus said to him, "Feed my lambs." A second time he said to him, "Simon son of John, do you love me?" He said to him, "Yes, Lord; you know that I love you." Jesus said to him, "Tend my sheep."

John 21:15-16

Today, the church remembers Bernard, Abbot of Clairvaux. Bernard was a Cistercian monk and later a person of great spiritual depth. Bernard was a writer that focused on who medieval spirituality affected the dimensions of a person's life. Secular leaders came to Bernard because of his peacekeeping skills. Bernard died in 1153. The passage today is Jesus encounter with his disciples after his resurrection. This is from the last portion of John's Gospel. This is what Jesus leaves Peter to live out. Peter is called to live out his love for Jesus in tending and feeding Jesus sheep. Do we nurture a relationship between our faith and our jobs, or do we put away our faith when we put on the badge? DO we connect what we believe with how we act? Does our study of the Bible lead us to service in the world? As we remember Bernard, we should reflect on how our faith is lived out.

God, Ruler of all peoples on earth, we thank you for sending witnesses of the faith like Bernard of Clairvaux to us. May we be challenged to live out our faith, as your Son, Jesus, challenged Peter. Amen.

AUGUST 21

For I (Paul) am convinced that neither death, nor life, nor angels, nor rulers, nor things present, nor things to come, nor powers, nor height, nor depth, nor anything else in all creation, will be able to separate us from the love of God in Christ Jesus our Lord.
Romans 8:38-39

When have you felt separated from God? Has it been something that you have done? Has it been something that has happened to you? Paul tells the church at Rome that there is nothing that can separate us. Paul tells us, that there is nothing in all creation that can keep us away from God. And this love relationship with God is made solid through Christ. Know that there is nothing that can separate you from the love of God, even when you think that it is possible.

God, Rock of our life, we give you thanks for sending your Son, Jesus Christ our Lord, so that we may never be separated from your love. Help us to rightly live in that love relationship with you. Amen.

AUGUST 22

By faith Abel offered to God a more acceptable (or greater) sacrifice than Cain's. Through this he received approval as righteous, God himself giving approval to his gifts; he died, but through his

168

faith he still speaks. By faith Enoch was taken so that he did not experience death; and "he was not found, because God had taken him." For it was attested before he was taken away that "he had pleased God." And without faith it is impossible to please God, for whoever would approach him must believe that he exists and that he rewards those who seek him. By faith Noah, warned by God about events as yet unseen, respected the warning and built an ark to save his household; by this he condemned the world and became an heir to the righteousness that is in accordance with faith.

Hebrews 11:4-7

We are a people of faith. We have seen throughout the history of our faith, what our faith can accomplish. We need to remember to remain faithful to God. We should keep God at the center of our life. We should follow the examples that our provided for us in the book of Hebrews. Listen to God, keep the faith, and follow in the way of Able, Enoch and Noah.

God, ruler of all creation, we give you thanks for sending faithful witnesses life Able, Enoch and Noah. Help us to be faithful to you and keep you at the center of our lives. Amen.

AUGUST 23

"You did not choose me but I (Jesus) chose you. And I appoint you to go and bear fruit, fruit that will last, so that the Father will give you whatever you ask him in my name. I am giving you these commands so that you may love one another."

John 15:16-17

Many times we forget who does the choosing. Being in a profession where we have control, we think we are always in charge. But we hear that it is not us who chooses Jesus, but Jesus who chooses us. We are not in control of this situation. Jesus has already chosen us. And Jesus gives us commands, not to only keep us in line, but that we may love one another. Today, thin about ways you can relinquish control to Jesus.

God, searcher of hearts, we give you thanks for knowing what is in our hearts. We are glad that you have chosen us, through the actions of your Son, Jesus. We are grateful that he is in control of our lives. Help us to live according to the commands that Christ has given to us. May we love one another, as you love us, enough to send your Son for us. Amen.

AUGUST 24

The Next day Jesus decided to go to Galilee. He found Philip and said to him, "Follow me." Now Philip was from Bethsaida, the city of Andrew and Peter. Philip found Nathanael and said to him, "We have found him about whom Moses in the law and also the prophets wrote, Jesus son of Joseph from Nazareth." Nathanael said to him, "Can anything good come out of Nazareth?" Philip said to him, "Come and see." When Jesus saw Nathanael coming toward him, he said to him, "Here is truly an Israelite in whom there is no deceit!" Nathanael asked him, "Where did you get to know me?" Jesus answered, "I saw you under the fig tree before Philip called you." Nathanael replied, "Rabbi, you are the Son of God! You are the King of Israel!" Jesus answered, "Do you believe because I told you that I saw you under the fig tree? You will see greater things than these." And he said to him, "Very truly, I tell you, you will see heaven opened and the angels of God ascending and descending upon the Son of Man."

John 1:43-51

Today, the church remembers Bartholomew, one of Jesus' apostles as listed in Matthew Mark and Luke. John uses the name Nathanael, and they are often believed to be the same person. Nathanael found Jesus with the help of another, Philip. And Nathanael realized that Jesus already knew him. How did you find Jesus? No matter how it happened, Jesus knew you before that moment. People may come to know that Jesus already knows them, through our actions. We must always follow Christ. We

170

never know when someone else will realize that they are known. Today, think about ways that we are to accept the invitation to follow Christ. How does that affect your life?

Almighty and everlasting God, you gave to Nathanael, the grace to believe and follow Christ. Help us in our following. Send your Holy Spirit to us, so that we may be instruments for you to tell the good news of Jesus. May others come to know that you already know them. Amen.

AUGUST 25

From one ancestor he made all nations to inhabit the whole earth, and he allotted the times of their existence and the bound-aries of the places where they would live, so that they would search for God and perhaps grope for him and find him – though indeed he is not far from each one of us. For 'In him we live and move and move and have our being'; as even some of your own poets have said, 'For we too are his offspring.'

Acts of the Apostles 17:26-28

It is not easy to see God in our lives. We get too clouded with other things. There are times when we grope, and search, and try to find God. We are not alone. There are many people in the world who are struggling to find God. But God is never far away from any of us. If fact, God is always right there with us, even when we don't see. We encounter many people who are searching. They have focused on things other than God, and cannot see God there, not very far away. Our task is to remind them that they are God's off-spring. We are to help them see that God is never far away. We are to help others who are searching, just like us. Today, reflect on how close God is to you. Then remember, that God is closer than that.

God, Shield of our fathers and mothers, we give you thanks for making us your offspring. We struggle with seeing you in our lives. Remain with us as we search, and grope, and struggle to see you. Stay with us during our struggles, as we find that you are closer to us than we know. Amen

AUGUST 26

There is one body and one spirit, just as you were called to the one hope of your calling, one Lord, one faith, one baptism, one God and Father of all, who is above all and through all and in all.

Ephesians 4:4-6

We know what is means to be a team. We are a bunch of people who make one shift, all the shifts makes a division, the different divisions make a department. Then all the departments make the "thin blue line" that connects us all. But we belong to a greater team. We are all members of the body of Christ by the one Holy Spirit. We all answer to the one Lord, in one faith, through our one baptism. Even though we do different tasks, we all worship the one God that we all confess. We know what it is like to be part of a whole that is greater than us.

God, Father of all, we give you thanks for all that you do for us. We rejoice in being included in the one family, as your children. Inspire us by the Holy Spirit, to continue in our calling of serving the body of your Son, our Lord, Jesus Christ. Amen

AUGUST 27

The Passover of the Jews was near, and Jesus went up to Jerusalem. In the temple he found people selling cattle, sheep, and doves, and the money changers seated at their tables. Making a whip of cords, he drove all of them out of the temple, both the sheep and the cattle. He also poured out the coins of the money changers and overturned their tables. He told those who were selling the doves, "Take these things out of here! Stop making my Father's house a marketplace!" His disciples remembered that it was written, "Zeal for your house will consume me." The Jews then said to him, "What sign can you show us for doing this?" Jesus answered them, "Destroy the temple, and in three days I will raise it up." The Jews then said, "This temple has been under construction for forty-six years, and will you raise it up in three days?" But he was speaking of the temple of his body. After he raised from the dead, his disciples remembered that he had said this; and they believed the scripture and the word that Jesus had spoken.

John 2:13-22

How have you felt when you were on a raid or executing a search warrant, or serving o high-risk arrest warrant? Everything is done swift and sure. It is rapid and with force. This is how Jesus enters and reacts in the temple. His movements are swift and sure. He uses force to drive out the people in the court. Jesus begins a new system of worshipping God. We no longer need to buy sacrifices to offer to God. God has received the sacrifice of his Son, once and for all. Jesus begins something new, in a swift and sure way. And after his resurrection, his disciples remembered what Jesus said and believed. Jesus has moved into your life in a swift and sure manner. Jesus continually cleans your house, sometimes with force. Jesus has brought you something new.

God, shining glory, we give you thanks for accepting the ultimate sacrifice for our sins, your Son. We know that Jesus continually cleanses us. May the Holy Spirit constantly work through us in your service. Amen.

AUGUST 28

Meanwhile Saul, still breathing threats and murder against the disciples of the Lord, went to the high priest and asked him for letters to the synagogues at Damascus, so that if he found any who belonged to the Way, men or women, he might bring them bound to Jerusalem. Now as he was going along and approaching Damascus, suddenly a light from heaven flashed around him. He fell to the ground and heard a voice saying to him, "Saul, Saul, why do you persecute me?" He asked, "Who are you, Lord?" The reply came, "I am Jesus, whom you are persecuting. But get up and enter the city, and you will be told what you are to do." The men who were traveling with him stood speechless because they heard the voice but saw no one. Saul got up from the ground, and though his eyes were open, he could see nothing; so they led him by the hand and brought him into Damascus. For three days he was without sight, and neither ate nor drank. Now there was a disciple in Damascus named Ananias. The Lord said to him in a vision, "Ananias." He answered, "Here I am , Lord" The Lord said to him, "Get up and go to the street called Straight, and at the house of Judas look for a man of Tarsus named Saul. At this moment he is praying, and he has seen in a vision a man named Ananias come in and lay his hands on him so that he might regain his sight." But Ananias answered, "Lord, I have heard from many about this man, how much evil he has done to your saints in Jerusalem; and here he has authority from the chief priests to bind all who invoke your name." But the Lord said to him, "Go, for he is an instrument whom I have chosen to bring my name before the Gentiles and kings and before the people of Israel; I myself will show him how much he must suffer for the sake of my name." So Ananias went and entered the house. He laid his hands on Saul and said, "Brother Saul, the Lord Jesus, who appeared to you on your way here, has sent me so that you may regain your sight and be filled with the Holy Spirit." And immediately something like scales fell from his eyes, and his sight was restored. Then he got up and was baptized, and after taking some food, he regained his strength. For several days he was with the disciples in Damascus, and immediately he began to proclaim Jesus in the synagogues, saying "He is the Son of God." All who heard him were amazed and said, "Is not this the man who made havoc in Jerusalem among those who invoked this name? And has he not come here for the purpose of bringing them bound before the chief priests?" Saul became increasingly more powerful and confounded the Jews who lived in Damascus by proving that Jesus was the Messiah.

Acts of the Apostles 9:1-22

Today, the church remembers Augustine Bishop of Hippo. Augustine died in 430c.e. Augustine wrote about his conversion experience in his autobiography, "Confessions". He, like Paul, had a memorable conversion experience. Did you have a conversion experience that opened your eyes to what God does for you? If you were raised in the church, baptized as an infant, can you have a conversion experience? We are called to have a continuous conversion. We should always be changing. We may have moments that are as memorable as Paul's of Augustine's. We may also have moments where our conversion is barely notices. Today, reflect upon the conversion that God brings to your life?

God, Source of all existence, we give you thanks for all you give to us. You cause conversion in our lives. May we all be continuously changed so that we may proclaim the name of Christ. Amen.

AUGUST 29

The LORD is gracious and merciful, slow to anger and abounding in steadfast love. The LORD is good to all, and his compassion is over all that he has made.

Psalm 145:8-9

We are always trying to wonder what God is like. But Scripture gives us glimpses of God. This passage reminds us that God is full of love for all of us. We, then, are to love others as God has loved us. We should strive to be gracious and merciful, slow to anger, abounding in steadfast love, and have love for everyone.

God, Source of all health, we give you thanks for being gracious, merciful, slow to anger, abounding in love and compassion. Help us to radiate the love that you give to us. Amen.

AUGUST 30

"And just as Moses lifted up the serpent in the wilderness, so must the Son of Man be lifted up, that whoever believes in him may have eternal life."

John 3:14-15

It is difficult for us to understand why God makes it so easy for us to be saved. God told Moses to put a serpent on a bronze pole. The people who looked at the serpent could be saved. Jesus was lifted up on a cross. The people who look at Jesus lifted could be saved. It is just that easy. Believing calls us into a certain life, but God knows that we cannot uphold all the laws all the time. We will stumble and fall in sin. But God loves us, and gave his Son, so that whoever believes may not perish, but have eternal life. Beginning today, look at Christ lifted up and believe.

God, Source of all true joy, we give you thanks for your love. You love us so much that you gave your Son to be lifted up. Send the Holy Spirit to us, to help us continually look to Christ lifted up for us. Amen.

AUGUST 31

"(Jesus said) When you are praying, do not heap up empty phrases as the Gentiles do; for they think that they will be heard because of their many words. Do not be like them, for your Father knows what you need before you ask him. Pray then in this way: 'Our Father in heaven, hallowed be your name. Your kingdom come. Your will be done, on earth as it is in heaven. Give us this day our daily bread (or our bread for tomorrow). And forgive us our debts, as we also have forgiven our debtors. And do not bring us to the time of trial (or into temptation), but rescue us from the evil one (or from evil).' For if you forgive others their trespasses, your heavenly Father will also forgive you; but if you do not forgive others, neither will your Father forgive your tres-

passes. (For the kingdom and the power and the glory are yours forever. Amen)

Matthew 6:7-15

How many times do we not know what to pray? We struggle for the words, our minds go blank, and we just don't know what to say. But remember, God knows what your prayers are. God knows what each one of us needs. Jesus gives us the Lord's Prayer, as a way to pray. This prayer covers all that we need. What things did Jesus ask for in this prayer? What do we usually ask for? We pray to be in conversation with God. God already knows our needs. If our images of God affect our prayers, how did Jesus' image of God as Father affect his prayer? What is our image of God? Whenever you feel the need to pray, and don't know what to pray, pray the prayer our Savior gave us. If our prayers reveal as much about us as about God, what do Jesus' requests reveal about him? Today, think about how and why we pray. How can we begin to pray the way Jesus taught us?

Our Father in Heaven, hallowed be your name. Your kingdom come. Your will be done, on earth as in heaven. Give us today our daily bread. And forgive us our sins, as we forgive those who sin against us. And save us from the time of trial, and deliver us from evil. For the kingdom, power and glory are yours, now and forever. Amen.

SEPTEMBER 1

The next day John again was standing with two of his disciples, and as he watched Jesus walk by, he exclaimed, "Look, here is the Lamb of God!" The two disciples heard him say this, and they followed Jesus. When Jesus turned and saw them following, he said to them, "What are you looking for?" They said to him, "Rabbi" (which translated means Teacher), "where are you staying?" He said to them, "Come and see." They came and saw where he was staying, and they remained with him that day. It was about four o'clock in the afternoon.

John 1:35-39

Have you ever found something that you didn't know you had lost? Or, have you found something you never knew you had? The disciples in this passage find Jesus, not knowing that they should be looking for him. We try to find so many things that we don't have or we don't need. We fill those holes in our lives with something that brings us up short. Jesus has already found you. Trust him, and walk with him for a little while. Jesus will help you find those things that you need to find.

God, Source of blessing, we give you thanks for all that you have given to us. We are able to find all the blessings that you send to us. The greatest blessing was sending Jesus into the world, so that we may find all that which we lack. Amen.

SEPTEMBER 2

Now there was a Pharisee named Nicodemus, a leader of the Jews. He came to Jesus by night and said to him, "Rabbi, we know that you are a teacher who has come from God; for no one can do these signs that you do apart from the presence of God." Jesus answered him, "Very truly, I tell you, no one can see the kingdom of God without being born from above (or born anew)." Nicodemus said to him, "How can anyone be born after having grown old? Can one enter a second time into the mother's womb and be born?" Jesus answered, "Very truly, I tell you, no one can enter the kingdom of God without being born of water and Spirit. What is born of the flesh is flesh, and what is born of the Spirit is spirit. Do not be astonished that I said to you, 'You must be born from above (or anew).' The wind (or spirit) blows where it chooses, and you hear the sound of it, but you do not know where it comes from or where it goes. So it is with everyone who is born of the Spirit." Nicodemus said to him, "How can these things be?" Jesus answered him, "Are you a teacher of Israel, and yet you do not understand these things? Very truly, I tell you, we speak of what we know and testify to what we have seen; yet you do not receive our testimony. If I have told you about earthly things and you do not believe, how can you believe if I tell you about heavenly things? No one has ascended into heaven except the one who descended from heaven, the Son of Man. ..."

John 3:1-13

What do you say to someone, when the come up to you with those questions that they have? They have been waited to see a law enforcement officer, to ask these questions that are the most difficult to answer. Some times, we may give them a quick, non-relative answer, and send them away. Many times, we try to answer, which leads us into an hour-long conversation. This may be how Jesus felt when Nicodemus came to him with his questions. Nicodemus had been wondering. What do we wonder about the message of Jesus? If you could meet Jesus and ask him something, what would it be? This is the conversation where Jesus gives Nicodemus, probably the most famous verse of the entire Bible, John 3:16. But Jesus gives that as an answer to Nicodemus questions. We should take the time to listen to people's questions. Our answers may be some of the most profound things they hear. We also need to ask Jesus our questions. And know that Jesus has an answer for us.

God, Source of eternal light, we give you thanks for sending your light into the world, Jesus. We have many questions about our faith. Send the Holy Spirit to us, that we may receive the answers to our questions. Allow us who are born of the Spirit, to help others who also may have questions. Amen.

SEPTEMBER 3

Now among those who went up to worship at the festival were some Greeks. They came to Philip, who was from Bethsaida in Galilee, and said to him, "Sir, we wish to see Jesus." Philip went and told Andrew; then Andrew and Philip went and told Jesus. Jesus answered them, "The hour has come for the Son of Man to be glorified. Very truly I tell you, unless a grain of wheat fall into the earth and dies, it remains just single grain; but if it dies, it bears much fruit. Those who love their life lose it, and those who hate their life in this world will keep it for eternal life. Whoever serves me must follow me, and where I am, there will my servant be also. Whoever serves me, the Father will honor. Now my soul is troubled. And what should I say – 'Father, save me from this hour?' No, it is for this reason that I have come to this hour. Father, glorify your name." Then a voice came from heaven, "I have glorified it, and I will glorify it again." The crowd standing there heard it and said that it was thunder. Others said, " An angel has spoken to him." Jesus answered, "This voice has come for your sake, not for mine. Now is the judgment of this world; now the ruler of this world will be driven out. And I, when I am lifted up from the earth, will draw all people to myself." He said this to indicate the kind of death he was to die.

John 12:20-33

What does God's voice sound like? Do we even think that God speaks to us? We may hear God's voice, but then we don't like what we hear. We deny God's words, we avoid carrying them out. We hold onto things we shouldn't and let go of things we ought to hold. Many times, we just don't even listen to hear God, because we don't want to know what God has to say to us. God does speak. We need to take the time to listen. God speaks to us through other people, through prayer, and through silence. Today, take some time and listen to what God has to say to you. And just think, someone else may hear God through your voice.

God, Source of good, we give you thanks for continually speaking to us. Help us to listen to your words. Send your Holy Spirit to us, to use us for your will. Amen.

SEPTEMBER 4

After this there was a festival of the Jews, and Jesus went up to Jerusalem. Now in Jerusalem by the Sheep Gate there is a pool, called in Hebrew (or Aramaic) Beth-zatha (or Bethesda, or Bethsaida), which has five porticoes. In these lay many invalids – blind, lame, and paralyzed (and waiting for the stirring of the water; for an angel of the Lord went down at certain seasons into the pool, and stirred up the water; whoever stepped in first after the stirring of the water was made well from whatever disease that person had. One man was there who had been ill for thirty-eight years. When Jesus saw him lying there and knew that he had been there a long time, he said to him, "Do you want to be made well?" The sick man answered him, "Sir, I have no one to put me into the pool when the water is stirred up; and while I am making my way, someone else steps down ahead of me." Jesus said to him, "Stand up, take you mat and walk." At once the man was made well, and he took up his mat and began to walk.

John 5:1-9

We go to situations and talk to people who just need to hear another perspective on how to get through. This lame man was struggling trying to be healed. Jesus comes to him with another perspective, and heals him. We show up, and people are trying to solve a problem with only one attempt at a solution. Many times, it takes us explaining to them that there are other options. Then, they may be able to heal the situation. We need to remember that we may not be able to heal every situation, like Jesus did. But, we may be able to offer some advice that allows others to see a new direction.

God, Source of health and strength, we give you thanks for all the options that you provide to us. Use us as a means to assist others in seeing new perspectives. Inspire us to hear new directions from others. Amen.

SEPTEMBER 5

"...I am not speaking of all of you; I know whom I have chosen. But it is to fulfill the scripture, 'The one who ate my bread (or ate bread with me) has lifted his heel against me.' I tell you this now, before it occurs, so that when it does occur, you may believe that I am he. Very truly, I tell you, whoever receives one whom I send receives me; and whoever receives me receives him who sent me."

John 13:18-20

We encounter people that are doing an act for someone else. This is commonplace. People send others to do their work. Many times it helps knowing whom they are working for, to get to the bottom of the situation. God sent Jesus into the world. Jesus now sends others into the world. Jesus says that if we listen to and respect the people he sends, and then God will be listened to and respected. Who do you represent? Who is sending you? The community you work for is represented in your presence. But Jesus is also represented when you show up. If Jesus sends you, and people accept you, then they accept Jesus. And if they accept Jesus, they accept God. We can act as the representative of Jesus in our words and deeds. Today, reflect on who sends you and whom you represent.

Sovereign God, we give you thanks for sending Jesus into this world. Help us to represent Jesus in our lives, so the others may receive him, and in turn, receive you. Amen.

SEPTEMBER 6

Consider your own call, brothers and sisters: not many of you were wise by human standards (or according to the flesh), not many were powerful, not many were of noble birth. But God chose what is foolish in the world to shame the wise; God chose what is weak in the world to shame the strong; God chose what is low and despised in the world, things that are not, to reduce to nothing things that are, so that no one (or no flesh) might boast in the presence of God. He is the source of your life in Christ Jesus, who became for us wisdom from God, and righteousness and sanctification and redemption, in order that, as it is written, "Let the one who boasts, boast in (or of) the Lord."

1 Corinthians 1:26-31

We need to consider our own calls from God. God called us to be law enforcement officers. We come from a variety of backgrounds. Many of us were not powerful, the smartest, the strongest, the richest of people. God calls us to live out our lives in this vocation, in service of God. People still look at us as law enforcement officers and people of the Christian faith, and call us foolish. How can we believe? But God has chosen us to take the message of the Gospel into places that need to hear it. God chooses people like us, just as has happened throughout history. Today, reflect on your call story. The story of how you became of law enforcement officer, the story of your faith, and the story of how your faith and law enforcement go together.

God, Staff and Support of the righteous, we give you thanks for sending your Son Christ Jesus as your wisdom to us. Send your Holy Spirit that we may live out our call to proclaim your Good News. My we be renewed by the righteousness, sanctification, and redemption provided us by Christ. Amen.

SEPTEMBER 7

They came to Jericho. As he and his disciples and a large crowd were leaving Jericho, Bartimaeus son of Timaeus, a blind beggar, was sitting by the roadside. When he heard that it was Jesus of Nazareth, he began to shout out and say, "Jesus, Son of David, have mercy on me!" Many sternly ordered him to be quiet, but he cried out even more loudly, "Son of David, have mercy on me!" Jesus stood still and said, "Call him here." And they called the blind man, saying to him, "Take heart; get up, he is calling you." So throwing off his cloak, he sprang up and came to Jesus. Then Jesus said to him, "What do you want me to do for you?" The blind man said to him, "My teacher, let me see again." Jesus said to him, "Go; your faith has made you well." Immediately he regained his sight and followed him on the way.

Mark 10:46-52

How many times have you been called to chase away someone who society considers "unwanted"? Citizens and community leaders do not want to see or hear from people who appear to be in dire straights. It doesn't present the type of place we want. So, we show up and do not listen to them. We either find a reason to arrest them, or we haul them off to the next place. How are they any different from Bartimaeus? These people have had difficulties in life that have brought them to this way of life. Many times, they are crying out for help, crying out for basic needs to survive. Do we listen, as Jesus did, or turn a deaf ear? Do we provide help and answer their cry, as Jesus did, or do we ignore them? These brothers and sisters need our help. And remember, they may be looking for the face of Christ in your eyes.

Strong God of Truth, we ask you to forgive when we have turned deaf ears, when we have acted in ignorance, when we have not cared properly for one of your children. Help us to do your work. Remind us our frailties when we look upon others as "unwanted". May we be your instruments of help. And may we see Christ in others eyes, as they may see Christ in ours. Amen.

SEPTEMBER 8

When he (Judas) had gone out, Jesus said, "Now the Son of Man has been glorified, and God has been glorified in him. If God has been glorified in him, God will also glorify him in himself and will glorify him at once. Little children, I am with you only a little longer. You will look for me; and as I said to the Jews so now I say to you, 'Where I am going, you cannot come.' I give you a new commandment, that you love one another. Just as I have loved you, you also should love one another. By this everyone will know that you are my disciples, if you have love for one another."

John 13:31-35

We have difficult times with loving others. Jesus gives us a "new commandment". We have been told to love others as we love ourselves. But now, Jesus commands us to love others as Christ loves us. Christ loves us enough to give up his life for us. We may even say to people that, "we put our life on the line for you." But putting our life on the line isn't all that is required in this new commandment. We are called to love them that much. As we encounter people, we are to love them with all that we have. It is through this action of love, that people will know that we are followers of Jesus.

God, Support of the innocent, we give you thanks for sending your Son to us. Jesus was innocent, but gave up his life out of love. May we follow the commandment Jesus gave us, to love others as he loves us. Send your Holy Spirit to us, that we may always love everyone that we meet. Amen.

SEPTEMBER 9

"...(Jesus says) If you abide in me, and my words abide in you, ask for whatever you wish, and it will be done for you. My Father is glorified by this, that you bear much fruit and become my disciples. As the Father has loved me, so I have loved you; abide in my love. If you keep my commandments, you will abide in my

love, just as I have kept my Father's commandments and abide in his love. I have said these things to you so that my joy may be in you, and that your joy may be complete.

John 15:7-11

"We don't believe in prayer." "Whenever I'm not sure about something, I just ask the Lord and he tells me exactly what I should do." Both of these comments assume something about what God does in prayer; some assume nothing happens, some assume everything happens. Most of us are somewhere in between these two extremes. We hear many different beliefs on what prayer does for us. But, we still may wonder to benefits of prayer. If you come upon a situation where someone is talking about prayer, enter into the discussion with him or her. Find out what they think. If they ask you to pray, do it. Even if you don't believe prayer will work, try it anyway. Maybe they are right. Jesus told us that God will answer our prayers. And God answers our prayers out of love. Today, take some time to think about your feelings on prayer. As you encounter others, be respectful of their beliefs on prayer. But, help them realize that God does answer prayer. You being there may be God answering someone's prayer.

God, true and only Light, we pray to you knowing that you hear us and that you answer our prayers. Hear our prayer when we call. Help us to learn to accept your intervention into our lives. May we know that we are always in constant communication with you. Amen.

SEPTEMBER 10

Rejoice in the Lord always; again I will say, Rejoice. Let your gentleness be known to everyone. The Lord is near. Do not worry about anything, but in everything by prayer and supplication with thanksgiving let your requests be made known to God. And the peace of God, which surpasses all understanding, will guard your hearts and your minds in Christ Jesus. Finally, beloved, whatever is true, whatever is honorable, whatever is just, whatever is pure, whatever is pleasing, whatever is commendable, if there is any excellence and if there is anything worthy of praise, think about (or take account of) these things. Keep on doing the things that you have learned and received and heard and seen in me, and the God of peace will be with you.

Philippians 4:4-9

We always want to be in control. When we arrive at a situation, we are in control. We are the ones that people look to make things right. Who do we look to make things right in our lives? We are supposed to give everything up in prayer. All our requests are to be made known to God, and we will have nothing to worry. Prayer is a way for us to let our lives be open to the direction of God. We open ourselves to God's love and purpose. The way this opening occurs, is through prayer. Today, make a commitment that you will give everything to God in prayer.

God, the world' Light, we give you thanks and offer to you our prayers. Send us your peace. Help us to know your purpose in our lives. Allow us to be instruments of your love in the world. Amen.

SEPTEMBER 11

"(The white-robed young man said)... But go, tell his disciples and Peter that he is going ahead of you to Galilee; there you will see him, just as he told you." So they went out and fled from the tomb, for terror and amazement had seized them; and they said nothing to anyone, for they were afraid.

Mark 16:7-8

An angel speaks to the woman at the tomb. What we know as the resurrection of Christ. And how do the women react, terror, amazement, fear and running away. They were confronted with an event that changed the entire world. Many times, we think people we jumping for joy at that moment. But the women and all of Jesus followers responded in the same way. We, too, are confronted with life-changing situations. One moment we can be driving along, the next moment we are in a life-and-death ordeal. How do we feel? Many times, terror, fear, amazement, and the desire to run away. The followers of Jesus were able to work through their emotions, and spread the Good News of this story. A story that exists to us. We, too, are able to work through our emotions. It is normal to feel that way in tense situations. But it is working through them, getting on the other side of them that matters. That way, all people involved may tell the story. But know that the way we are able to get through it is because of the risen Christ, who walks with us, wherever we go.

God, Father of our risen Lord, we give you thanks for resurrecting Jesus so that we may have life with you. Be with us in our times of terror, fear, amazement and flight. Help us to work through those tense moments that present themselves to us. May we know that the risen Christ walks with us. Send your Holy Spirit to us, so that we may continue to tell the story of the Good News. Amen.

SEPTEMBER 12

"(Jesus said) If another member of the church sins against you, go and point out the fault when the two of you are alone. If the member listens to you, you have regained that one. But if you are not listened to, take one or two others along with you, so that every word may be confirmed by the evidence of two or three witnesses. If the member refuses to listen to them, tell it to the church; and if the offender refuses to listen even to the church, let such a one be to you as a Gentile and a tax collector. Truly I tell you, whatever you bind on earth will be bound in heaven, and whatever you loose on earth will be loosed in heaven. Again, truly I tell you, if two of you agree on earth about anything you ask, it will be done for you by my Father in heaven. For where two or three are gathered in my name, I am there among them."

Matthew 18:15-20

We are agents of discipline for society. But Christ specifically gave us instructions on how to discipline among followers. But how often do we follow Christ's instructions? Many times we talk behind peoples' backs, we ignore them, we discount them, we heap judgment upon them. Is that the proper way for followers to act? We should also take this action into our lives with people who are not necessarily followers of Jesus. This is just the proper way for people to act. Go to them face to face when you are alone. Then take two or three. Then go to the larger group with which you are both associated. You would be surprised how much is worked out using this method. Today, reflect upon the people with which you have an issue. Then, begin to go to them, one on one, to resolve the issue. Remember, where two or three are gathered in his name, so Christ will be. If you and someone else are together, Christ is there with you.

God, Reconciler of all, we give you thanks for sending your Son as an example of how to live in right relationships. Help us to work out our differences in the proper manner. Be with us as we go to others. Be with us as others come to us with an offense. May we all be together with Christ among us. Amen.

SEPTEMBER 13

"(Jesus said) Therefore I tell you, do not worry about your life, what you will eat or what you will drink, or about your body, what you will wear. Is not life more than food, and the body more than clothing? Look at the birds of the air; they neither sow nor reap nor gather into barns, and yet your heavenly Father feeds them. Are you not of more value than they? And can any of you by worrying add a single hour to your span of life (or add one cubit to your height)? And why do you worry about clothing? Consider the lilies of the field, how they grow; they neither toil nor spin, yet I tell you, even Solomon in all his glory was not clothed like one of these. But if God so clothes the grass of the field, which is alive today and tomorrow is thrown

into the oven, will he not much more clothe you – you of little faith? Therefore do not worry, saying, 'What will we eat?' or 'What will we drink?' or 'What will we wear?' For it is the Gentiles who strive for all these things; and indeed your heavenly Father knows that you need all these things. But strive first for the kingdom of God and his righteousness, and all these things will be given to you as well.

Matthew 6:25-33

We work so hard to provide ourselves with the things of life. We work extra duty and overtime to pay for all those things that we think we need. We worry about what we have, don't have, and can't pay for. But Jesus tells us not to worry. God will provide us with everything that we need. Notice that what God knows we need and what we think we need may be two different things. God will ensure that the necessities of life will be taken care. It is the excesses that we worry about. God tells us not to worry. And maybe we need to realize that we don't need them. We need to strive for a simpler life. By needing less, we may work fewer hours, allowing us to spend more time with family and friends. We may be able to take better care of ourselves physically, mentally, emotionally, and spiritually. And isn't that what God knows we really need. Today, reflect upon the worries of your life. Do you really need those things? Do you really have to worry about that? Make your life simpler.

God, Provider of all our needs, we thank you for giving us all that we need. Help us to evaluate our lives and what is important. Strengthen us to not worry and put our trust in you. Amen.

SEPTEMBER 14

Let the same mind be in you that was in Christ Jesus, who, though he was in the form of God, did not regard equality with god as something to be exploited, but emptied himself, taking the form of a slave, being born in human likeness. And being found in human form, he humbled himself and became obedient to the point of death – even death on a cross. Therefore God also highly exalted him and gave him the name that is above every name, so that at the name of Jesus every knee should bend, in heaven and on earth and under the earth, and every tongue should confess that Jesus Christ is Lord, to the glory of God the Father.

Philippians 2:5-11

Today, the church celebrates Holy Cross Day. Holy Cross Day dates back to 335CE in which Constantine built a basilica on what was believed to be the place of the crucifixion of Jesus. The cross is the primary symbol of Christianity. We need to ask ourselves, "Does the cross have a central place in my life? Does my church focus on the cross in its worship, teaching, preaching and ministry to the world? We make the sign of the cross over ourselves in remembrance of our baptism. As you reflect on the role of the cross in your life, make the sign of the cross over yourself. Remember that you are baptized into a death like Jesus' and into a resurrection like his.

Almighty God, your Son Jesus was lifted high upon a cross so that the whole world may be drawn to him. Send you Holy Spirit to us, so that we may pick up our cross and follow him. All this we do because Christ died for our salvation. Amen.

SEPTEMBER 15

(Jesus said) "Do not let your hearts be troubled. Believe in God, believe also in me."

John 14:1

We drive around with a troubled heart. We wonder if God hears our prayers. We wonder if Jesus is really with in difficult times. Often, there are specific answers to specific prayer requests. When these occur, we should recognize them, and give thanks back to God. But just as many times, there are vague, unidentified effects of prayer. Many times, we only see these types of answers when we look back at situations. We may only see part of the answer. There may even be times that we see nothing, and we begin to wonder is we are even connected with prayer at all. God is there for us, and we should believe God will act. In the same way, Jesus is there for us, and Jesus will act in our lives. We should not walk around with troubled hearts, but we should offer everything up in prayer.

God, our hearts are troubled. We come to you in prayer, to interact in our lives. We believe in you, and Your Son Jesus, and the Holy Spirit. We believe that you answer prayers. Help us to see the answers that you send to us. Amen.

SEPTEMBER 16

I (John) write these things to you who believe in the name of the Son of God, so that you may know that you have eternal life. And this is the boldness we have in him, that if we ask anything according to his will, he hears us. And if we know that he hears us in whatever we ask, we know that we have obtained the requests made of him.

1 John 5:13-15

What does this passage require? We who believe in Christ are to ask anything according to his will. What does this passage promise? It promises that if we ask according to Christ's will, he will hear us. And if we know he hears us, we know that we obtain what we ask. Is this consistent with your Christian experience? Many times, we ask things according to our own will, and not according to the will of Christ. The greatest answer given us is that we will have eternal life. Everything else, we need to offer up in prayer, according to Christ's will. Today, offer up your requests to Christ and ask that his will be done. And it will.

God, source of all boldness, we give you thanks for sending your Son, so that we who believe may have eternal life. Send your Holy Spirit to us, so that we may empty ourselves. May we ask everything according to the will of Christ. And may we also know that all ask according to Christ's will is obtained. Amen.

SEPTEMBER 17

"(Jesus said) I am the Good Shepherd. The good shepherd lays down his life for the sheep. The hired hand, who is not the shepherd and does not own the sheep, sees the wolf coming and runs away – and the wolf snatches them and scatters them. The hired hand runs away because a hired hand does not care for the sheep. I am the good shepherd. I know my own and my own know me, just as the Father knows me and I know the Father. And I lay down my life for the sheep. I have other sheep that do not belong to this fold. I must bring them also, and they will listen to my voice. So there will be one flock, one shepherd. For this reason the Father loves me, because I lay down my life in order to take it up again. No one takes it from me, but I lay it down of my own accord. I have power to lay it down, and I have power to take it up again. I have received this command from my Father."

John 10:11-18

This is a very familiar and very soothing passage of Scripture, Jesus is the Good Shepherd. But where do we find ourselves as law enforcement officers in this passage. Many times, we think we are the shepherd, who enters into people's lives at times of need, and help them with their difficulties. Sometimes, this may be true. But how many times do we act like the hired hand? We come in, and because we don't care or we don't have any attachment, we leave without completing our duty. We have left these people in danger, just as the hired hand leaves the sheep to the wolves. There may be times tat we come into a situation that is unfamiliar to us, and we may need guidance. We may have to go to another as a sheep relies on the shepherd. But, how many times are we really the wolf? We come into situations with the purpose to do harm. We may even come in as wolves in sheep's clothing. Acting like we want to help, but really there to be destructive. We need to remember that we are members of Jesus' flock. And we are given the task of helping care for Christ's sheep. All that we do should be in the name of Christ. And we should always remember that we, too, are sheep that need a shepherd, the Good Shepherd.

God, we give you thanks for sending your Son to be our Good Shepherd. May we always walk in a way that tends to Christ's flock. May we also realize that we too are sheep who need guidance. Amen.

SEPTEMBER 18

But now in Christ Jesus you who once were far off have been brought near by the blood of Christ. For he is our peace; in his flesh he has made both groups into one and has broken down the dividing wall, that is, the hostility between us. He has abolished the law with its commandments and ordinances, that he might create in himself one new humanity in place of the two, thus making peace, and might reconcile both groups to God in one body (or reconcile both of us in one body for God) through the cross, thus putting to death the hostility through it (or in him, or in himself). So he came and proclaimed peace to those who were near; for through him both of us have access in one Spirit to the Father.
Ephesians 2:13-18

Today, the church remembers Dag Hammarskjold. Hammarskjold was a Swedish diplomat and humanitarian who served as Secretary General of the United Nations. Hammarskjold was killed in a plane crash on September 18, 1961, while on his way to negotiate a cease-fire between U.N. and Katanga forces. It was not until after his death that the publications of his personal journal, "Markings", revealed his deep Christian faith. "Markings" revealed that Hammarskjold's life involved his strong personal spirituality with his diplomacy. How often do we as law enforcement officers, feel like diplomats. We are called into situations that involve negotiating a peaceful resolution between hostile parties. Many times, we come to the quickest solution to just stop the whole situation.

We threaten the individuals to bring them to understanding. How would Dag Hammarskjold handle our profession? We need to implement our spirituality into our diplomacy. We should not look for the easiest solution, but work for a solution that brings us all into one body with Christ. This means a little more involvement on our part. This leads us to look at negotiating situations through the lens of the cross. Today, begin to resolve situations through Christ.

God, source of all peace, all thoughts of peace and truth come from you. Kindle in the hearts of all your children the love of peace, and guide with your wisdom all who are in conflict, so that your Kingdom will go forward in peace and the earth will be filled with the knowledge of your love. Help us to be more like your servant Dag Hammarskjold, who brought together his faith and his diplomacy. Amen.

SEPTEMBER 19

By contrast, the fruit of the Spirit is love, joy, peace, patience, kindness, generosity, faithfulness, gentleness, and self-control. There is no law against such things.

Galatians 5:22-23

When we pray, we should ask to receive the fruits of the Spirit. We need to ask the Holy Spirit to remove all the vices of our life and replace them with the fruits. When we encounter people, we should interact with them through these fruits. Today, pray to remove your vices removed and filled with the fruits.

God, giver of all good gifts, we thank you for sending the Holy Spirit to us, to fill us with the fruits. Remove the vices of our life. And forgive us, through Christ, of all the sins we have committed through these vices. Amen.

SEPTEMBER 20

Truly, O people of Zion, inhabitants of Jerusalem, you shall weep no more. He will surely be gracious to you at the sound of your cry; when he hears it, he will answer you. Though the Lord may give you the bread of adversity and the water of affliction, yet your Teacher will not hide himself any more, but your eyes shall see your Teacher. And when you turn to the right or turn to the left, your ears shall hear a word behind you, saying, "This is the way; walk in it." Then you will defile your silver-covered idols and your gold-plated images. You will scatter them like filthy rags; you will say to them, "Away with you!"

Isaiah 30:19-22

Our job places us face-to-face with people who are crying, calling out, and feeling afflicted. There are times in our lives when we feel the same way. We may feel that there is no hope. But, there is hope for the afflicted. Isaiah tells us that God does hear our cries and our callings. And that even though there are times of difficulty, God answers us. God allows us to shake off our afflictions. We may be the instruments through which others are able to scatter their afflictions. We need to pray to shake off ours. Prayer is a discipline that teaches us to give up control and look for another direction. God will give us this new direction. Prayer is not the last ditch effort of the hopeless, but the beginning of a conversation where healing can occur. Today, pray for the removal of your afflictions, and listen for God's answer.

God, Sender of the Teacher, we give you thanks for hearing our cries and our calls. Help us to let go of control, and listen for your directions. Send the Holy Spirit to us, that we may be able to follow the direction, out of affliction that you give us. May we be instruments of the Great Teacher, Your Son, and Jesus Christ. Amen.

SEPTEMBER 21

As Jesus was walking along, he saw a man called Matthew sitting at the tax booth; and he said to him, "Follow me." And he got up and followed him. And as he sat at dinner (or reclined) in the house, many tax collectors and sinners came and were sitting (or were reclining) with him and his disciples. When the Pharisees saw this, they said to his disciples, "Why does your teacher eat with tax collectors and sinners?" But when he heard this, he said, "Those who are well have no need of a physician, but those who are sick. Go and learn what this means, 'I desire mercy, not sacrifice.' For I have come to call not the righteous but sinners."

Matthew 9:9-13

Today, the church remembers Matthew, the apostle and evangelist. Matthew is also called Levi, in some of the accounts of his discipleship. Matthew was a tax collector for the Roman government. Being a tax collector, Matthew was considered an outcast and traitor to his people. Jesus' association with tax collectors and sinners was considered scandalous to the religious leaders. But Matthew did wonderful things in his ministry. Matthew becomes an apostle for Jesus. There are many times that we as law enforcement officers are seen as outcasts and traitors to our community. But, as followers and disciples of Jesus, we are able to do wonderful things for God's Kingdom. We need to focus our life on Christ. Our jobs put us in contact with people who need to know God is active in their lives. We may become the apostle and evangelist for our situations, just as Matthew was for his. Even though we may be despised, Jesus came to us, too.

Almighty God, your Son, Jesus, called a despised tax collector to be one of His apostles. Help us to respond to your transforming call, like Matthew. May we realize that even the despised can do your work, through the power of the Holy Spirit. Amen.

SEPTEMBER 22

(Jesus said) "I am the true vine, and my Father is the vinegrower. He removes every branch in me that bears no fruit. Every branch that bears fruit he prunes to make it bear more fruit. You have already been cleansed by the word that I have spoken to you. Abide in me as I abide in you. Just as the branch cannot bear fruit by itself unless it abides in the vine, neither can you unless you abide in me. I am the vine, you are the branches. Those who abide in me and I in them bear much fruit, because apart from me you can do nothing. Whoever does not abide in me is thrown away like a branch and withers; such branches are gathered and thrown into the fire, and burned.

John 15:1-6

Jesus tells us that we need pruned. God constantly trims, cuts, opens, and prunes us, so that we may bear more fruit. Being pruned is difficult for us. We don't want to think that we need to change a little. But, it is better for the whole vine if all the branches are pruned. We also learn that we are all connected. We are not a bunch a branches lying around separately. We are branches connected to the same vine. We are all connected, and we affect each other. It is just like working on a law enforcement department. We all need to do through revision to help the entire department accomplish its mission. The same is true for the Kingdom of God. Today, ask yourself how God is pruning you?

God, the great Vine grower, we give you thanks for connecting us to the true Vine, Jesus. Help us to realize that we are connected to each other. Change us so that we may always produce more fruit for the Kingdom. Send your Holy Spirit to us that we may be changed to better benefit all believers. Amen.

SEPTEMBER 23

Not that I have already obtained this or have already reached the goal (or have already been made perfect); but I press on to make it my own, because Christ Jesus has made me his own. Beloved, I do not consider that I have made it my own (or my own yet); but this one thing I do: forgetting what lied behind and straining forward to do what lies ahead, I press on toward the goal for the prize of the heavenly (or upward) call of God in Christ Jesus. Let those of us then who are mature be of the same mind; and if you think differently about anything, this too God will reveal to you. Only let us hold fast to what we have attained.

Philippians 3:12-16

We who go into law enforcement tend to be driven people. We want to accomplish everything, as quick and as best as possible. But then we are upset when we don't accomplish the goals or accomplish them in the time we expected. We spend a lot of time looking back on past failures and looking forward to what we should be doing. As Christians, we are called to press on to the goal God has given us through Christ. We are called to forget what lies behind us. The goal we are to focus on is a divine goal. Don't get caught up in the need to accomplish everything and a fast-track timeline. Take your time. Today let go of all the things in your past that weighs you down. Focus your sight on the call God has placed you. Christ has revealed a purpose. That is the goal we press on toward.

God, Revealer of all, we thank you for sending your Son, Christ Jesus, into the world to issue us a heavenly call. Help us to let go of the past and to focus forward on the goal you have set before us. Our prayers, O God, flow from what we are not. Your goal through Christ makes us what we are. Send your Holy Spirit to us that we may continue to press on. Amen.

SEPTEMBER 24

I waited patiently for the LORD; he inclined to me and heard my cry. He drew me up from the desolate pit (or the pit of tumult), out of the miry bog, and set my feet upon a rock, making my steps secure. He put a new song in my mouth, a song of praise to our God. Many will see and fear, and put their trust in the LORD. Happy are those who make the LORD their trust, who do not turn to the proud, to those who go astray after false gods. You have multiplied, O LORD my God, your wondrous deeds and your thoughts towards us; none can compare with you. Were I proclaim and tell of them, they would be more than can be counted.

Psalm 40:1-5

As law enforcement officers, we find many people bogged down in the miry pit. How often have we also found ourselves there? But there is hope. God can remove us from the pit and place a new song in our mouth. With this new song, we can tell others that it is possible to get out. We are to put our trust in the Lord. The next time you find someone in the pit, tell him or her the story of how God pulled you out. Also, be willing to listen to others' stories, it may be God sending a message to you.

O Lord our God, we give you thanks for pulling us from the pit. Help us to put our trust in you. May we always be willing to tell our story to others, who may need to hear your saving words. Amen.

SEPTEMBER 25

(Jesus said) "You are my friends if you do what I command you. I do not call you servants any longer, because the servant does not know what the master is doing; but I have called you friends, because I have made known to you everything that I have heard from my Father."

John 15:14-15

What is the first song you may have learned in Sunday school–"What a Friend we have in Jesus"? How true that song really is. We spend much of our time at work by ourselves. It seems like we are on our own. We come home, and it may feel like we can't talk to anyone. No one understands what we go through or can understand what is going on with us. It appears that we don't have any friends outside of work to talk to. If we talk to anyone, it is probably someone from work. But we do have a friend in Jesus. Jesus tells his disciples in the upper room that they are his friends. So are we. Jesus has revealed everything to us. He does this out of love and friendship. Jesus is someone that we can talk to about what is on our mind. Jesus may also provide us with family and friends that will also listen to us. We just have to give it a chance.

Heavenly Father, we give you thanks for sending your Son into the world to be our friend. We realize that you have revealed everything to us through Christ. Send your Holy Spirit so that we may see all the friends we have in our lives. Help us to talk to our friends so that we may live a healthier life. Amen.

SEPTEMBER 26

Then when you call upon me and come and pray to me, I will hear you. When you search for me, you will find me; if you seek me with all your heart.

Jeremiah 29:12-13

We know what it means to search for someone. Our job teaches us how to properly track, search and find someone. God gives us the instruction on how to find Him. It is much easier than tracking someone through the woods. All we have to do is pray. Call on God in pray, and you will find God. God will hear you. Spend some time today, seeking, searching, and calling upon the Lord. God will hear you and find you. Open up your heart to God.

God, Hearer of our call, thank you for hearing us when we pray to you. Send your Holy Spirit to us so that we may find you and open our heart to you. Amen.

SEPTEMBER 27

They went to a place called Gethsemane; and he said to his disciples, "Sit here while I pray." He took with him Peter and James and John, and began to be distressed and agitated. And he said to them, "I am deeply grieved, even to death; remain here, and keep awake." And going a little farther, he threw himself on the ground and prayed that, if it were possible, the hour might pass from him. He said, "Abba, Father, for you all things are possible; remove this cup from me; yet, not what I want, but what you want." He came and found them sleeping; and he said to Peter, "Simon, are you asleep? Could you not keep awake one hour? Keep awake and pray that you may not come into the time of trial (or into temptation); the spirit indeed is willing, but the flesh is weak." And again he went away and prayed, saying the same words. And once more he came and found them sleeping, for their eyes were very heavy; and they did not know what to say to him. He came a third time and said to them, "Are you still sleeping and taking rest? Enough! The hour has come; the Son of Man is betrayed into the hands of sinners. Get up, let us be going. See, my betrayer is at hand."

Mark 14:32-42 ·

Here we see that even Jesus took time to pray in a difficult situation. Jesus wanted to make sure that he was doing God's will. In many situations, we do not have the time to pray to God that we do the right thing. But there are situations where we do have time. In those instances, stop and take the time to offer the situation in prayer. Listen for God's will. We should also pray that we do God's will in those instances when we don't feel we have time to pray. Jesus gave us the Lord's Prayer. We pray, "Your kingdom come, your will be done". We also pray, "Save us from the time of trial." These are the same words Jesus uses in the garden. Whenever possible, take time to pray for God's guidance in difficult situations. Make sure that what you do is what God desires, and not the outcome only you desire.

Abba, Father, we struggle with difficult decisions, just as Jesus did in the Garden. Help us to know your will for us. Send your Holy Spirit to us that we may remain in prayer and come to know your will. Amen.

SEPTEMBER 28

(Jesus prayed) "I have made your name known to those whom you gave me from the world. They were yours, and you gave them to me, and they have kept your word. Now they know that everything you have given me is from you; for the words that you gave to me I have given to them, and they have received them and know in truth that I came from you; and they have believed that you sent me. I am asking on their behalf; I am not asking on behalf of the world, but on behalf of those who you gave me, because they are yours. All mine are yours, and yours are mine; and I have been glorified in them. And now I am no longer in the world, but they are in the world, and I am coming to you. Holy Father, protect them in your name that you have given me, so that they may be one as we are one. While I was with them, I protected them in your name that you have given me. I guarded them, and not one of them was lost except the one destined to be lost, so that the scripture might be fulfilled. But now I am coming to you, and I speak these things in the world so that they may have my joy made complete in themselves. I have given them your word, and the world has hated them because they do not belong to the world. I am not asking you to take them out of the world, but I ask you to protect them from the evil one. They do not belong to the world, just as I do not belong to the world. Sanctify them in the truth; your word is truth.

John 17:6-17

How many times does a new officer come on, and they go out and buy a new car, or a new house, or buy a lot of expensive things? We get tied up in the material things of this world.

We work extra to make more money to buy more things. We live in a world that focuses on what we have. Jesus prayed that we be protected from the evil one. Jesus realized that his disciples would remain in the world, but should not give in to the world. Jesus' prayer holds true for us today. We are called to be Jesus' disciples in the world. We belong here, but we do not belong to it. We belong to a kingdom of love. If we act in love, the world will hate us because we do not conform to culture. Today, reflect upon what you have, and see if you live your life in the world or of the world.

God, Giver of the Word, we thank you for hearing Jesus' prayer for us. Guide us to continue being his disciples in this world. Help us to not give in to culture and belief in materialism. Send your Holy Spirit to us, that we may be protected from the evil one, as we continue to bring your message of love to this world. Amen.

SEPTEMBER 29

And war broke out in heaven; Michael and his angels fought against the dragon. The dragon and his angels fought back, but they were defeated, and there was no longer any place for them I heaven. The great dragon was thrown down, that ancient serpent, who is called the Devil and Satan, the deceiver of the whole world – he was thrown down to the earth, and his angels were thrown down with him. Then I (John) heard a loud voice in heaven proclaiming, "Now have come the salvation and the power and the kingdom of our God and the authority of his Messiah (or Christ), for the accuser of our comrades (or brothers) has been thrown down, who accuses them day and night before our God. But they have conquered him by the blood of the Lamb and by the word of their testimony, for they did not cling to life even in the face of death. Rejoice them, you heavens and those who dwell in them! But woe to the earth and the sea, for the devil has come down to you with great wrath, because he knows that his time is short!"

Revelation 12:7-12

Today, the church remembers St. Michael and all angels. Michael is an archangel who led the battle in heaven against the angels of the dragon. Michael is the patron saint of police officers. As Michael was the defender of the faith in heaven, we are also called to defend the faith here on earth. We should always stand up in defense of what is right in the name of the Lamb. Many of us wear St. Michael's medals to remind us of this duty.

Everlasting God, You have created and an order of ministries of heavenly beings and earthly beings. Grant that, as your angels always serve and worship you in heaven, may they also serve you in helping and defending us here on earth. Be with us, as we continue in the battle against evil, and defend all for which you stand. Amen.

SEPTEMBER 30

(Jesus said) "Again, the kingdom of heaven is like a net that was thrown into the sea and caught fish of every kind; when it was full, they drew it ashore, sat down, and put the good into baskets but threw out the bad. So it will be at the end of the age. The angels will come out and separate the evil from the righteous and throw them into the furnace of fire, where there will be weeping and gnashing of teeth. Have you understood all this? They answered, "Yes". And he said to them, "Therefore every scribe who has been trained for the kingdom of heaven is like the master of a household who brings out of his treasure what is new and what is old."

Matthew 13:47-52

Today, the church remembers Jerome, a translator and teacher who died in 420ce. Jerome is known for translating the Scriptures from the original Hebrew and Greek into Latin. Latin was the common language of the time. This allowed more people to begin to read the Scriptures themselves, for the first time. Jerome's translation, called the "Vulgate", remained the standard Latin translation for the next 1500 years. What version or translation of the Bible do you read? Do you use the same one all the time, or do you refer to different ones. How often do you read the Bible? We need to be reading the Bible everyday. Today, begin to set aside a specific time and read from the Bible. Get into the habit of reading Scripture every day.

God, Giver of the Word, your Holy Spirit gives different gifts to different people. We praise you for the gifts you bestow upon us. We thank you for sending servants like Jerome, so that we may have a fuller knowledge of Scripture to guide our life. Help us to read your Word everyday. Amen.

OCTOBER 1

Answer me when I call, O God of my right! You gave me room when I was I distress. Be gracious to me, and hear my prayer. How long, you people, shall my honor suffer shame? How long will you love vain words, and seek after lies? Selah But know that the LORD has set apart the faithful for himself; the LORD hears when I call to him. When you are disturbed (or are angry), do not sin; ponder it on your beds, and be silent. Selah Offer right sacrifices, and put your trust in the LORD. There are many who say, "O that we might see some good! Let the light of your face shine on us, O LORD!" You have put gladness in my heart more than when their grain and wine abound.

Psalm 4:1-7

Psalm 4 is a lament, a prayer for deliverance from personal enemies. We hear a cry for help. We hear a rebuke for those who falsely accuse. And the accused is assured of the Lord's help. The psalm writer includes many emotions in the Psalm. Prayer is bringing our very thought before God. God knows what we feel. Prayer is bringing those feelings and thoughts to the One who cares the most. What emotions are you feeling? Take some time today, and offer those feelings to God. Cry out for help. You will receive assurance of the Lord's help.

Lord, Hearer of our cry, we give you thanks for listening to us. We know our feeling and thoughts and deeds are in need of help. Send us your assurance. Help us to offer our prayers to you. Send Your Holy Spirit so that we may continue to pray. May we always rest in the assurance that you gave to us in Your Son, Jesus Christ our Lord. Amen.

OCTOBER 2

O LORD, in the morning you hear my voice; in the morning I plead my case to you, and watch.

Psalm 5:3

The Bible is full of references to prayer in the morning and in the evening, when you rise and when you lie down. At the beginning and end of the day, we can often find a few minutes of quiet time to pray. Maybe this is a time to pray with your family. It may be a time to pray alone. Sometimes, lying in bed, and praying may help you get to sleep. Praying as you lie in bed as you wake up, may help start the day off right. Today, try to start praying as you go to bed and when you wake up.

O Lord our God, hear us when we pray to you. May our prayers help us to sleep and help us to rise. May we rest in the peace that you provide. Amen.

OCTOBER 3

As soon as they left the synagogue, they entered the house of Simon and Andrew, with James and John. Now Simon's mother-in-law was in bed with fever, and they told him (Jesus) about her at once. He came and took her by the hand and lifted her up. Then the fever left her, and she began to serve them. That evening, at sundown, they brought to him all who were sick or possessed with demons. And the whole city was gathered around the door. And he cured many who were sick with various diseases, and cast out many demons; and he would not permit the demons to speak, because they knew him. In the morning, while it was still very dark, he got up and went out to a deserted place, and there he prayed. And Simon and his companions hunted for him. When they found him, they said to him, "Everyone is searching for you." He answered, "Let us go on to the neighboring towns, so that I may proclaim the message there also; for that is what I came to do." And he went throughout Galilee, proclaiming the message in their synagogues and casting out demons.

Mark 1:29-39

From the very beginning of his ministry, Jesus took time to pray. Jesus had done much ministry in this passage. He was preparing to go out and do more. In preparation, he went out, by himself, and began to pray. Whenever we begin a difficult task or a long project, do we take time to pray? We need to pray for strength, guidance, endurance, and all the wisdom to accomplish the task. We should do this every day. Some of us may feel that there is no time for prayer in the morning. We have hectic schedules, many people to get out the door, too much to do. But even as we wake up, we can greet God and remind ourselves of God's presence. Many of us work different hours that we don't wake up in the morning, but sleep and wake to different times of the day. Whenever your daily cycle begins, we can take time to include God into our daily routine. It really makes a difference if we ask for what we need most during that time before we step out into the world and all the coming day has to bring. Today, begin to pray to God as soon as you begin your daily cycle, whenever that may be.

God, Source of guidance, we ask you to be with us as we begin our daily cycle. Help us to pray at the beginning of our day, so that we may include you in everything that we do. May we serve your kingdom as Christ, going out, proclaiming the Good News, healing the sick, and casting out demons. All of this we do through the power of the Holy Spirit. Amen.

OCTOBER 4

Make a joyful noise to the LORD, all the earth. Worship the LORD with gladness; come into his presence with singing.
Psalm 100:1-2

We are to be happy in our worship to God. How do you feel when you worship the Lord? God calls us t be vocal about our singing of praises. Today, think of the things that you are thankful for God giving you. Take some time today and worship God for all your gifts. Make a joyful noise to God. Be glad with what God has provided for you. Sing a song of thanksgiving to God.

Almighty God, giver of all good gifts, we give you thanks for all we received. May you hear our loud praises of you. May you hear noise of celebration in your name. Amen.

OCTOBER 5

Set a guard over my mouth, O LORD; keep watch over the door of my lips. Do not turn my heart to any evil, to busy myself with wicked deeds in company with those who work iniquity; do not let me eat of their delicacies.

Psalm 141:3-4

How many times do we let our mouths get the best of us during a day. Our lips utter things that are of a sinful nature. Our speech because a wicked deed. During our daily prayers, we should ask God to give us strength to speak well of everything. We should pray that we not speak evil of anyone else, or ourselves. Today, ask God to clean up our speech, language, and the way we talk.

God, we thank you for constantly watching over us. Help us to always speak well of everything. May we use language that glorifies you. Help us to always speak of others in the best light. Amen.

OCTOBER 6

(Jesus said) "You have heard that it was said, 'You shall love your neighbor and hate your enemy.' But I say to you, Love your enemies and pray for those who persecute you, so that you may be children of your Father in heaven; for he makes his sun rise on the evil and on the good, and sends rain on the righteous and on the unrighteous.

Matthew 5:43-45

Many people hate us and persecute us because of what we wear to work everyday. They would just as soon kill us as speak to us. It is easy to divide into "us" and "them". And we give "them" nasty names and we hate them back. And we justify this in our own minds. But, Jesus tells us that this is not right. Not only are we not to hate them, we are to love them. This is a difficult thing, loving your enemies. But, we are children of God.

And we are called to see the blood of Christ in the eyes of everyone we encounter, even our enemies.

All-loving Father, we give you thanks for loving us enough to send your Son to us, that we may learn your ways. Send your Holy Spirit to us, that we may be filled with love, and in turn, love our neighbors and our enemies. Strengthen us in those times where we fall short in loving others. Forgive us when we hate. Help us to live a righteous life. Amen.

OCTOBER 7

Do not rejoice over me, O my enemy; when I fall, I shall rise; when I sit in darkness, the LORD will be a light to me.

Micah 7:8

Many of us work nights, and can relate to the metaphor Micah is using here. As we sit in darkness, we have lights to light our way. As we sit in the darkness of our lives, the Lord lights our way. Many times, we drive around, thinking about the darkness that pervades our lives. But God is with us through the dark and light. God provides us with a way to see the right direction, and follow it. Tonight, as you sit in the dark, think about the ways God has given you direction to follow during the dark times of your life. If you are in one now, pray that you receive God's light.

God, Light of our life, we give you thanks for being with us, even in the difficult times. Point the direction out of the darkness, so that we may walk in your light. Amen.

OCTOBER 8

Do not deceive yourselves. If you think that you are wise in this age, you should become fools so that you may become wise. For the wisdom of this world is foolishness with God. For it is written, "He catches the wise in their craftiness," and again, "The Lord knows the thoughts of the wise, that they are futile."

1 Corinthians 3:18-20

Do you remember your Field Training Officer telling you to forget everything you learned in the academy? Your FTO said they would teach you the way things really are. Here you are feeling like you know everything about law enforcement, and they tell you that you are a fool. This is what Paul is talking about here. We should never get to a point where we think we know everything about God, the faith, or Christianity. The more we learn, the more we should act like we don't know. It is only in emptying ourselves that we are able to learn more. When we think we have all knowledge, we close our minds to other learning. Continually become a fool so that you may become wise.

God, Give of all Knowledge, we give you thanks for all that you reveal to us. We are not able to fully understand you. Help us to empty ourselves with knowledge, so that we may learn more of what you have to teach us. All of this is done by the power of the Holy Spirit, through your great revelation, Jesus Christ our Lord. Amen.

OCTOBER 9

These twelve Jesus sent out with the following instructions: "Go nowhere among the Gentiles, and enter no town of the Samaritans, but go rather to the lost sheep of the house of Israel. As you go, proclaim the good news, 'The kingdom of heaven has come near (or is at hand).' Cure the sick, raise the dead, cleanse the lepers, cast out demons. You received without payment; give without payment. Take no gold, or silver, or copper in your belts, no bag for your journey, or two tunics, or sandals, or a staff; for laborers deserve their food. Whatever town or village you enter, find out who in it is worthy, and stay there until you leave. As you enter the house, greet it. If the house is worthy, let your peace come upon it; but if it is not worthy, let your peace return to you. If anyone will not welcome you or listen to your words, shake off the dust from your feet as you leave that house or town. Truly I tell you, it will be more tolerable for the land of Sodom and Gomorrah on the day of judgment than for that town.

Matthew 10:5-15

Jesus sent his disciples out with very specific instructions. Jesus sends us out into the world. We encounter many of the same people that Jesus sent his original disciples out to encounter. We are called to do all of the same things. We are to act in the same way in our faith. And we are not supposed to make a profit on doing ministry. So, as you enter each situation at work, at home, or just out and about; think about how Jesus would want you take act. How can you be a disciple of Christ in that situation?

God, Sender of Your Son, we go out into the world as He has sent us. May we fulfill the entire ministry we are to accomplish. May we continue to proclaim the Good News. Send your Holy Spirit to us, so that we may be strengthen in our work. Amen.

OCTOBER 10

The LORD is my shepherd, I shall not want. He makes me lie down in green pastures; he leads me beside still waters (or waters of rest); he restores my soul (or life). He leads me in right paths (or paths of righteousness) for his name's sake.

Psalm 23:1-3

God is good to us. Find a comfortable place to sit. Get settled, in a chair or on the floor. Think back over your day; what you did, what happened to you, what went well, what didn't go so well. Is there anything you wish you could do again? Ask for what you need. God doesn't have to do things over because of falling short. God provides everything to us. Pray for God's forgiveness. May the conversation is about help you need in making a situation right in your life. Maybe you need assistance in doing things differently than you had before. Take some time, and ask God in prayer.

Almighty God, we give you thanks for everything you provide in our lives. You know that answers to our prayers before we ask. Send your help to us. May we always to turn you to make our lives right. Amen.

OCTOBER 11

For thus says the Lord GOD: I myself will search for my sheep, and will seek them out. As shepherds seek out their flocks when they are among their scattered sheep, so I will seek out my sheep. I will rescue them from all the places to which they have been scattered on a day of clouds and thick darkness. I will bring them out from the peoples and gather them from the countries, and will bring them into their own land; and I will feed them on the mountains of Israel, by the watercourses, and in all the inhabited parts of the land. I will feed them with good pasture, and the mountain heights of Israel shall be their pasture; there they shall lie down in good grazing land, and they shall feed on rich pasture on the mountains of Israel. I myself will be the shepherd of my sheep, and I will lie down, says the Lord God. I will seek the lost, and I will bring back the strayed, and I will bind up the injured, and I will strengthen the weak, but the fat and the strong I will destroy. I will feed them with justice.

Ezekiel 34:11-16

Did God provide for you today? Did anything special happen to you? Was there an experience that affected you deeply. God lives in the events of our lives. God want you to discover all that you need. God provides for you. Today, think about what God may have wanted you to discover.

Lord God, we give you thanks for all that you provide us. We feed from the good pastures and we have your Son, as our Good Shepherd. Help us to find all that you want us to discover. May we be nourished by your word to go out into the world to serve your kingdom. Amen.

OCTOBER 12

On the holy mount stands the city he founded; the LORD loves the gates of Zion more than all the dwellings of Jacob. Glorious things are spoken of you, O city of God. Selah. Among those who know me I mention Rahab and Babylon; Philistia too, and Tyre, with Ethiopia - "This one was born there." They say. And of Zion it shall be said, "This one and that one were born in it": for the Most High himself will establish it. The LORD records, as he registers the peoples, "This one was born there." Selah. Singers and dancers alike say, "All my springs are in you."

Psalm 87:1-7

God speaks wonderful things for you. Now, count your blessings, remembering the things for which you are grateful. Thank God for all of it, and for your very life itself. There are many who might say, "Oh, that we might see some good!" Be one of those who recognizes good when you see it, and give thanks for it.

God, founder of the cities, we give you thanks for our many blessings. We remember that all things come from you. Help us to recognize the good in all things. Be with us in this life, so that we may be with you at the gates of heaven. Amen.

OCTOBER 13

Jesus went on with his disciples to the villages of Caesarea Philippi; and on the way he asked his disciples, "Who do people say that I am?" And they answered him, "John the Baptist; and others, Elijah; and still others, one of the prophets." He asked them, "But who do you say that I am?" Peter answered him, "You are the Messiah." And he sternly ordered them not to tell anyone about him.

Mark 8:27-30

Like Peter, we know the true identity of Jesus. We are called to follow him, and be one of his disciples. We should evaluate ourselves everyday. Take some time when you get home, at the end of your day, whenever that may be. Evaluate your discipleship for the day. Before you fall asleep, think back over the day. Converse with God, asking the Holy Spirit to show you what you may have missed in the business of the day. Ask Jesus how your discipleship is going. Ask God if you did everything that was asked of you during the day. Spend some time in prayer, before you go to sleep. Try this either laying in bed, or sitting quietly in a chair. Take some time to look over your day. Then, leave your day with God. This one is over, tomorrow begins a new day. Put your trust in God, and be at peace.

God, our ultimate trust, we know the true identity of your Son. Send your Holy Spirit to us, that we may continue to be disciples. We offer up this day to you. Show us all that we can do for your kingdom. Forgive us for our shortcomings. May we begin a new day tomorrow. Amen.

OCTOBER 14

As they came near the village to which they were going, he (Jesus) walked ahead as if he were going on. But they urged him strongly, saying, "Stay with us, because it is almost evening and the day is now nearly over." So he went in to stay with them. When he was at the table with them, he took bread, blessed and broke it, and gave it to them. Then their eyes were opened, and they recognized him; and he vanished from their sight. They said to each other, "Were not our hearts burning within us while he was talking to us on the road, while he was opening the scriptures to us?" That same hour they got up and returned to Jerusalem; and they found the eleven and their companions gathered together. They were saying, "The Lord has risen indeed, and he has appeared to Simon!" Then they told what had happened on the road, and how he had been made known to them in the breaking of the bread.

Luke 24:28-35

People sitting down together, breaking and sharing bread, seeing in a new way. Jesus shared himself in the breaking of the bread at the Last Supper. Here he reveals himself to the disciples at the evening meal on the first Easter Sunday. We are also invited to share and reveal ourselves with those at our table. An evening meal may be the only time when the family is able to get together. Remember, that Jesus is there with us at the meal. In the presence of Christ, let us spend time with one another.

Almighty God, honor guest at all meals, we give you thanks for providing us with the food we need. We thank you for sending your son to eat with us. We also give thanks for the time we are able to share at meals with our family and friends. Bless that time. Amen.

OCTOBER 15

He also told this parable to some who trusted in themselves that they were righteous and regarded others with contempt: "Two men went up to the temple to pray, one a Pharisee and the other a tax collector. The Pharisee, standing by himself, was praying thus, 'God, I thank you that I am not like other people: thieves, rogues, adulterers, or even like this tax collector. I fast twice a week; I give a tenth of all my income.' But the tax collector, standing far off, would not even look up to heaven, but was beating his breast and saying, 'God, be merciful to me, a sinner!'... "

Luke 18:9-13

As law enforcement officers, we tend to talk a lot. We do not need to use a lot of words when we pray. The tax collector in this story used one short sentence. He did not try to use a lot of words to inform God; he wasn't trying to impress others; he may not of been trying to feel more spiritual. He just said what was on his heart. At any time of the day or night, this prayer can be as effective as any other. This prayer becomes a reminder of who we are as Christians. We are dependant on grace and we trust in God. In the New Testament, the word "mercy" means not only forgiveness, but also the outward acts rising from Jesus' compassion; feeding, teaching, and healing. Today, find a comfortable position where you are, close your eyes, breathe, and then begin to pray this simple prayer.

Lord Jesus, Son of God, have mercy on me, a sinner. Amen.

OCTOBER 16

Blessed be the God and Father of our Lord Jesus Christ, who has blessed us in Christ with every spiritual blessing in the heavenly places, just as he chose us in Christ before the foundation of the world to be holy and blameless before him in love. He destined us for adoption as his children through Jesus Christ, according to the good pleasure of his will, to the praise of his glorious grace that he freely bestowed on us in the Beloved. In him we have redemption through his blood, the forgiveness of our trespasses, according to the riches of his grace that he lavished on us. With all wisdom and insight he has made known to us the mystery of his will, according to his good pleasure that he set forth in Christ, as a plan for the fullness of time, to gather up all things in him, things in heaven and things on earth. In Christ we have obtained an inheritance (or been made a heritage), having been destined according to the purpose of him who accomplishes all things according to his counsel and will, so that we, who were the first to set our hope on Christ, might live for the praise of his glory. In him you also, when you have heard the word of truth, the gospel of your salvation, and had believed in him, were marked with the seal of the promised Holy Spirit; this is the pledge of our inheritance toward redemption as God's own people, to the praise of his glory.

Ephesians 1:3-14

Bless appears three times in the first verse of this passage. What blessings do you have? Many of us think that we do not have many blessings. But as we begin to look, we see that God has provided us with many blessings. God gives us every blessing that we receive. Through Christ, God will continue to bless us. We are blessed. We are marked with the seal of the promised Holy Spirit. Through Christ, we are inheritors of God's kingdom. Today, reflect upon the many blessings you have received.

God, Most Blessed, we thank you for the many blessings that you have provided for us. As we are marked with the Holy Spirit, may we go out and proclaim the good news of Christ to the world. Amen.

OCTOBER 17

After leaving the synagogue he (Jesus) entered Simon's house.
Now Simon's mother-in-law was suffering from a high fever, and
they asked him about her. Then he stood over her and rebuked
the fever, and it left her. Immediately she got up and began to
serve them. As the sun was setting, all those who had any who
were sick with various kinds of diseases brought them to him;
and he laid his hands on each of them and cured them. Demons
also came out of many, shouting, "You are the Son of God!" But
he rebuked them and would not allow them to speak, because
they knew that he was the Messiah (or the Christ).

Luke 4:38-41

Our work habits, our stress, our way of life, contributes to
sickness and illness. Law enforcement officers tend to get sick
often and easily. We don't take care of ourselves. We are called
to be whole, even physically. Jesus did many healings, even
Peter's mother-in-law. We need to take care of ourselves. We
need to regularly go to the doctor and follow their instructions.
Christ wants us to be physically fit so that we can go out into the
world in service. If you have any ailment, take care of it.

Jesus, great healer, make us whole. Help us to be physically
fit. Heal us when we are sick. Send the Holy Spirit to us so that
we may be strengthened to serve God. Amen.

OCTOBER 18

Since many have undertaken to set down an orderly account of the
events that have been fulfilled among us, just as they were handed on
to us by those who from the beginning were eyewitnesses and servants
of the word. I too decided, after investigating everything carefully
from the very first (or for a long time), to write an orderly account for
you, most excellent Theophilus, so that you may know the truth con-
cerning the things about which you have been instructed.

Luke 1:1-4

Today, the church remembers St. Luke, the evangelist. Luke was the author of both the Gospel According to Luke and the Acts of the Apostles. Paul calls Luke the "beloved physician". Little else is known of Luke's life. Luke's symbol is a winged ox. Luke was a physician who told the good news of Jesus. You are a law enforcement officer who is to tell the good news of Christ. We use our vocations as a means to proclaim the Gospel. You, too, should decide to be an evangelist.

Almighty God, you inspired your servant Luke the physician to reveal in his orderly account the love and healing power of your Son, Jesus. Give your church the same love and power to heal. Send your Holy Spirit to us, that we may also be inspired to proclaim the good news of Christ. Amen.

OCTOBER 19

But I have calmed and quieted my soul, like a weaned child with its mother; my soul is like the weaned child that is with me (or my soul within me is like a weaned child).

Psalm 131:2

We should live our lives as actions of humble submission to God's will and guidance. Calm and quiet your soul. Our souls race with noise and movement. We should be like a weaned child with its mother, calm and peaceful. Today, take some time to calm and quiet your soul.

Loving God, hold me close. Send your Holy Spirit to me, to help me calm and quiet my soul. Amen.

OCTOBER 20

(Jesus Said) "I have said these things to you while I am still with you. But the Advocate (or Helper), the Holy Spirit, whom the Father will send in my name, will teach you everything, and remind you of all that I have said to you. Peace I leave with you; my peace I give to you. I do not give to you as the

world gives. *Do not let your hearts be troubled, and do not let them be afraid.*

John 14:25-27

Jesus came to bring peace to the world. Jesus also brings peace to our lives. We should not let our hearts be troubled about issues that arise. We should also not be afraid to enter into any situation. Christ said that God would send the Holy Spirit to us. God will teach us everything that we need to know. We need to have faith in the work of God. We must also remember that as peace officers, we may be the Holy Spirit working in other peoples' lives. We may be the instrument that God uses to teach. We may be the way that others' are taught what Jesus said. Be open to the work of God, both in your life and through your life.

Spirit of God, give us peace. Remind us of all the Christ has taught us. May we not be troubled or afraid. Amen.

OCTOBER 21

After this Jesus went to the other side of the Sea of Galilee, also called the Sea of Tiberias. A large crowd kept following him, because they saw the signs that he was doing for the sick. Jesus went up the mountain and sat down there with his disciples. Now the Passover, the festival of the Jews, was near. When he looked up and saw a large crowd coming toward him, Jesus said to Philip, "Where are we to buy bread for these people to eat?" He said this to test him, for he himself knew what he was going to do. Philip answered him, "Six months' wages would not buy enough bread for each of them to get a little." One of his disciples, Andrew, Simon Peter's brother, said to him, "There is a boy here who has five barley loaves and two fish. But what are they among so many people?" Jesus said, "Make the people sit down." Now there was a great deal of grass in the place, so they sat down, about five thousand in all. Then Jesus took the loaves, and when he had given thanks, he distributed them to those who were seated; so also the fish, as much as they wanted. When they were satisfied, he told his disciples, "Gather up the fragments left over, so that nothing may be lost." So they gathered them up, and from the fragments of the five barley loaves, left by those who had eaten, they filled twelve baskets. When the people saw the sign that he had done, they began to say, "This is indeed the prophet who is to come into the world." When Jesus realized that they were about to come and take him by force to make him king, he withdrew again to the mountain by himself. When evening came, his disciples went down to the sea, got into the boat, and started across the sea to Capernaum. It was now dark, and Jesus had not yet come to them. The sea became rough because a strong wind was blowing. When they had rowed about three or four miles, they saw Jesus walking on the sea and coming near the boat, and they were terrified. But he said to them, "It is I (or I am); do not be afraid." Then they wanted to take him into the boat, and immediately the boat reached the land toward which they were going.

John 6:1-21

Can you hear the fear in the disciples' voices? We don't have enough money, we don't have enough food. He is walking on the sea! The disciples displayed fear, even in the presence of Jesus. When do you hear fear in your voice? We work in a profession that is filled with time to be afraid. Do we show it? We live life, full of situations that cause us to fear. Do we display it? Fear is a natural emotion. Jesus understands fear. But, when we turn the focus from ourselves, our knowledge, our understanding of how things are done; and we turn to Christ to do the work, our fears are taken away. Today, think about the things in your life that cause you to be afraid. Release them to Christ, to have him show you the way.

God, answer to all fears, we give you thanks for sending you Son, Jesus, into the world, to show us how to live our lives. Send your Holy Spirit to us, that we may focus on Christ, and follow him. Amen.

OCTOBER 22

Let my prayer be counted as incense before you, and the lifting up of my hands as an evening sacrifice.

Psalm 141:2

In the evening, it is a good way to release the troubles of the day, by praying. Place your trust in God that all you have done is good. Begin to settle down from the day by reading the Bible, saying prayers, and turning everything over to God. This will help you start a new day fresh and renewed.

God, hearer of all prayers, hear us as we send our prayers to you, like incense. May we lift our hands to you in prayer, turning over all that we have. Amen.

OCTOBER 23

The whole assembly kept silence, and listened to Barnabas and Paul as they told of all the signs and wonders that God had done through them among the Gentiles. After they finished speaking, James replied, "My brothers, listen to me. Simeon has related how God first looked favorably on the Gentiles, to take from among them a people for his name. This agrees with the words of the prophets, as it is written, 'After this I will return, and I will rebuild the dwelling of David, which has fallen; from its ruins I will rebuild it, and I will set it up, so that all other peoples may seek the Lord – even all the Gentiles over whom my name has been called. Thus says the Lord, who has been making these things known from long ago (Known from of old are all his works).' Therefore I have reached the decision that we should not trouble those Gentiles who are turning to God, but we should write to them to abstain only from things polluted by idols and from fornication and from whatever has been strangled and from blood. For in every city, for generations past, Moses has had those who proclaim him, for he has been read aloud every sab-bath in the synagogues." Then the apostles and the elders, with the consent of the whole church, decided to choose men from among their members and to send them to Antioch with Paul and Barnabas. They sent Judas called Barsabbas, and Silas, leaders among the brothers, ...

Acts of the Apostles 15:12-22

Today, the church remembers James of Jerusalem. James became a leader in the early church in Jerusalem. James is identified as the brother of our Lord, Jesus. James was instrumental in the decision made at the Council. This moment changed the church forever. Tradition holds that James was martyred for his faith. Did James set out to be a hero, or was he just doing his job? We work in a profession, that gets lifted up as heroes, from time to time. But are we really heroes, or are we just doing our job? Sometimes, it is difficult to live with a hero status. Like James, we need to keep our feet on the ground, and make sound decisions. Don't let the "hero" talk go to head. Keep grounded in all that you do.

God, sender of heroes throughout history, we thank you for sending people like James to this world, to help us make right decisions. Send your Holy Spirit to us, as we work in dangerous places. Help us to keep grounded in Christ. May we always make decision for the best of your children, our brothers and sisters. Amen.

OCTOBER 24

My eyes are awake before each watch of the night, that I may meditate on your promise.

Psalm 119:148

How many of us work the night watch? We are the ones who stay alert while the others sleep. What do we do with that time we work at night. We have lots of time just to ourselves. Take some time to think about the promises God has made to you. Take time to think and prayer, during those moments when your full atten-

226

tion is not on a specific task; waiting in line or stopped in traffic, when your energy level drops. Some of the best times to talk to God are when you are confused, depressed or grieved. We sit by ourselves hour-after-hour in our feelings. Why not take time during those night hours to talk with God. God promises to listen.

God, keeper of all watches, we give you thanks for watching over us at night. Be with us as we protect others while they rest. Send your Holy Spirit to us during those times, so that we may release to you our feelings. May we always find Christ, even in the dark. Amen.

OCTOBER 25

So, whether you eat or drink, or whatever you do, do everything for the glory of God.

1 Corinthians 10:31

We need to remember that, even though we are law enforcement officers, we are still doing God's work. God called us into this profession. This is our ministry. Everyone that we interact with needs to hear and see the Good News Christ brings.

Dear God, open our eyes so that we may see that all we do is for your glory. Open our hearts, that we may show Christ to everyone that we meet. Guide our steps, that by the power of the Holy Spirit, we may continue to walk in your ways. Amen.

OCTOBER 26

The cup of blessing that we bless, is it not a sharing in the blood of Christ? The bread that we break, is it not a sharing of the body of Christ? Because there is one bread, we who are many are one body, for we all partake of the one bread.

1 Corinthians 10:16-17

When we enter in to prayer relationship with God, we find out that we can also be helpful to others. We realize that we are connected to each other. We are the one body. Pray can help you feel better. Pray connects you consciously to God. Pray transforms you in ways you may not imagine. And prayer can help you deal with your difficulties so you can use your energy for others. Do you know of anyone who may need your help? Do you know about their prayer life? Take a risk and ask them. Begin to share in that one body. We are connected. Today, think of one person to engage. Now, go to them. You may be the answer to their prayers.

Almighty God, we give you thanks for sending your Son into this world. He gave us the bread and cup of life, so that we may His one body. Send your Holy Spirit to us, that we may realize our connectedness. Be with us as we talk with others about their difficulties. Amen.

OCTOBER 27

My mouth is filled with your praise, and with your glory all day long.

Psalm 71:8

We as law enforcement officers hear all types of language everyday. We, too, have our own language. Many times, our language is not always the best. We say things we shouldn't. We curse and swear. We comment on things about which, we should remain silent. Our words do not always match what we do or who we are. Our mouths should be filled with praise of God, and our words should bring God glory. Today, pay attention to what you say. Make sure your words are offering praise and glory to God.

Precious God, You are the One who is to receive praise and glory. Forgive us for the way we speak, the language we use, and our manner of speech. Fill our mouths with Your praise, and allow us to bring glory to you. Amen.

OCTOBER 28

Beloved, do not believe every spirit, but test the spirits to see whether they are from God; for many false prophets have gone out into the world. By this you know the Spirit of God: every spirit that confesses that Jesus Christ has come in the flesh is from God, and every spirit that does not confess Jesus (or does away with Jesus, or dissolves Jesus) is not from God. And this is the spirit of the antichrist, of which you have heard that it is coming; and now it is already in the world. Little children, you are from God, and have conquered them; for the one who is in you is greater than the one who is in the world. They are from the world; therefore what they say is from the world, and the world listens to them. We are from God. Whoever knows God listens to us, and whoever is not from God does not listen to us. From this we know the spirit of truth and the spirit of error.

1 John 4:1-6

Today, the church remembers Simon and Jude, apostles of Jesus. We know little about both Simon and Jude. But both of them confessed Jesus as living in the flesh. They both listened to Jesus. These two apostles were from God, and spoke God's word. We may be like Simon and Jude. Little may be known about us in the future. But we still have to listen to the Holy Spirit; confess the life, death and resurrection of Jesus; and know God. When we speak about God in truth, people will listen to us. We need to be talking about our faith, just as Simon and Jude did long ago. And like them, we do it, not out of personal gain, but to proclaim what God has done for us. We will probably not be famous, and we will be in fantastic company.

God, we thank you for sending us people like Simon and Jude. We pray that we, too, may be faithful and zealous in our mission. Amen.

OCTOBER 29

See that none of you repays evil for evil, but always seek to do good to one another and to all. Rejoice always, pray without ceasing, give thanks in all circumstances; for this is the will of God in Christ Jesus for you. Do not quench the Spirit. Do not despise the words of the prophets (or despise prophecies), but test everything; hold fast to what is good; abstain from every form of evil.

1 Thessalonians 5:15-22

We live in a world where retaliation is the answer. Too many times, we see law enforcement officers getting into trouble, because they retaliated on someone. They were not able to control themselves. They let their emotions get the better of them. It is difficult to let go of those feelings. We can when we place out feelings in Christ. Always be willing to pray. Always give thanks to God, no matter what the circumstance. Allow the Holy Spirit to work in your life. When you feel emotions raging inside of you, take some time to refocus on the good. Then proceed where God leads you.

God, Greatest Good, we give you thanks for everything in our lives. Send your Holy Spirit to us, that we may do your will through Christ. Hear our prayers in times of difficulty, that we may be able to overcome evil. Help us to always rejoice in you. Amen.

OCTOBER 30

(Jesus said) "And whenever you pray, do not be like the hypocrites; for they love to stand and pray in the synagogues and at the street corners, so that they may be seen by others. Truly I tell you, they have received their reward. But whenever you pray, go into your room and shut the door and pray to your Father who is in secret; and your Father who sees in secret will reward you (openly).

Matthew 6:5-6

The kinds of prayer that are best for one person are not necessarily the best for someone else. Discovering your own ways of praying nourishes your relationship with God. We see that Jesus tells us not to pray like others do. Close your eyes, take a few deep breaths, and take some time for yourself with God. Lay aside all the things that your experienced during the day. Today, work on finding out the best way for you to pray. Where is the place? What do you say? What do you use to help you concentrate? Work all of these things out, so that everyday, your feel comfortable to talk with God.

God, answer to all prayers, we give you thanks for listening to us. Send your Holy Spirit to us, that we may feel comfortable in talking to you. Your Son, Jesus, was the example of how we are to talk to you. Help us be more like Jesus. Amen.

OCTOBER 31

Submit yourselves therefore to God. Resist the devil, and he will flee you. Draw near to God, and he will draw near to you. Cleanse your hands, you sinners, and purify your hearts, you double-minded. Lament and mourn and weep. Let your laughter be turned into mourning and your joy into dejection. Humble yourselves before the Lord, and he will exalt you.

James 4:7-10

Sometimes, we make praying a very difficult task. We need to make it much more simple. Christians throughout the centuries have struggled with making prayer simple. The best way is to just "draw near to God." Open yourself up. God will hear you. It doesn't matter when or where. God has drawn near to you.

God, in the midst of our noisy, busy lives, we thank you for drawing near to us. Hear us and be with us as we draw near to you. Walk with us in those times when we do not draw near to you. Help us to humble ourselves before you. We thank you for the blessings of quiet time that you send. It is peaceful to be with you and others in the quiet of our lives. Amen.

NOVEMBER 1

When Mary came where Jesus was and saw him, she knelt at his feet and said to him, "Lord, if you had been here, my brother would not have died." When Jesus saw her weeping, and the Jews who came with her also weeping, he was greatly disturbed in spirit and deeply moved. He said, "Where have you laid him?" They said to him, "Lord, come and see." Jesus began to weep. So the Jews said, "See how he loved him!" But some of them said, "Could not he who opened the eyes of the blind man have kept this man from dying?" Then Jesus, again greatly disturbed, came to the tomb. It was a cave, and a stone was lying against it. Jesus said, "Take away the stone." Martha, the sister of the dead man, said to him, "Lord, already there is a stench because he has been dead four days." Jesus said to her, "Did I not tell you that if you believed, you would see the glory of God?" So they took away the stone. And Jesus looked upward and said, "Father, I thank you for having heard me. I knew that you always hear me, but I have said this for the sake of the crowd standing here, so that they may believe that you sent me." When he had said this, he cried with a loud voice, "Lazarus, come out!" The dead man came out, his hands and feet bound with strips of cloth, and his face wrapped in a cloth. Jesus said to them, "Unbind him, and let him go."

John 11:32-44

Today, the church celebrates All Saints Day. We remember all the baptized people of God, both dead and alive. We are all saints, and we all make up the body of Christ. We remember our dearly departed. And we celebrate knowing that we live under the promise of seeing them again in eternal life. Today, think about all the Christians that have been in your life. Take some time, and think about the contributions they made in your formation. If they are still alive, call them, write them a letter. Let them know that you are thinking of them.

Ever-Living God, we are all united in your church, the body of Christ. We give you thanks for sending others to show us how to live in the faith. Be with us during our times of grief. Send your Holy Spirit to us, until that time that we may all be reunited. Amen.

NOVEMBER 2

Wisdom has built her house, she has hewn her seven pillars. She has slaughtered her animals, she has mixed her wine, she has also set her table. She has sent out her servant-girls, she calls from the highest places in the town, "You that are simple, turn in here!" To those without sense she says, "Come, eat of my bread and drink of the wine I have mixed. Lay aside immaturity and live, and walk in the way of insight."

Proverbs 9:1-6

We go through a lot training in this profession. We go through the academy. We have a field training program, in-service training, more classes. Some of us even get college degrees in these areas. After awhile, we get full of ourselves, that we know all there is to know. It is at that time, that we should read this passage from Proverbs. We are called to come to God's house as simple people. Our minds should be open to learning what God has to teach us. Not full of our own knowledge. God is the source of all wisdom. God has built a house for us and invited us to a feast. God has send people out to us to get us to come in. And God feeds us with the common food of bread and wine, the food that everyone could afford. The same bread and wine that Jesus chooses to use as his Body and blood in Communion. As soon as you feel yourself at a high place, remember that we are called to be simple.

All-knowing God, Giver of all wisdom, we thank you for inviting us to your house. We give thanks for the gifts that Christ gives to us in his body and blood. We give thanks for the Holy Spirit in our life, reminding us to be simple. Amen.

NOVEMBER 3

Now when they heard this, they were cut to the heart and said to Peter and to the other apostles, "Brothers, what should we do?" Peter said to them, "Repent, and be baptized every one of you in the name of Jesus Christ so that your sins may be forgiven; and you will receive the gift of the Holy Spirit. For the promise is for you, for your children, and for all who are far away, everyone whom the Lord our God calls to him." And he testified with many other arguments and exhorted them, saying, "Save yourselves from this corrupt generation." So those who welcomed his message were baptized, and that day about three thousand persons were added. They devoted themselves to the apostles' teaching and fellowship, to the breaking of the bread and prayers.

Acts of the Apostles 2:37-42

There are many times that we feel we are alone. But being baptized means that we are members of a larger community. We are part of fellowship that we have with all who believe. We are called to live our lives in fellowship. Whatever affects one member, affects us all. Those who were baptized in this passage of Acts devoted themselves to four things: apostles' teaching, fellowship, Holy Communion, and praying. The "breaking of the bread" is what we now call Holy Communion. We should receive Communion as often as we are able. We should constantly be reading the Bible and the teachings of the church. We should have a purposeful prayer life. And we should be in fellowship with others. If you do not have a worshipping community at this time, you need to find one. Find one that has worship at times that your schedule allows regular attendance. Get involved with the life of a community of faith.

Gracious God, we give you thanks for the church that you maintain. Send the Holy Spirit to us, to guide us to finding the community of faith that meets our needs. As the body of Christ, we need to be with others who are baptized in the name of the Father, and of the Son, and of the Holy Spirit. Amen.

NOVEMBER 4

I have passed out of mind like one who is dead; I have become like a broken vessel. For I hear the whispering of many- terror all around! - as they scheme together against me, as they plot to take my life. But I trust in you, O LORD; I say, "You are my God." My times are in your hand; deliver me from the hand of my enemies and persecutors.

Psalm 31:12-15

We work in a profession where people hate us just because we wear a uniform to work. Some people would rather kill us than look at us. When we pray, tell God the situation you find yourself. You may say that is silly. You might think that you would never say things like that in a prayer. The people who prayed this Psalm were in touch with a lot of the same feelings. God wants to hear how we really are doing. So, tell God how you feel: oppressed, fearful, in conflict, mad, mentally exhausted, emotionally strained.

All-Knowing God, hear us as we tell you how we really are. We put our trust in you. Help us through the difficult times. We walk a difficult path. Protect us as we do your work. Amen.

NOVEMBER 5

Blessed be the God and Father of our Lord Jesus Christ! By his great mercy he has given us a new birth into a living hope through the resurrection of Jesus Christ from the dead, and into an inheritance that is imperishable, undefiled, and unfading, kept in heaven for you, who are being protected by the power of God through faith for a salvation ready to be revealed in the last time. In this you rejoice, even if now for a little while you have had to suffer various trials, so that the genuineness of your faith - being more precious than gold that, though perishable, is tested by fire - may be found to result in praise and glory and honor when Jesus Christ is revealed.

1 Peter 1:3-7

Our own birthday is a special day for us. We may take time to look back on the year or several years. We use birthdays to mark stages of life. Our baptism was a birthday also. It was the day we were given a new birth into a living hope of eternal life. This is also something to celebrate. We live under the promises of God. This is something to celebrate everyday. Our days now are living out our new life. Today, and every day from now on, gives thanks to God for the promises God has given to us through Christ.

Giving God, we thank you for all you have promised. We rejoice and praise you for our new life. We give you thanks for sending your Son, Jesus, so that we may have these promises. Send your Holy Spirit to us, that we may continue to walk in the new life you have given us. Amen.

NOVEMBER 6

Bless the Lord, O my soul, and all that is within me, bless his holy name. Bless the Lord, O my soul, and do not forget all his benefits - who forgives all your iniquity, who heals all your diseases, who redeems your life from the Pit, who crowns you with steadfast love and mercy, who satisfies you with good as long as you live so that your youth is renewed like the eagle's.

Psalm 103:1-5

We should be grateful for all the gifts God gives to us. We should offer God praise and adoration. When you pray, give praise to God for what God has given to you. Today, think about all the good gifts God has bestowed on you, and give praise.

Blessed Lord, we give you thanks for all that you have given to us. Forgive us for not always giving you the praise and adoration you deserve. Amen.

NOVEMBER 7

Likewise the Spirit helps us in our weakness; for we do not know how to pray as we ought, but the very Spirit intercedes (for us) with sighs too deep for words.

Romans 8:26

We find it difficult to pray. But we need to remember that God already knows what we need. And the Holy Spirit helps us in our weakness. Whether our weakness is praying, or any other weakness, the Holy Spirit works for us. The Holy Spirit is able to communicate in ways that words could not. Today, release your weaknesses, and have to Holy Spirit speak for you.

All-knowing God, we give you thanks for sending the Holy Spirit to us. There are times when we are not able to speak the words we need to say. May the Holy Spirit continue to communicate on our behalf. Amen.

NOVEMBER 8

Finally, be strong in the Lord and in the strength of his power. Put on the whole armor of God, so that you may be able to stand against the wiles of the devil. For our (or your) struggle is not against enemies of blood and flesh, but against the rulers, against the authorities, against the cosmic powers of this present darkness, against the spiritual forces of evil in the heavenly places. Therefore take up the whole armor of God, so that you may be able to withstand on that evil day, and having done everything, to stand firm. Stand therefore, and fasten the belt of truth around your waist, and put on the breastplate of righteousness. As shoes for your feet put on whatever will make you ready to proclaim the gospel of peace. With all these (or in all circumstances), take the shield of faith, with which you will be able to quench all the flaming arrows of the evil one. Take the helmet of salvation, and the sword of the Spirit, which is the word of God.

Ephesians 6:10-18

As law enforcement officers, we are all to familiar with the need to wear armor. We put our body armor and uniform on everyday. We carry several pieces of equipment that protect us. We also have other equipment in case the need more armor. As Christians, God supplies us with holy armor to protect us from evil. We wear the belt of truth, our holy duty belt, so that we are always truthful and do not lie. We wear the breastplate of righteousness like our ballistic vest, protecting our heart and vital organs. We do not let our emotions get the best of us. We are clothed with the righteousness of Christ. We wear footgear, like our boots, to carry us to all parts, proclaim the Good News of the Gospel of peace. We carry a shield of faith, much like carrying a body bunker or ballistic shield. We do not let insults, setbacks and temptations take control of us. Our faith allows us to make confession and believe in the victory of Christ over evil. The helmet of salvation, our hat, protects our minds from doubting God's saving work for us. Nothing can separate us from the love of God. The sword of the Spirit, the Word of God, is our weapon as Christians. This is the only offensive piece that we carry. The Word of God is what we use to overcome evil. And we should use, and read and study the Word as much as possible. We practice with our firearms and other intermediate weapons. We should involve our self in the Word. God provides us with this armor to us. It should not be stored away. Everyday from now on, when your get dressed for work, putting on your duty gear, make sure you put on each piece of God's armor along with it.

God, Provider of our holy armor, we thank you for providing us with the equipment to wage spiritual battle against evil. Send you Holy Spirit to us, that we may always have all our armor and use it properly. All of this is done in the name of your Son, Jesus Christ, who has already won the victory over sin, death, and devil. Amen.

NOVEMBER 9

First of all, then, I urge that supplications, prayers, intercessions, and thanksgivings be made for everyone,

1 Timothy 2:1

There are things we should try to include whenever we pray. They are listed in this passage; supplications, prayers, intercessions and thanksgivings. We should always thank God for everything we receive. We should always communicate with God in prayer. We should always ask God to help us in our situations. And we should ask God act in the lives of others. We learn that prayer is what binds us as a community. It is praying for each other that helps us along the way. Martin Luther wrote in his *Treatise on Good Works*, "[C]ommon prayer is precious and the most powerful, and it is for its sake that we come together ... the Christian church on earth has no greater power or work against everything that may oppose it than such common prayer." By praying together and for each other, we work to defeat everything that may oppose us. So today, begin to include supplications, intercessions and thanksgivings in your prayers.

God, hearer of all prayers, we give you thanks for all that you have provided us. We ask you to act in our life, and in the lives of all your children. Amen.

NOVEMBER 10

The LORD is near to all who call on him, to all who call on him in truth.

Psalm 145:18

There may be times in our lives when we feel like God is not close to us. We feel alone and alienated. But the Psalmist reminds us that God is always close to us. It is during times when we feel alone that we need to call on God the most. It is when we feel we are alienated, that we need to talk with God. And God is always there to listen. Sometimes, that communication is best done with others. As we gather with others, we find out that we are not alone. So today, call on God in truth.

Lord God, we thank you for always being close to us. Lead us to others with whom we may pray together. Lead others to us, so that we may be with them. Amen.

NOVEMBER 11

Sing praises to the LORD, O you his faithful ones, and gives thanks to his holy name. For his anger is but for a moment; his favor is for a lifetime. Weeping may linger for a night, but joy comes with the morning.

Psalm 30:4-5

There are many passages in the Bible about giving thanks in all circumstances, even the most difficult. Many times, it is tough for us to give thanks situations are not positive. But God is still with us during those times. We receive God's favor for an eternity. God will help us get through the difficult times. Don't wait until the trouble is over to give God thanks. Give God thanks and praise, even in the midst of trouble, because God will get you through this.

Holy God, we give you thanks for all that you have done for us. We may be in times of trouble and difficulty right now. But, your favor is for a lifetime. And your promise us, joy on the other side of our trials. Amen.

NOVEMBER 12

I do not cease to give thanks for you as I remember you in my prayers.

Ephesians 1:16

Who do you give thanks for in your life? What people along the way have helped you? Prayer is way to give these people thanks for the assistance they have offered you. Many times, we do not thank them for their help. Take some time today, and think of the people you are thankful are in your life. If you are able, verbally thank them. If not, take some prayer time to offer thanksgiving to God, for sending them into your life.

God, Sender of all, we give you thanks for sending people into our lives to help us along the way. Continue sending others, to guide us when we need it most. May you also use us in the lives of others. Amen.

NOVEMBER 13

First of all, then, I urge that supplications, prayers, intercessions, and thanksgivings be made for everyone, for kings and all who are in high positions, so that we may lead a quiet and peaceable life in all godliness and dignity. This is right and is acceptable in the sight of God our Savior, who desires everyone to be saved and to come to the knowledge of the truth. For there is one God; there is also one mediator between God and humankind, Christ Jesus, himself human, who gave himself a ransom for all - this was attested at the right time. For this I was appointed a herald and an apostle (I am telling the truth [in Christ], I am not lying), a teacher of the Gentiles in faith and truth.

1 Timothy 2:1-7

Christ called us to be his disciples. But many times, we may wonder why God calls us at such a time as this. We see some of the best and some of the worst this world has to offer. Why is it that God calls us now? Timothy receives a letter that states that all that God has done has happened at the right time. God calls us specific at this time, to be workers for the kingdom. God has a plan, and everything in God's plan, including us, happens at just the right time.

God, keeper of all time, we give you thanks for sending your Son, Christ Jesus, as a mediator between you and us. Help us to understand that all that you done is done in the right time. Send your Holy Spirit to us, that we may continue in Christ, even in a world and a time such as this. Amen.

NOVEMBER 14

Are any among you sick? They should call for the elders of the church and have them pray over them, anointing them with oil in the name of the Lord.

James 5:14

How many people do we come upon that are physically, mentally, emotionally and spiritually sick? One of the best things we can do is pray for them. Along with and medical attention we get to them, we should also attend to them within the church. Today, think of all the people who may need your prayer for their spiritual, mental emotional and physical well-being. Pray for them. Find out if they are connected to a faith community, and ask that church to get in touch with them also.

God, healer of all, we give you thanks for the healing touch you send to us. Continue make us whole. Hear the prayers of those we offer to you, and those who are known but to you. Send the Holy Spirit to them, so that they may also be made whole in Christ. Amen.

NOVEMBER 15

While Peter was kept in prison, the church prayed fervently to God for him.

Acts of the Apostles 12:5

Part of our job, is putting people in prison. But, that does not mean that they should be excluded from the Christian community. We tend to forget those who are in jails and prisons. When we are in a position that we place someone in custody, take a moment and pray for them. Think of all the people you can remember in jails and prison, and take some time today to pray for them all.

Almighty God, many of your children have spent time in jails and prisons all over this world. We lift them up to you at this time. Help us to remember them and keep them in our prayers. Amen.

NOVEMBER 16

Hannah prayed and said, "My heart exults in the LORD; my strength is exulted in my God. My mouth derides my enemies, because I rejoice in my victory. There is no Holy One like the LORD, no one besides you; there is no Rock like our God. Talk no more so very proudly, let not arrogance come from your mouth; for the LORD is a God of knowledge, and by him actions are weighed. The bows of the mighty are broken, but the feeble gird on strength. Those who were full have hired themselves out for bread, but those who are hungry are fat with spoil. The barren has borne seven, but she who has many children is forlorn. The LORD kills and brings to life; he brings down to Sheol and raises up. The LORD makes poor and makes rich; he brings low, he also exults. He raises up the poor from the dust; he lifts the needy from the ash heap, to make them sit with princes and inherit a seat of honor (He grants the vow of the one who vows, and blesses the years of the just.). For the pillars of the earth are the LORD's, and on them he has set the world. He will guard the feet of his faithful ones, but the wicked shall be cut off in darkness; for not by might does one prevail. The LORD! His adversaries shall be scattered; the Most High will thunder in heaven. The LORD will judge the ends of the earth; he will give strength to his king, and exult the power of his anointed."

1 Samuel 2:1-10

This passage is known as the Song of Hannah. Hannah prays this prayer to God. It is a song of thanksgiving to God. God is over all people. No matter where people are in their life, God is still watching over them. Our job causes us to meet people who are at the extremes. We need to remember that God is over everyone we encounter, regardless of their station in life. We should also give thanks to God, in prayer, for all that God has given to us.

Most High God, we give you thanks for all that you have given to us. We remember that you are the God of all creation. Help us to see everyone we encounter as your children. May we always be thankful to you. Amen.

NOVEMBER 17

We always give thanks to God for all of you and mention you in our prayers, constantly remembering before our God and Father your work of faith and labor of love and steadfastness of hope in our Lord Jesus Christ.

1 Thessalonians 1:2-3

Who do you remember has done the work of faith in God? Who has been a labor of love in the Lord? Who maintains a steadfast hope in Jesus Christ? Do others believe this about you? Today, spend some time thinking about the people who have affected your faith life. Give thanks to God for these people. And always remember, that someone maybe looking at you in that same way.

God, Father of our Lord Jesus Christ, we give you thanks for sending people to us, as examples of how to live our lives. May we always remember these actions in our hearts. Help us to be a work of faith, a labor of love, and a steadfast hope in Christ. Amen.

NOVEMBER 18

I pray that the God of our Lord Jesus Christ, the Father of glory, may give you a spirit of wisdom and revelation as you come to know him, so that, with the eyes of your heart enlightened, you may know what is the hope to which he has called you, what are the riches of his glorious inheritance among the saints, and what is the immeasurable greatness of his power for us who believe, according to the working of his great power.

Ephesians 1:17-19

As law enforcement officers, we come to believe that we have great power. When we see abuse by law enforcement, it is usually because of the way power was abused. But, those of us who believe in God, come to the greatness of true power. God gives us the wisdom and revelation to realize it is God, not us, who have the power. God makes this known by God's power. If we think we have a lot of power, how much greater must God's power be? Today, take some time to reflect upon the power of God. How has God been powerful in your life? And then remember, God may be working God's great power in you, so that someone else may see.

God, Father of glory, we give you thanks for our Lord Jesus Christ. Send your Holy Spirit to us, that we may continually have the wisdom and revelation to see your power in the world. Help us to live our lives out of your immeasurable power. Amen.

NOVEMBER 19

I (Paul) thank my God every time I remember you, constantly praying with joy in every one of my prayers for all of you, because of your sharing in the gospel from the first day until now.
Philippians 1:3-5

As law enforcement officers, we become very close to the people we work with every day. The become not only our co-workers, but our partners. We place our lives in their hands. We spend a lot of time with them. Paul may have felt these same things with the people at Philippi. Do we have the same feelings for those that we work with in sharing the Gospel? Today, think about those who are your partners in sharing the Good News. Remember them in your prayers.

God, we thank you for providing partners to keep us safe. We also thank you for sending partners to help us in sharing the Gospel with the work. May we always remember each other as we do you. Amen.

NOVEMBER 20

And this is my prayer, that your love may overflow more and more with knowledge and full insight to help you to determine what is best, so that in the day of Christ you may be pure and blameless,
Philippians 1:9-10

How do we know what is best on the job? Our training, experience, knowledge and perception help us to try to determine what the right course of action is. How do we know what is best on our Christian journey? God gives us all the tools we need to complete our tasks. God gives us the knowledge of what we should do. Christ came into this world as a physical example of the true love of the Triune God. Christ's love for us allows us to continue on our journey, in love for others. The Holy Spirit gives us insight into the directions we should follow. We receive our training, experience, knowledge and perception through God.

God of love, we give you thanks for the knowledge you give to us. We give you thanks for the love you share with us. We give you thanks for the insight you provide to us. May we always determine what is best. Amen.

NOVEMBER 21

And he (Jesus) said to them, "Suppose one of you has a friend, and you go to him at midnight and say to him, 'Friend, lend me three loaves of bread; for a friend of mine has arrived, and I have nothing to set before him.' And he answers, from within, 'Do not bother me; the door has already been locked, and my children are with me i bed; I cannot get up and give you anything.' I tell you, even though he will not get up and give him anything because he is his friend, at least because of his persistence he will get up and give him whatever he needs. So I say to you, Ask, and it will be given you; search and you will find; knock, and the door will be opened for you. For everyone who asks receives, and everyone who searches finds, and for everyone who knocks, the door will be opened. Is there anyone among you who, if your child asks for (bread, will give a stone; or if your child asks for) a fish, will give a snake instead of a fish? Or if the child asks for an egg, will give a scorpion? If you then, who are evil, know how to give good gifts to your children, how much more will the heavenly Father give the Holy Spirit (from heaven) to those who ask him!"

Luke 11:5-13

The Bible suggests that at every turn in our journey, if we pray, we will be changed. But this only happens when we are honest with God. We need to pray to God as we are, asking what we need. We often begin prayer by beginning with ordinary things. Ordinary, every day things are just as important as any-thing. This is an expression of who we really are. And remember that Jesus tells us that God already knows anyway. So we might as well be honest. But, the more we ask God, the more we under-stand what we really need. And God gives us the gifts of nearness, and peace, and protection, and the Holy Spirit. Jesus tells us that we just have to ask. So today, take so time in prayer with God, as you really are, asking for what you really need.

Heavenly Father, we give you thanks for all the good gifts you send to us. Jesus tells us to ask for what we need. Hear us even as you already know. Send the Holy Spirit to us, to help us in our journey. Amen.

NOVEMBER 22

"Be still, and know that I am God! I am exulted among the nations, I am exulted in the earth."

Psalm 46:10

As law enforcement officers, we are active people, we always want to do something. But there are times when the best tactic is to stop and listen. We listen to what is going on in a place. We listen to hear people moving. We listen to hear the siren of our partner responding to us. As Christians, we want to be active people. But there are times in our journey when we should just stop and listen. Many times, we are afraid of what we may hear if we do listen. God may ask us to do more. Sometimes, we don't listen because we are afraid that we won't hear anything. God communicates with us all the time. God tells us what is best for us. We just need to be still, and know that God is God. Today, take some time to stop and listen. Go somewhere quiet. Try to clear the place of all distractions. Try to clear your mind of all the noises, and just listen to God.

God, the One who is exulted among the nations and in the earth, we give you thanks for communicating with us. We know that you watch over us. We are people who are afraid to stop, afraid to listen for fear of what we might hear, and afraid to listen for fear that we won't hear anything at all. Be with us in these times. Amen.

NOVEMBER 23

When the LORD restored the fortunes of Zion (or brought back those who returned to Zion), we were like those who dream. Then our mouth was filled with laughter, and out tongue with shouts of joy; then it was said among the nations, "The LORD has done great things for them." The LORD has done great things for us, and we rejoiced. Restore our fortunes, O LORD, like the watercourses in the Negeb. May those who sow in tears reap with shouts of joy. Those who go out weeping, bearing the seed for sowing, shall come home with shouts of joy, carrying their sheaves.

Psalm 126:1-6

It is during this time of year, when the winter darkness comes sooner in the day, that we take time to give thanks. We give thanks for all sorts of things. Traditionally, we gave thanks for the harvest and the abundant crops. Now we are thankful for many things in our lives. We also know that God provides all things to us. As we take time to offer thanks with one another, offer thanks to God for all we have received. And begin today to offer thanks to God everyday.

Lord God, Provider of all, we give you thanks for all that you have provided us. We acknowledge that you are the source of all that we receive. May we continue to be blessed by your gifts. Amen.

NOVEMBER 24

The Lord said: Because these people draw near with their mouths and honor me with their lips, while their hearts are far from me, and their worship of me is a human commandment learned by rote; so I will again do amazing things with this people, shocking and amazing. The wisdom of their wise shall perish, and the discernment of the discerning shall be hidden.

Isaiah 29:13-14

There are many times at our jobs that people tell us things, and we act like we believe them and will do what they say, but then go off with no intention of doing it. Sometimes, it is from the people we encounter who expect us to do something outside of ability. Sometimes, it is our supervisors telling us we have to do something according to regulation. We shake our heads, smile, then go back doing what we want. We do this with God also. Sometimes, we say prayers and offer thanks. We tell God that we are going to change. Then, we go off with no intention of changing. God wants us to make a new relationship. One that is not superficial. God will even help us accomplish this new relationship. God is going to do amazing things with us, even when our hearts are not right.

Amazing God, forgive us when we do not act as we speak. Help us when are hearts are far away from you. We pray that you change us in shocking ways. May we always draw near to you. Amen.

NOVEMBER 25

O give thanks to the LORD, for he is good; for his steadfast love endures forever. Let the redeemed of the LORD say so, those he redeemed from trouble and gathered in from the lands, from the east and from the west, from the north and from the south. Some wandered in desert wastes, finding no way to an inhabited town; hungry and thirsty, their souls fainted within them. Then they cried to the LORD in their trouble, and he delivered them from their distress; he led them by a straight way, until they reached an inhabited town. Let them thank the LORD for his steadfast love, for his wonderful works to humankind. For he satisfies the thirsty, and the hungry he fills with good things.

Psalm 107:1-9

We encounter people in various forms of trial in their lives. We find people who have come from all over. We try to help them in their troubles. Sometimes we succeed, sometimes we do not. We wander around ourselves in times of difficulty. God's steadfast love for us helps us through our troubles. God walks with us during the difficult times. God will help us in our thirsts and in our hungers. God will deliver us from distress. Today, take some time to thank God for the steadfast love that we receive. Offer up to God all the prayers of trials you may have. And remember, God may be using you to help someone else in their trials. God not only does good things for you, but also does good things with you.

Almighty God, we give you thanks for your steadfast love. Be with us when we hunger and thirst. Be with us when we wander in distress. Use us to accomplish your good things. Amen.

NOVEMBER 26

Then Pilate entered the headquarters (or the praetorium) again, summoned Jesus, and asked him, "Are you the King of the Jews?" Jesus answered, "Do you ask this on your own, or did others tell you about me?" Pilate replied, "I am not a Jew, am I?

Your own nation and the chief priests have handed you over to me, what have you done?" Jesus answered, "My kingdom is not from this world. If my kingdom were from this world, my followers would be fighting to keep me from being handed over to the Jews. But as it is, my kingdom is not from here." Pilate asked him, "So you are a king?" Jesus answered, ""You say that I am a king. For this I was born, and for this I came into the world, to testify to the truth. Everyone who belongs to the truth listens to my voice."

John 18:33-37

For some denominations, the Sunday before the start of Advent is the last Sunday of the liturgical year. This Sunday is often called Christ the King Sunday. In this passage from John, we hear that Jesus kingdom is not from this world. We know that Jesus' kingdom is a much different place than here. Jesus came into this world so that we may share in his Kingdom. Christ is your king. Today, give thanks that Christ came into the world so that you may enjoy his kingdom.

Almighty and everlasting God, it is your desire to restore all thing to you Son, Jesus Christ. You have anointed Christ as a king of all creation. Grant that all of us, who are divided by the power of sin, may be united under one kingdom, and by the gentle rule of our Savior, Jesus Christ, who reigns with you and the Holy Spirit. Amen.

NOVEMBER 27

Let the words of my mouth and the meditation of my heart be acceptable to you, O LORD, my rock and my redeemer.

Psalm 19:14

Many of us may hear this verse at the beginning of a sermon. Pastors use this as a prayer to God, that they may rightly preach the living word of God. What a task! But, shouldn't we all be proclaiming the living word of God. Our profession causes our language to deteriorate very rapidly. Would we want God to hear us talk like that? Well, God does hear us. So do others. Our language must always represent who we are. Always remember that God listens to us. Today, ask yourself if your language is acceptable to God.

O God, our rock and our redeemer, we give you thanks for listening to us. Forgive us when our language may not represent us as your children. May our words always be acceptable to you. Amen.

NOVEMBER 28

O that you would tear open the heavens and come down, so that the mountains would quake at your presence - as when fire kindles brushwood and the fire causes water to boil - to make your name known to your adversaries, so that the nations might tremble at your presence! When you did awesome deeds that we did not expect, you came down, the mountains quakes at your presence. From ages past no one has heard, no ear has perceived, no eye has seen any God besides you, who works for those who wait for him. You meet those who gladly do right, those who remember you in your ways. But you were angry, and we sinned; because you hid yourself we transgressed. We have all become like one who is unclean, and all our righteous deeds are like a filthy cloth. We all fade like a leaf, and our iniquities, like the wind, take us away. There is no one who calls on your name, or attempts to take hold of you; for you have hidden your face from us, and have delivered (or melted) us into the hand of our iniquity. Yet, O LORD, you are our Father; we are the clay, and you are our potter; we are all the work of your hand. Do not be exceedingly angry, O LORD, and do not remember iniquity forever. Now consider, we are all your people.

Isaiah 64:1-9

It seems like culture and society start the Christmas season earlier and earlier each year; shopping, sales, commercials, hectic life. But, the time before Christmas in the church is called Advent. We prepare ourselves for the birth of Jesus. We are waiting for the Christ child. We are making ready ourselves. With the birth of Jesus, all that Isaiah spoke about did change. God did reveal. God came to us. We can now approach God. In Advent, we wait and make ready for this miraculous event to occur. Today, try to focus on God, and avoid the cultural hustle and bustle around you, even if it is only for a few moments every day.

God, the Almighty Potter, we give you thanks for making yourself known to us. We sin. Please forgive us. Help us as we ready our selves for your Son. Be with us as we wait for the baby Jesus. Amen.

NOVEMBER 29

For God alone my soul waits in silence, for my hope is from him. He alone is my rock and my salvation, my fortress; I shall not be shaken. On God rests my deliverance and my honor; my mighty rock, my refuge is in God. Trust in him at all times, O people; pour out your heart before him; God is a refuge for us. Selah

Psalm 62:5-8

Sometimes during this Advent season, we may wait in silence for God. God will come to us. God is our rock, our salvation, our fortress. We do meaning things while we wait. Gregory of Nazianzus once wrote, "Lord, as I read your words, let me hear your speaking. As I reflect on each page, let me see your image. And as I seek to put your precepts into practice, let my heart be filled with joy." Today, take some time in silence to reflect upon who God is for you.

O God, our rock, our fortress, our salvation, we give you thanks for giving us refuge. Help us to give up ourselves and put our trust in you. Forgive us when we don't. Come to us, as we wait. Amen.

NOVEMBER 30

One of the two who heard John [the baptist] speak and followed him was Andrew, Simon Peter's brother. He first found his brother Simon and said to him, "We have found the Messiah (which is translated Anointed [or Christ])." He brought Simon to Jesus, who looked at him and said, "You are Simon son of John. You are to be called Cephas (which is translated Peter [or rock])."

John 1:40-42

Today, the church remembers the apostle Andrew. Part of Andrew's calling was to bring others to meet Jesus. Andrew brought his brother, other friends, even the boy with five loaves and two fish. How good are we at inviting others to meet Jesus? Do we tell others about our relationship with Jesus? Today, as we enter Advent and move toward Christmas, tell others your story about meeting Jesus. You may even be moved to take someone with you to meet him.

Almighty God, the apostle Andrew answered your call by taking others to meet your Son, Jesus. May we be inspired by the Holy Spirit to continue in the same ministry. May others come to know you, through Christ, by the power of the Holy Spirit, and on the arm of a friend. Amen.

DECEMBER 1

The young man said to him (Jesus), "I have kept all these (commandments) from my youth; what do I still lack?" Jesus said to him, "If you wish to be perfect, go, sell your possessions, and give the money to the poor, and you will have treasure in heaven; then come, follow me." When the young man heard this word, he went away grieving, for he had many possessions. Then Jesus said to his disciples, "Truly I tell you, it will be hard for a rich person to enter the kingdom of heaven. Again I tell you, it is easier for a camel to go through the eye of a needle then for someone who is rich to enter the kingdom of God." When the disciples heard this, they were greatly astounded and said, "Then who can be saved?" But Jesus looked at them and said, "For mortals it is impossible, but for God all things are possible."

Matthew 19:20-26

We struggle with passages like this. As law enforcement officers, we work overtime, special duty, court time; just to make more money. Then we buy all sorts of things. There are many times that Jesus tells us things we really don't want to hear. We want to find out the level of proof necessary for us to get into heaven. And then Jesus tells us. We wonder how any of us can get there. On our own, we can't, we will always fall short. But, with God all things are possible. We need to depend, utterly, on God. Today, reflect upon the way we try to accumulate things. Is that how Jesus would want us to use are riches?

God, One for whom all things are possible, we fall short of the standard your Son Jesus set for us. Forgive us our shortcomings. Send the Holy Spirit to us, that we may be able to use our riches for the your Kingdom. Help us to trust and depend on you. Amen.

DECEMBER 2

My child, if you accept my words and treasure up my command-
ments within you, making your ear attentive to wisdom and
inclining your heart to understanding; if you indeed cry out for
insight, and raise your voice for understanding; if you seek it like
silver, and search for it as for hidden treasures - then you will
understand the fear of the LORD and find the knowledge of God.
Proverbs 2:1-5

As people of this time, we search for knowledge. We are always
interested in knowing more. God gives us the way to understand. In
our prayer life, we are able to work at accepting God's word and
treasuring God's commandments. Through prayer we are able to
hear wisdom and bring understanding. Through our prayers, we are
able to ask for insight and explain our understanding to God. We
need to seek this relationship with God like we would search for precious metals. Continue in developing your prayer life.

Lord God, we give you thanks for being your children. Help
us to come to understanding of what you desire for us. Help us in
our prayers to you. Hear us as we cry. May we continue in fear
and love of you. Amen.

DECEMBER 3

So Joshua did as Moses told him, and fought with Amalek, while
Moses, Aaron, and Hur went up to the top of the hill. Whenever
Moses held up his hand, Israel prevailed; and whenever he low-
ered his hand, Amalek prevailed. But Moses' hands grew weary;
so they took a stone and put it under him, and he sat on it. Aaron
and Hur held up his hands, one on one side, and the other on the
other side; so his hands were steady until the sun set.
Exodus 17:10-12

How many times have you been out directing traffic, with
your hands in the air for a long time? When your hands are high

and people can see you, there is some order to the traffic flow. But when you get tired, and your hands go down, chaos sets in. People don't know where to go. We may be able to sympathize with Moses in this passage. We look for someone to come and relieve us. Even when we are out there with our hands high, God is with us, supporting us. When we start to get tired, God is still with us, supporting us. God will send people to help us accomplish our task. Sometimes we refuse the help, we want to do it all ourselves. But we need to accept the help when it comes. It may be an answer from God to our prayer.

God, our greatest support, we give you thanks for being with us when it is easy, and when we are in difficult times. Thank you for sending others to us, the we may gain assistance in our work. Help us to continue doing the work of your kingdom. Amen.

DECEMBER 4

Hear, O Israel: The LORD is our God, the Lord alone (or The LORD our God is one LORD, or The LORD our God, the LORD is one, or The LORD is our God, the LORD is one). You shall love the LORD your God with all your heart, and with all your soul, and with all your might. Keep these words that I am commanding you today in your heart. Recite them to your children and talk about them when you are at home and when you are away, when you lie down and when you rise. Bind them as a sign on your hand, fix them as an emblem on your forehead, and write them on the doorposts of your house and on your gates.

Deuteronomy 6:4-9

What do we love most of all? Many times it is a person, possession, or a desire. God gives us specific instructions on how our relationship with God is suppose to be. We are to love God with everything that we have. God loves us that much. We are to give everything we have to God. All else in our life is secondary. When we put our lives in focus, we are able to overcome all obstacles.

Lord God, thank you for loving us. Help us as we try to love you with everything we have. Strengthen us to keep your commandments. Forgive us when we fall short. Amen.

DECEMBER 5

Therefore the LORD himself will give you a sign. Look, the young woman (or the virgin) is with child and shall bear a son, and shall name him Immanuel (that is God with us).

Isaiah 7:14

As we move through Advent and closer to Christmas, we remember that God is now with us in Jesus. God has given us a sign of love in sending Jesus into the world. Today, think about the ways the Triune God is with you.

Lord God, we give you thanks for sending your Son, Jesus to us. We know that you are with us. May the Holy Spirit continue to work in our lives, so that others may know that you are with them. Amen.

DECEMBER 6

(Jesus said) "But understand this: if the owner of the house had known in what part of the night the thief was coming, he would have stayed awake and would not have let his house be broken into. Therefore you also must be ready, for the Son of Man is coming at an unexpected hour. Who then is the faithful and wise slave, whom his master has put in charge of his household, to give the other slaves their allowance of food at the proper time? Blessed is that slave whom his master will find at work when he arrives. Truly I tell you, he will put that one in charge of all his possessions.

Matthew 24:43-47

Today, the church remembers Nicholas, Bishop of Myra. Nicholas is one of the most beloved saints, but we know little about him, except for the legends we have of him. According to the tradition of the church, Nicholas devoted his life to good works, was generous to the poor, and died peacefully in 342. His gift giving exploits are legendary. It is Nicholas, that we get the legend of jolly Ole St. Nick, St. Nicholas, Santa Claus. It is in the tradition of Nicholas that Santa Claus visits and brings gifts during Christmas. Today, think of the gifts that people have given you. Think about the simple gifts you may give others.

Almighty God, you have raised up faithful bishops of your church, like Nicholas. May the memory of their service be a source of joy for us and encouragement to our faith. May we continue to serve you and confess your name in the world. May we be strong in bringing others the good gifts of your love. Amen.

DECEMBER 7

In those days a decree went out from Emperor Augustus that all the world should be registered. This was the first registration and was taken while Quirinius was governor of Syria. All went to their own towns to be registered. Joseph also went from the town of Nazareth in Galilee to Judea, to the city of David called Bethlehem, because he was descended from the house and family of David. He went to be registered with Mary, to whom he was engaged and who was expecting a child. While they were there, the time came for her to deliver her child.

Luke 2:1-6

As we continue in this season of Advent, we move closer to the birth of Jesus. Joseph and Mary had a difficult road to go, before Jesus was born. But God was with them during this whole time. And God's work came out of their difficulties. Many times, it may seem that our road may be difficult. We may not be able to see how God is working through our difficulties. But, God is with us. And God does work through us, even during the difficult times.

God of all creation, we give you thanks for the birth of your Son, Jesus. As you were with Joseph and Mary, be with us during our times of difficulty. Send the Holy Spirit to us, that we may be able to continue on the road you have set before us. Amen.

DECEMBER 8

In those days John the Baptist appeared in the wilderness of Judea, proclaiming, "Repent, for the kingdom of heaven has come near (or is at hand)." This is the one of whom the prophet Isaiah spoke when he said, "The voice of one crying out in the wilderness: 'Prepare the way of the Lord, make his paths straight.'" Now John wore clothing of camel's hair with a leather belt around his waist, and his food was locusts and wild honey. Then the people of Jerusalem and all Judea were going out to him, and all the region along the Jordan, and they were baptized by him in the river Jordan, confessing their sins. But when he saw the Pharisees and the Sadducees coming for baptism, he said to them, "You brood of vipers! Who warned you to flee from the wrath to come? Bear fruit worthy of repentance. Do not presume to say to yourselves, 'We have Abraham as our ancestor'; for I tell you, God is able from these stones to raise up children to Abraham. Even now the axe is lying at the root of the trees; every tree therefore that does not bear good fruit is cut down and thrown into the fire. I will baptize you with (or in) water for repentance, but one who is more powerful than I is coming after me; I am not worthy to carry his sandals. He will baptize you with (or in) the Holy Spirit and fire. His winnowing fork is in his hand, and he will clear his threshing floor and will gather his wheat into the granary; but the chaff he will burn with unquenchable fire." Then Jesus came from Galilee to John at the Jordan, to be baptized by him. John would have prevented him, saying, "I need to be baptized by you, and do you come to me?" But Jesus answered him, "Let it be so now; for it is proper for us in this way to fulfill all righteousness." Then he consented. And when Jesus had been baptized, just as he came up from the water, suddenly the heavens were opened to him and he saw the Spirit of God descending like a dove and alighting on him. And a voice from heaven said, "This is my Son, the Beloved, with whom I am well pleased."

Matthew 3:1-17

As we prepare for Christmas, we remember that John the Baptist came before Jesus to prepare the way. It was John who announced Jesus. And it was John who baptized Jesus. Jesus baptism was the birth of his ministry. Can you remember who prepared the way for you? Do you remember your baptism, your birth into Christ? Many people in our lives announce Jesus to us. God uses many people to proclaim the Good News of his Son. Today, think about the people who have announced Jesus to you. And remember, God may be using you to announce Jesus to someone else.

God, Voice from Heaven, we thank you for your beloved Son. Though the power of the Holy Spirit, we were born into Christ at our baptism. Strengthen us in our baptismal call. May we go out into the world, announcing Christ. Amen.

DECEMBER 9

Comfort, O comfort my people, says your God. Speak tenderly to Jerusalem, and cry to her that she has served her term, that her penalty is paid, that she has received from the LORD's hand double for all her sins. A voice cries out: "In the wilderness prepare the way of the LORD, make straight in the desert a highway for our God. Every valley shall be lifted up, and every mountain and hill be made low; the uneven ground shall become level, and the rough places a plain. Then the glory of the LORD shall be revealed, and all people shall see it together, for the mouth of the LORD has spoken."

Isaiah 40:1-5

The prophet Isaiah spoke of a time when God would change the whole world, that the world, as known, would be totally different. We as Christians, see John the Baptist as the herald that announces the Lord. And Jesus is the one, through whom God is revealed. Christ makes everything in our world different. God is revealed in Christ and by the power of the Holy Spirit. We wait for the birth of our Lord once again.

Lord, the glory that has been revealed, we thank you for sending your Son to us. You have made the world entirely different than it was. May we go out, with the Holy Spirit, into the world, as the heralds, announcing the second coming of your Son, Jesus Christ. Amen.

DECEMBER 10

As it is written in the prophet Isaiah, "See, I am sending my messenger ahead of you, who will prepare your way; the voice of one crying out in the wilderness: 'Prepare the way of the Lord, make his paths straight.'" John the baptizer appeared (or John was baptizing) in the wilderness, proclaiming a baptism of repentance for the forgiveness of sins. And people from the whole Judean countryside and all the people of Jerusalem were going out to him, and were baptized by him in the river Jordan, confessing their sins. Now John was clothed with camel's hair, with a leather belt around his waist, and he ate locusts and wild honey. He proclaimed, "The one who is more powerful than I is coming after me; I am not worthy to stoop down and untie the thong of his sandals. I have baptized you with water; but he will baptize you with the Holy Spirit." In those days Jesus came from Nazareth of Galilee and baptized by John in the Jordan. And just as he was coming up out of the water, he saw the heavens torn apart and the Spirit descending like a dove on him. And a voice came from heaven, "You are my Son, the Beloved; with you I am well pleased."

Mark 1:2-11

John the Baptist prepared the way for Jesus. John's appearance may have been strange for some people. People may have been put off by how he looked. He probably wasn't the picture people had in mind for the herald announcing the messiah. People look at us in strange ways. We wear distinctive clothing. We stick out in public. We sit down to eat at a restaurant, and people stare at us while we eat. But we have a message to proclaim, also. We announce Jesus, just as John did. When you proclaim the truth, people will listen, no matter what you look like. Allow people to overcome your appearance, and let them talk to you about the difficult issues in their lives. Some may even confess their sins to you. And, as strange looking as you may be, you may have the opportunity to announce Jesus to them.

Lord, Voice from heaven, we thank you for sending your Son to us. By the same Spirit that descended like a dove on Jesus, may we be inspired to proclaim Christ. Help us to be confident in our message, so that others may overcome our appearance, and hear the truth of the Good News. Amen.

DECEMBER 11

Here is my servant, whom I uphold, my chosen, in whom my soul delights; I have put my spirit upon him; he will bring forth justice to the nations. He will cry or lift up his voice, or make it heard in the street; a bruised reed he will not break, and a dimly burning wick he will not quench; he will faithfully bring forth justice. He will not grow faint or be crushed until he has established justice in the earth; and the coastlands wait for his teaching.
Isaiah 42:1-4

We move closer to the birth of Jesus. Jesus changed the world. We hear the words from the prophet Isaiah. Jesus had the Spirit of God upon him. Jesus brought forth justice to the nations, and for all the earth. Christ has come into the world to make all things right. As we wait to celebrate his birth, how has Jesus changed your life? How can Jesus continue to change your world?

Almighty God, we thank you for sending your Son to this world, to bring forth justice. As the Holy Spirit rested upon Jesus, may it rest upon us as we do your work. Amen.

DECEMBER 12

In the fifteenth year of the reign of Emperor Tiberius, when Pontius Pilate was governor o fJudea, and Herod was ruler of Galilee, and his brother Philip was ruler of the region of Ituraea and Trachonitis, and Lysanias ruler of Abilene, during the high priesthood of Annas and Caiaphas, the word of God cam to John son of Zechariah in the wilderness. He went into all the region around the Jordan, proclaiming a baptism of repentance for the forgiveness of sins, as it is written in the book of the words of the prophet Isaiah, "The voice of one crying out in the wilderness: 'Prepare the way of the Lord, make his paths straight. Every valley shall be filled, and every mountain and hill shall be made low, and the crooked shall be made straight, and the rough ways made smooth; and all flesh shall see the salvation of God.'" John said to the crowds that came out to be baptized by him, "You brood of vipers! Who warned you to flee from the wrath to come? Bear fruits worthy of repentance. Do not begin to say to yourselves, 'We have Abraham as our ancestor'; for I tell you, God is able from these stones to raise up children of Abraham. Even now the ax is lying at the root of the trees; every tree therefore that does not bear good fruit is cut down and thrown into the fire." And the crowds asked him, "What then should we do?" In reply he said to them, "Whoever has two coats must share with anyone who has none; and whoever has food must do likewise." Even tax collectors came to be baptized, and they asked him, "Teacher, what should we do?" He said to them, "Collect no more than the amount prescribed for you." Soldiers also asked him, "And we, what should we do?" He said to them, "Do not extort money from anyone by threats or false accusation, and be satisfied with your wages." As the people were filled with expectation, and all were questioning in their hearts concerning John, whether he might be the Messiah, John answered all of them by saying, "I baptize you with water; but one who is more powerful than I is coming; I am not worthy to untie the thong of hi sandals. He will baptize you with the Holy Spirit and fire. His winnowing fork is in his hand, to clear his threshing floor and to gather the wheat into his granary; but the chaff he will burn with unquenchable fire." So, with many other exhortations, he proclaimed the good news to the people. But Herod the ruler, who had been rebuked by him because of Herodias, his brother's wife, and because of all the evil things that Herod had done, added to them all by shutting up John in prison. Now when all the people were baptized, and when Jesus also had been baptized and was praying, the heaven was opened, and the Holy Spirit descended upon him in bodily form like a dove. And a voice came from heaven, "You are my Son, the Beloved; with you I am well pleased."

Luke 3:1-22

In Luke's account of this passage, we see more of John's activity. We see that the good news means everything will be turned upside-down. Could you imagine that happening in our time? We would no longer need to do our jobs, because everyone and everything would be as it should be. We are called to give when we have. We are called to be fair at all times. And through Christ, every valley will be filled and every mountain made low. The crooked will be made straight and the rough made smooth. And all flesh will see the salvation of God. Everything will be as it should be.

God, Source of our salvation, we thank you for sending prophets like John, and sending your Son, Jesus. We thank you for sending the Holy Spirit. May we continue to work for your kingdom, making everything equal and as it should be. Forgive us when we fall short. Amen.

DECEMBER 13

Paul said, "John baptized with the baptism of repentance, telling the people to believe in the one who was to come after him, that is, in Jesus.

Acts of the Apostles 19:4

Even in the early years of the church, it was remembered that John spoke of the one who was to come, and to be baptized in his name. Today, while in this season of Advent, we should tell people to be baptized in the name of the one to come.

Almighty God, may we be remembered for telling the Gospel story. Inspire us to continue to tell others our faith. Be with of as we go into the world, calling people to baptism in the name of the Father, Son and Holy Spirit. Amen.

DECEMBER 14

As they went away, Jesus began to speak to the crowds about John: "What did you go out into the wilderness to look at? A reed shaken by the wind? What then did you go out to see? Someone dressed in soft robes? Look, those who wear soft robes are in royal palaces. What then did you go out to see? A prophet? Yes, I tell you, and more than a prophet. This is the one about whom it is written, 'See, I am sending my messenger ahead of you, who will prepare your way before you.' Truly I tell you, among those born of women no one has arisen greater than John the Baptist; yet the least in the kingdom of heaven is greater than he. From the days of John the Baptist until now the kingdom of heaven has suffered violence and the violent take it by force. For all the prophets and the law prophesied until John came; and if you are willing to accept it, he is Elijah who is to come. Let anyone with ears listen!"

Matthew 11:7-15

Even Jesus acknowledged the importance of John the Baptist coming before him. With the life, death and resurrection of Jesus, all the laws and the prophets are fulfilled. We can understand Jesus' description of the kingdom of heaven being acted upon violently. There are times when we, as law enforcement are acted upon violently. But God's Kingdom is able to overcome all obstacles. And we should tell other about the coming of God's Kingdom.

Almighty God, you sent the law and the prophets, then you sent your Son. Be with us, send your Holy Spirit to us, as we await the coming of your kingdom. Amen.

DECEMBER 15

Then his (John's) father Zechariah was filled with the Holy Spirit and spoke this prophecy: "Blessed be the Lord God of Israel, for he looked favorably on his people and redeemed them. He has raised up a mighty savior for us in the house of David, as he spoke through the mouth of his holy prophets from old, that we would be saved from our enemies and from the hand of all who hate us. Thus he has shown the mercy promised to our ancestors, and has remembered his holy covenant, that oath that he swore to our ancestor Abraham, to grant us that we, being rescued from the hands of our enemies, might serve him without fear, in holiness and righteousness before him all our days. And you, child, will be called a prophet of the Most High; for you will go before the Lord to prepare his ways, to give knowledge of salvation to his people by the forgiveness of their sins. By the tender mercy of our God, the dawn from on high will break upon us, to give light to those who sit in darkness and in the shadow of death, to guide our feet into the way of peace." The child grew and became strong in spirit, and he was in the wilderness until the day he appeared publicly to Israel.

Luke 1:67-80

This passage in Luke is called the Song of Zechariah. John was born a few months before Jesus. John the Baptist would eventually prepare the way of the Lord. Jesus did accomplish all that Zechariah prophesied. Christ will do all of this in our lives. With the birth of Jesus, the entire world was changed. As we continue to approach Christmas, think of the way Jesus has changed your life.

God Most High, we give you thanks for sending prophets like Zechariah and John to prepare the way of your Son. Help us to hear the prophets of today who speak your word. Guide us when we do not hear them. May we be filled with the Holy Spirit, that we may proclaim your glorious deeds to the world. Amen.

DECEMBER 16

Now concerning the times and the seasons, brothers and sisters, you do not need to have anything written to you. For you yourselves know very well that the day of the Lord will come like a thief in the night. When they say, "There is peace and security", then suddenly destruction will come upon them, as labor pains come upon a pregnant woman, and there will be no escape! But you, beloved, are not in darkness, for that day to surprise you like a thief; for you are all children of light and children of the day; we are not of the night or of darkness. So then let us not fall asleep as others do, but let us keep awake and be sober; for those who sleep sleep at night, and those who are drunk get drunk at night. But since we belong to the day, let us be sober, and put on the breastplate of faith and love, and for a helmet the hope of salvation. For God has destined us not for wrath but for obtaining salvation through our Lord Jesus Christ, who died for us, so that whether we are awake or asleep we may live with him. Therefore encourage one another and build up each other, as indeed you are doing.

1 Thessalonians 5:1-11

We are all too familiar with the thief in the night. We have worked those third shifts, trying to stay awake. We know if we would dose off, something would happen. And it is during those times when everything seems quite, that we expect something to happen. Thieves don't call ahead to let us know when and where they are coming. When Jesus returns, it will be much the same. The Apostle Paul want us to act the same way in waiting for the Lord. There will not be any calling ahead, letting us know when and where. We are just suppose to remain vigilant. We should not let ourselves drift away in the ways of the world. Just when you think everything is going along just fine, be prepared.

Lord God, we give you thanks for sending your Son, Jesus, to us. Be with us as we await his return. Send the Holy Spirit to us that we may be vigilant in our wait. Amen.

DECEMBER 17

Then Jesus was lead by the Spirit into the wilderness to be tempted by the devil. He fasted forty days and forty nights, and afterwards he was famished. The tempter came and said to him, "If you are the Son of God, command these stones to become loaves of bread." But he answered, "It is written, 'One does not live by bread alone, but by every word that comes from the mouth of God.'" Then the devil took him to the holy city and placed him on the pinnacle of the temple, saying, "If you are the Son of God, throw yourself down; for it is written, 'He will command his angels concerning you.' and 'On their hands they will bear you up, so that you will not dash your foot against a stone.'" Jesus said to him, "Again it is written, 'Do not put the Lord your God to the test.'" Again the devil took him to a very high mountain and showed him all the kingdoms of the world and their splendor; and he said to him, "All these I will give you, if you will fall down and worship me." Jesus said to him, "Away with you, Satan! for it is written, 'Worship the Lord your God, and serve him only.'" Then the devil left him, and suddenly angels came and waited for him.

Matthew 4:1-11

When is it that we are tempted the most? It is usually when we are fatigued. Jesus has been in the wilderness forty days and nights. He is famished. It is in this moment that Satan tempts Jesus. Will work in professions that lead to fatigue. We work long hours. We deal with circumstances that try us physically, mentally, emotionally, and spiritually. We may not eat properly or exercise on a regular basis. It is in those moments of fatigue, that we too, may be tempted. They may be small or large, but they all take a toll on us. Try to alleviate the amount of time you feel fatigued. Take care of yourself. But in those times when you are fatigued, be aware of the dangers and temptations that may present themselves to you.

God, we give you thanks for sending your Son into this world to defeat Satan. Send the Holy Spirit to us, that we may be able to overcome temptation. Be with us when we are fatigued, so that we may continue on the path. Amen.

DECEMBER 18

And the Spirit immediately drove him into the wilderness. He was in the wilderness forty days, tempted by Satan; and he was with the wild beasts; and the angels waited on him.

Mark 1:12-13

It is in the wilderness that Jesus is tempted. What is your wilderness? When is it that your feel that you are out on your own? Jesus was out on his own, or so it seemed. Jesus was able to overcome Satan. Jesus is with us when we are in our wilderness. We are not alone in our trials. Jesus will help us overcome. Today, think about what causes you to be in the wilderness, and come up with ways to have Jesus help you overcome your trials.

God, sender of angels, we thank you for sending your Son, Jesus to us. Send the Holy Spirit to us that we may be able to overcome Satan in our wilderness of trials. Amen.

DECEMBER 19

Jesus, full of the Holy Spirit, returned from the Jordan and was led by the Spirit in the wilderness, where for forty days he was tempted by the devil. He ate nothing at all during those days, and when they were over, he was famished. The devil said to him, "If you are the Son of God, command this stone to become a loaf of bread." Jesus answered him, "It is written, 'One does not live by bread alone.'" Then the devil said to him, "To you I will give their glory and all authority; for it has been given over to me, and I give it to anyone I please. If you, then, will worship me, it will all be yours." Jesus answered him, "It is written, 'Worship the Lord your God, and serve him only.'" Then the devil took him to Jerusalem, and placed him on the pinnacle of the temple, saying to him, "If you are the Son of God, throw yourself down from here, for it is written, 'He will command his angels concerning you, to protect you,' and 'On their hands they will bear you up, so that you will not dash your foot against a stone.'" Jesus answered him, "It is said, 'Do not put the Lord your God to the test.'" When the devil had finished every test, he departed from him until an opportune time.

Luke 4:1-13

We find Jesus being tempted for forty days. The devil offers that which Jesus hungers. The devil offers Jesus authority if Jesus would worship him. The devil finally tries to get Jesus to perform a task just to prove who he is. What tempts you? What are the things that your hunger for, that may be a temptation? What do you worship? What would you do to get authority? What actions would you take just to show who you are? These are the issues that tempt us in our lives. We need to stay firm in not giving in to temptations. Giving in to temptation corrupts our lives. And even if you succeed, do not think you have overcome temptation. The devil only left Jesus until an opportune time. Temptation will come back to us also.

Lord God, we give you thanks for sending your Son to overcome the temptations of the devil. Send the Holy Spirit to us that we may also overcome the temptation in our lives. May we realize that avoiding temptation is a life-long battle. Forgive us for those times that we give in to temptation. And when we do, put us back on the right path. Amen.

DECEMBER 20

Since, then, we have a great high priest who has passed through the heavens, Jesus, the Son of God, let us hold fast to our confession. For we do not have a high priest who is unable to sympathize with our weaknesses, but we have one who in every respect has been tested (or tempted) as we are, yet without sin. Let us therefore approach the throne of grace with boldness, so that we may receive mercy and find grace to help in time of need.

Hebrews 4:14-16

This passage realizes that we are still tested and tempted. We cannot overcome all temptation on our own. Jesus can sympathize with us because he, too, was tempted. Jesus understands how we feel in those times of need. Jesus is our high priest that is able to give us mercy for past sins, and to grant us grace for present and future needs. Today, make confession to God of everything that tempts you. You will feel the mercy and grace, and the Holy Spirit will be with you always.

God of mercy and grace, we give you thanks for sending your Son, so that he may be able to sympathize with our testing. Be with us during those times of trial, that we may be able to overcome temptation. In those times when we are not able, send the Holy Spirit to us. Amen.

DECEMBER 21

(Jesus said) "... And you know the way to the place where I am going." Thomas said to him, "Lord, we do not know where you are going. How can we know the way?" Jesus said to him, "I am the way, and the truth, and the life. No one comes to the Father except through me. If you know me, you will know my Father also. From now on you do know him and have seen him."

John 14:4-7

Today, the church remember Thomas the apostle. We remember Thomas on the winter solstice, the shortest day of the year. We will now begin to see more light as we await the arrival of spring and summer. Thomas needed to see to believe. Thomas invites us to see the light of Advent as we await the coming of a Savior, Jesus. As Jesus said to Thomas, he also says to us, "I am the way, and the truth, and the life."

God of night and day, we give you thanks for the seasons, as we celebrate the entire cycle of your creation. We give thanks for sending your Son, Jesus into the world so that we may also know you. Send the Holy Spirit to us, that we may be able to follow the Way, and the Truth, and the Life. Amen.

DECEMBER 22

He (God) humbled you by letting you hunger, then by feeding you with manna, with which neither you nor your ancestors were acquainted, in order to make you understand that one does not live by bread alone, but by every word that comes from the mouth of the LORD.

Deuteronomy 8:3

One of the greatest temptations we run into is the over use of pride and self-sufficiency. We work in profession where it is only us out there. We are by ourselves most of the time. If anything gets done, and done right, we do it ourselves. But we do rely on another. We cannot do anything ourselves. There are times when we turn to God for help. God reminds us that we should always turn to God. Everything we do is viewed through God's word to us. Sometimes, we have to learn difficult lessons to remind us of our relationship with God.

God, giver of manna, we thank you for all you have given us. Forgive us when we believe we can do everything on our own. Help us to live in a deeper relationship with you. Amen.

DECEMBER 23

As he (Jesus) walked by the Sea of Galilee, he saw two brothers, Simon, who is called Peter, and Andrew his brother, casting a net into the sea - for they were fishermen. And he said to them, "Follow me, and I will make you fish for people." Immediately they left their nets and followed him. As he went from there, he saw two other brothers, James son of Zebedee and his brother John, in the boat with their father Zebedee, mending their nets, and he called them. Immediately they left the boat and their father, and followed him.

Matthew 4:18-22

Jesus entered into relationships with normal fishermen. They because Jesus' first disciples. Jesus has entered into a relationship with us. Many would see us as normal people. But Jesus uses us to go out into the world to be fishers of people. Because of our profession, we have the opportunity to meet a variety of people in different places in life. Jesus uses us to talk to others about our faith.

God, we give you thanks for sending your Son, Jesus so that we may have a relationship with you. Send the Holy Spirit to us, that we may go out into the world, and become fishers of people. Forgive us when we do not follow, but help us back onto the path. Amen.

DECEMBER 24

And she (Mary) gave birth to her firstborn son and wrapped him in bands of cloth, and laid him in a manger, because there was no place for them in the inn. In that region there were shepherds living in the fields, keeping watch over their flock by night. Then an angel of the Lord stood before them, and the glory of the Lord shone around them, and they were terrified. But the angel said to them, "Do not be afraid; for see - I am bringing you good news of great joy for all people: to you is born this day in the city of David a Savior, who is the Messiah (or the Christ), the Lord. This will be a sign for you: you will find a child wrapped in bands of cloth and lying in a manger." And suddenly there was with the angel a multitude of the heavenly host, praising God and saying, "Glory to God in the highest heaven, and on earth peace among those whom he favors (or goodwill among people)!" When the angels had left them and gone into heaven, the shepherds said to one another, "Let us go now to Bethlehem and see this thing that has taken place, which the Lord has made known to us." So they went with haste and found Mary and Joseph, and the child lying in a manger. When they saw this, they made known what had been told them about this child; and all who heard it were amazed at what the shepherds told them. But Mary treasured all these words and pondered them in her heart. The shepherds returned, glorifying and praising God for all they had heard and seen, as it had been told them.

Luke 2:7-20

Every year we celebrate the birth of our Savior. There are many times in our lives that we may feel terrified. But as the angel spoke to the shepherds, he hear the same words, "Do not be afraid." Today, remember that Jesus was born as a Savior, the Messiah, the Christ. Remember that God is with us, and we do not need to be afraid.

Almighty God, you broke through the darkness by sending the Light to this world. Help us to walk in the light of your Son, by the power of the Holy Spirit. Amen.

DECEMBER 25

In the beginning was the Word, and the Word was with God, and the Word was God. He was in the beginning with God. All things came into being through him, and without him not one thing came into being. What has come into being in him was life, and the life was the light of all people. The light shines in the darkness, and the darkness did not overcome it. There was a man sent from God, whose name was John. He came as a witness to testify to the light, so that all might believe through him. He himself was not the light, but he came to testify to the light. The true light, which enlightens everyone, was coming into the world. he was in the world, and the world came into being through him; yet the world did not know him. He came to what was his own, and his own people did not accept him. But to all who received him, who believed in his name, he gave power to become the children of God, who were born, not of blood or of the will of the flesh, or of the will of man, but of God. And the Word became flesh and lived among us, and we have seen his glory, the glory as of a father's only son, full of grace and truth.

John 1:1-14

The Christmas message is found in this prologue of the Gospel of John. Today, we celebrate the Word becoming flesh and dwelling among us. This day, we remember that God is now with us. God's Son, Jesus was born into humanity. We now see the true light of Christ. Our darkness has been pierced. And the darkness cannot overcome the light. Today, celebrate the birth of Christ, and rejoice that God the Father, God the Son, and God the Holy Spirit, are active in your life.

Almighty God, we celebrate the birth of your Son. We thank you for all you have done. May we always walk in the true light. Help us when we stray. Be with us as we lift high the songs and hymns which proclaim our faith. Amen.

DECEMBER 26

Stephen, full of grace and power, did great wonders and signs among the people. Then some of those who belonged to the synagogue of the Freedmen (as it was called), Cyrenians, Alexandrians, and others of those from Cilicia and Asia, stood up and argued with Stephan. But they could not withstand the wisdom and the Spirit with which he spoke. Then they secretly instigated some men to say, "We have heard him speak blasphemous words against Moses and God." They stirred up the people as well as the elders and the scribes; then they suddenly confronted him, seized him, and brought him before the council. They set up false witnesses who said, "This man never stops saying things against this holy place and the law; for we have heard him say that this Jesus of Nazareth will destroy this place and will change the customs of Moses handed on to us." And all who sat in the council looked intently at him, and they saw that his face was like the face of an angel. Then the high priest asked him, "Are these things so?" And Stephen replied: "Brothers and fathers, listen to me. ..."

Acts of the Apostles 6:8-7:2a

Today, the church remembers Stephen the deacon and first martyr of the Christian Church. The joy of Christmas and the birth of Jesus are contrasted by the harshness of the world as we remember Stephen. How many times have we had people bring false accusations against us? We work in a high profile profession. And people do not mind trying to harm us with half-truths and lies. Stephan was in this same situation. But even as have was being tried, he brought the Good News of Jesus to his accusers. Today, remember that even those who falsely accuse you are in need of hearing God's love for them. Try to not become vindictive and hurtful, but be filled with the Holy Spirit.

O Lord, we give you thanks for sending messengers like Stephen into the world. Help us to love our enemies and seek forgiveness from those who want to hurt us. Fill us with the Holy Spirit, so that, like Stephen, we may proclaim the Good News of your Son, Jesus, even in the face of lies and deceit. Amen.

DECEMBER 27

Peter turned and saw the disciple whom Jesus loved following them; he was the one who had reclined next to Jesus at the supper and had said, "Lord, who is it that is going to betray you?" When Peter saw him, he said to Jesus, "Lord, what about him?" Jesus said to him, "If it is my will that he remain until I come, what is that to you? Follow me!" So the rumor spread in the community (among the brothers) that this disciple would not die. Yet Jesus did not say to him that he would not die, but, "If it is my will that he remain until I come, what is that to you?" This is the disciple who is testifying to these things and has written them, and we know that his testimony is true. But there are also many other things that Jesus did; if every one of them were written down, I suppose that the world itself could not contain the books that would be written.
John 21:20-25

Today, the church remembers John, the apostle and evangelist. John is traditionally believed to be the author of the fourth Gospel, three epistles that bear his name, and the book of Revelation. John is also assumed to be the "beloved disciple" because Jesus entrusted the care of his mother, Mary, to John at the cross. John's Gospel is filled with expressions of love. John was unique in his telling of the Good News of Jesus. We should go out into the world, proclaiming the Good News of Christ's love for all of us. We should tell others how much God loves the world. We should remind others that the Holy Spirit will be with us always.

Merciful Lord, let the brightness of your light shine on your children. May we all be instructed by the words of John. Help us to walk in the light of your truth, as found in your Son Jesus, so that we may attain eternal life. Send the Holy Spirit to us during those times when we are in darkness, that we might be able to follow your love. Amen.

DECEMBER 28

Now after they (the wise men) had left, an angel of the Lord appeared to Joseph in and dream and said, "Get up, take the child and his mother, and flee to Egypt, and remain there until I tell you; for Herod is about to search for the child, to destroy him." Then Joseph got up, took the child and his mother by night, and went to Egypt, and remained there until the death of Herod. This was to fulfill what had been spoken by the Lord through the prophet, "Out of Egypt I have called my son." When Herod saw that he had been tricked by the wise men, he was infuriated, and he sent and killed all the children in and around Bethlehem who were two years old or under, according to the time that he had learned from the wise men. Then was fulfilled what had been spoken through the prophet Jeremiah, "A voice was heard in Ramah, wailing and loud lamentation, Rachel weeping for her children; she refused to be consoled, because they are no more."

Matthew 2:13-18

Today, the church remembers the Holy Innocents. These are the children who were slaughtered by Herod, in an attempt to kill Jesus. We see the use of institutional violence in this passage. We, as law enforcement, are in a difficult situation. We need to make sure that we are not party to institutional violence. The order doesn't always have to come from the top of government. If we informally decide to oppress a certain group of people, we are accomplishing the same as Herod was trying to do. We need to make sure that we view everyone as the same, and do not cause violence upon any group.

O God, today we remember the slaughter of the holy innocents of Bethlehem by the order of Herod. We pray that you receive all innocent victims into your arms with mercy. Send the Holy Spirit to disrupt all plans institutional violence. May we be filled with justice, love, and peace, as we learned from your Son, Jesus. Amen.

DECEMBER 29

Jesus went out again beside the sea; the whole crowd gathered around him, and he taught them. As he was walking along, he saw Levi son of Alphaeus sitting at the tax booth, and he said to him, "Follow me." And he got up and followed him. And as he sat at dinner in Levi's house, many tax collectors and sinners were also sitting with Jesus and his disciples - for there were many who followed him. When the scribes and Pharisees saw that he was eating with sinners and tax collectors, they said to his disciples, "Why does he eat (and drink) with tax collectors and sinners?" When Jesus heard this, he said to them, "Those who are well have no need for a physician, but those who are sick; I have come to call not the righteous but sinners."

Mark 2:13-17

How much do you feel like an outcast? When you are out, and the discussion gets to what you do for a living, do people look at you different when they know you are in law enforcement? There have been different professions throughout history that have had this stigma. Now it is law enforcement, in Jesus' day, it was tax collectors. In this passage, we see Jesus eating with those who are the outcasts of their time, tax collectors and sinners. Jesus' spent much time with the outcasts. Jesus spends time with the outcasts now. Remember that God does not see you as an outcast.

God, the great physician, we give you thanks for coming to all of us, even those who are seen as outcasts. Be with us as we struggle with sin in our daily lives. Send the Holy Spirit that we may be reminded that you do not cast us out. Help us to be more like your Son, Jesus, who would eat with anyone. Amen.

DECEMBER 30

Once while Jesus was standing beside the lake of Gennesaret, and the crowd was pressing in on him to hear the word of God, he saw two boats there at the shore of the lake; the fishermen had gone out of them and were washing their nets. He got into one of the boats, the one belonging to Simon, and asked him to put out a little way from the shore. Then he sat down and taught the crowds from the boat. When he had finished speaking, he said to Simon, "Put out into the deep water and let down your nets for a catch." Simon answered, "Master, we have worked all night long but have caught nothing. Yet if you say so, I will let down the nets." When they had done this, they caught so many fish that their nets were beginning to break. So they signaled their partners in the other boat to come and help them. And they came and filled both boats, so that they began to sink. But when Simon Peter saw it, he fell down at Jesus' knees, saying, "Go away from me, Lord, for I am a sinful man!" For he and all who were with him were amazed at the catch of fish that they had taken; and so also were James and John, sons of Zebedee, who were partners with Simon. Then Jesus said to Simon, "Do not be afraid; from now on you will be catching people." When they had brought their boats to the shore, they left everything and followed him.

Luke 5:1-11

This great haul was unexpected from these men. They came in after a day of fishing. They did not expect to encounter Jesus and fill two boats with fish. Jesus' makes himself known in our lives at unexpected times. Just when you think you have things figured out, something changes. God provides everything in our lives.

Jesus walks with us all of the time, and makes himself known with it is necessary. The Holy Spirit is always present with us, filling us with the love of God. So, expect the unexpected to happen.

God, worker of all miracles, we give you thanks for meeting all our needs. May Jesus continually make himself known in our lives, even when we do not expect it. May the Holy Spirit make all things known to us. Amen.

DECEMBER 31

O LORD, our Sovereign, how majestic is your name in all the earth! You have set your glory above the heavens. Out of the mouth of babes and infants you have founded a bulwark because of your foes, to silence the enemy and the avenger. When I look at your heavens, the work of your fingers, the moon and the stars that you have established; what are human beings that you are mindful of them, mortals that you care for them? Yet you have made them a little lower than God, and crowned them with glory and honor. You have given them dominion over the works of your hands; you have put all things under their feet, all sheep and oxen, and also the beasts of the field, the birds of the air, and the fish of the sea, whatever passes along the paths of the seas. O LORD, our Sovereign, how majestic is your name in all the earth!
Psalm 8:1-9

As we ready for a new year, how can we not celebrate God's glory. We see God's glory in the night sky, in all creation, in God's love for us. God's has also given us the responsibility to care for all creation. Today, reflect upon the past year, and how you have changed. God has been at work in you. Give thanks to God!

Eternal God, you have placed us in a world of space and time. You bless us with your love in all the events of our lives. Send the Holy Spirit to us, so that in this new year we may known your presence and see your love at work. May we also be guided to proper dominion over your creation. And may we look forward to the coming of your Son, Jesus Christ, the Light of the world. Amen.